Poem and Music in the German Lied
from Gluck to Hugo Wolf

Poem and Music in the German Lied
from Gluck to Hugo Wolf

Jack M. Stein

Harvard University Press Cambridge, Massachusetts 1971

To Judy and Janie

Preface

Most lied analyses, even in the few instances where critical attention is paid to the words, are written from the point of view of the music. My approach has been from the poem, in the conviction that this change of direction provides new insights. In discussing both poems and music, I have tried to keep the interested nonspecialist in mind. Musical illustrations are indispensable, but they have been made as uncomplicated as possible, and I have avoided technical terminology as much as I could. As a result, music specialists may on occasion find explanations and descriptions that could have been taken for granted, just as the literary scholar may sometimes come across explicit elaborations that to him seem self-evident. The thoroughness with which the different lieder are treated, as well as the proportionate attention given to words or music in each instance, varies greatly, in part to avoid monotony and repetitiousness, but chiefly to bring out what I considered most essential.

Portions of this study appeared in preliminary form in the following journals: *PMLA (Publications of the Modern Language Association), Monatshefte, Journal of Aesthetics and Art Criticism, Musical Quarterly,* and *Comparative Literature.* Subsequent discussions and exchanges of opinion, both public and private, were invaluable in developing the analyses to their present state. With pleasure I acknowledge my indebtedness to the Guggenheim and the Kendall Foundations, whose financial assistance greatly facilitated the completion of this study. It is difficult to express in words the debt of gratitude I owe to Hilde von Gronicka for the many happy hours we spent during the 1950's in learning and performing, for ourselves and friends, a large repertoire of eighteenth and nineteenth century lieder. Without the insights provided by that intense study, this book would never have been attempted.

Cambridge, Mass.
September 1970   J.M.S.

Contents

Poem and Music in the German Lied

from Gluck to Hugo Wolf

Introduction

Potentially the lied, or art song, is a miniature *Gesamtkunstwerk* or fusion of two arts, poetry and music. But it differs from other composite musical forms in a significant feature: one of its components, the verse, was originally an independent work, complete in itself, created in most cases without thought of musical setting—indeed, having poetic-musical elements of its own.

Other composite forms, notably opera, often involve an adaptation of a previously existing work, but not an absorption of it unchanged into the larger unit. There are a few exceptions, such as Richard Strauss's *Salome*, which uses a German translation of Oscar Wilde's French original. Alban Berg's musical drama on Georg Büchner's *Woyzeck*[1] is another example, as is his *Lulu*, a setting of Frank Wedekind's plays *Der Erdgeist* and *Die Büchse der Pandora*. But even these are not quite parallel to the lied, because in all cases the text is shortened, sometimes drastically, to give the musical work a manageable length.[2]

Robert Schumann made a fine (and sadly neglected) cantata of excerpts from Goethe's *Faust I* and *II*; Beethoven used part of Schiller's "An die Freude" for the finale of his Ninth Symphony. There are many such examples, but none of them incorporates unchanged an entire work, as does the lied with the lyric poem. Even Richard Wagner's musical dramas are not like the lied in this respect, for his texts, though some were published separately before the music had been written, were clearly intended from the outset to be part of the larger unit. The same is true of the famous collaborations between poet and composer, as between Hugo von Hofmannsthal and Richard Strauss, or Paul Claudel and Darius Milhaud.

The lied, then, is the only composite musical form that regularly makes use of an entire work of art, albeit a miniature one, as an integral part. Aesthetically this is a critical factor, which implies certain responsibilities on the part of the composer toward the poem. The fate of the poem in the larger form, and the manifold ways in which, both theoretically and in practice, song writers have attempted to handle this relationship, is the subject of this book. I attempt to analyze, through individual lieder, just how lyric poetry and music are combined, what problems are inherent in the form, and whether there is an ideal way to effect this combination.

The 1750's is the starting point. In these years the so-called First Berlin School of song composers broke with the baroque-rococo past and started the tradition that was to culminate in the great songs of the nineteenth century. During the entire second half of the eighteenth century many song composers made a studied effort to achieve a balance between word and tone in the lied. Johann Friedrich Reichardt and Friedrich Zelter, the leading song writers of the later 1700's, produced a larger number of settings that achieve a delicate blend of poem and music than have any other composers before or since. The great composers of the second half of the eighteenth century—Gluck, Haydn, and Mozart—were interested only peripherally in the lied. Of the three, Gluck's contributions to the development of the form are by far the most important, although his songs have been forgotten. Beethoven, as always, is a powerful transitional figure who, though less important in song than in almost all other divisions of music, made significant contributions to its development.

With Schubert a new era in song composition began. The fact that his forms evolved from those of his predecessors does not basically alter the fact that he changed the character of the lied more than any other composer, and that it remained as he had changed it (with variations and further developments) for the entire nineteenth century. But with this change in character came critical alterations in the relation between the music and the poetry. In general, the songs improved, but the word-tone problems became more acute.

In Schubert, as in Schumann, Brahms, and Wolf, the music in the lied dominates over the poem, so that the temptation is great for the listener or performer to pay little attention to the words. The increased assertiveness of the music, however, did not come about because the composer himself held the poem in low regard. There is abundant evidence that Schubert and his major successors consistently strove for a proper musical interpretation of the poem, which they considered of primary importance. It follows that the listener or performer who is willing to pay particular attention to the poem can come a good deal closer to experiencing nineteenth century song as the composers intended than can one who takes the easier, more prevalent course of basking in the beauty of the musical phrases.

In lieder before Schubert, the texture of the music is seldom so rich that the primacy of the poem is threatened. From Schubert on, however, the listener who wants to hear the song as a potential synthesis of poem and music must overcome formidable obstacles. The chief difficulty is the simple fact that the words often do not come distinctly through the complex of musical sounds. It is usually necessary to follow a printed text. Though the words are frequently supplied in song recitals or on recordings, here too there are hazards. Seldom in such instances is the text printed as a poem in its own right, with careful attention to strophic form and to the way that the poet meant it to look on the page. The words are usually copied directly from the song itself, without reference to the original. It is therefore difficult, sometimes impossible, to reconstruct the form of the poem from a nineteenth century song. One example can stand for many. Here are the first two stanzas of the poem "Der Kuss" by Ludwig Hölty, taken from the jacket of a recording of Brahms's song of the same name:

Unter Blüten des Mais spielt' ich mit ihrer Hand,
Koste liebend, koste liebend mit ihr,
Schaute mein schwebendes Bild im Auge des Mädchens,
Raubt' ihr bebend den ersten Kuss.

Zuckend fliegt nun der Kuss,
Wie ein versengend Feu'r
Mir durch Mark und Gebein.
Du, die Unsterblichkeit durch die Lippen mir sprüht,
Wehe, wehe mir Kühlung zu.[3]

These are certainly the words, but this is not the poem. Hölty wrote an asclepiadic ode, which is a quite different entity when written as the poet wanted it:

Unter Blüten des Mais spielt' ich mit ihrer Hand,
Koste liebend mit ihr, schaute mein schwebendes
Bild im Auge des Mädchens,
Raubt' ihr bebend den ersten Kuss.

Zuckend fliegt nun der Kuss wie ein versengend Feu'r
Mir durch Mark und Gebein. Du, die Unsterblichkeit
Durch die Lippen mir sprüht,
Wehe, wehe mir Kühlung zu.

Of the problems in word-tone relationship, the caliber of the composer's interpretation of the poem assumes major significance beginning with Schubert. In the eighteenth century, because of the relatively unassuming quality of most musical settings, the composer's interpretation of the poem was not so critical, though examples are plentiful of his failure fully to understand a poem. But when the composer does as much interpreting as did nineteenth century song writers, there is every justification for calling him to account for its quality. In this regard I know of no major composer, not to speak of minor ones, who is above criticism. It is not that a composer's interpretation of a poem must conform to the original intention of the poet. Regardless of what the poet wanted to communicate, once the poem has been set on paper, it becomes an independent entity, subject to a variety of readings.[4] The composer has every right to his own interpretation. But his case is unique in that his way of looking at the poem becomes explicit in his musical setting. By limiting the poem to his one interpretation, the song reduces the poem's intrinsic scope.[5]

Furthermore, in his song the composer puts the adequacy or inadequacy of his interpretation on permanent record. Schubert's six songs to poems of Heine are a case in point. Every one is a misinterpretation of Heine. Now Schubert composed these songs only a year after the poems had appeared, and Heine has since proved troublesome to interpret. No one could possibly expect Schubert to have understood Heine as he is only now beginning to be known, over a hundred years afterward. But the composer's picture of the poet is firmly fixed in six important works of art, and it cannot be altered to accommodate new insights. Although a lyric poem offers no obstacle to new readings, songs set the poem in a mold that cannot adjust to fuller comprehension or increased perspectives in literary analysis. Thus, Schubert's Heine songs must stand as faulty interpretations of one of Germany's greatest poets. While an understanding of the poems has deepened, the songs have remained exactly the same. As this gulf grows between poem and song, in a certain way the song loses in stature.

Not much has been written about the lied from the point of view of the poem. There is, in fact, a widespread cliché that second-rate verse is better material for songs than great poems. Behind this notion lies the feeling that fine poetry does not need a musical setting; although one may not mind having inferior poetry tampered with by a composer, one resists on principle letting anything so drastic happen to the great poems of Goethe and Mörike. In view of the caliber of most musical settings of great lyric poetry, this hesitance is justified. And if one prefers to listen to a song without paying attention to the words, it is helpful if the poem is not disturbingly high in quality. But there is a considerable minority of excellent musical-poetic syntheses employing the greatest lyric poems, and these in fact represent the highest pinnacle of song literature.

Books on the song are invariably a great deal more involved with music than words. Usually the poem is uncritically accepted. It is hard on readers with a strong interest in lyric poetry to find commentators treating Schmidt von Lübeck's wretched poem "Der Wanderer," for example, on an equal footing with the greatest poems in the German language, as is the case in the overwhelming majority of musicological analyses of song.[6] There are a very few exceptions. Richard Capell's *Schubert's Songs*, a highly regarded work, has a brief introductory chapter on the poets, but after that, the music gets the lion's share of attention. Eric Sams in his *The Songs of Hugo Wolf* devotes considerable attention to the poems, but even so the music remains the chief focus. Thrasybulos Georgiades has produced an elaborate work entitled *Schubert: Musik und Lyrik,* in which he attempts, unsuccessfully in my view, to show a wholly new relationship between poem and music in Schubert's songs. Yet in his book, too, while the musical analysis is complex, the treatment of the poetry is relatively superficial. In 1969 a new volume by Eric Sams appeared, *The Songs of Robert Schumann,* parallel in its approach to the earlier work on Wolf. The only study I know which offers a song analysis that does full justice to the poem as well as the music, discussing both aspects in detail and with equal professional competence, is an unpublished dissertation by Harry E. Seelig, "Goethe's 'Buch Suleika' and Hugo Wolf: A Musical-Literary Study."[7]

Though it is assumed in literature on the song that the composer should attempt to capture the mood of the poem and to observe its rhythmic pattern, shaping the musical line in accordance with these requirements, the precise nature of the word-tone relationship is not examined. Discussions of the merits of strophic versus through-composed settings seldom are searchingly critical of the relation between word and tone. Through-composing, being a later and more complex phenomenon, is almost always thought to represent potentially a more precise way of blending poem and music, since it gives the composer the opportunity to be more meticulous in his musical delineation of textual details—though it is refreshing to read Donald Tovey's remark, "No modern musical criterion is shallower than that which regards as lazy and primitive the setting of different stanzas of a poem to the same melody."[8]

There is need for a study of the song form that makes no such assumptions and which will examine basic questions about the form, such as whether it is desirable, or indeed possible, for the composer to match the poetic rhythm with a vocal melody and a piano accompaniment; to what extent a composer can properly give special musical treatment to certain passages or words in the poem without throwing the work off balance; what happens to the poetic-musical elements already contained in the poem; and how faithfully a particular composer has interpreted a poem.[9] Such an approach inevitably involves value judgments. Even when documentation is complete and analysis detailed, on aesthetic matters there can never be absolute proof, nor even total agreement. In his *Nicomachean Ethics* Aristotle writes, "It is the mark of an educated man to seek only so much exactness in each type of inquiry as may be allowed by the nature of the subject matter." I therefore do not claim interpretive infallibility in the analyses that follow. On the contrary, I gladly acknowledge that other practiced eyes and ears could react quite differently in individual instances. My aim is merely to call attention to the manifold varieties of aesthetic balance between poem and music in the lied, without insisting that the reader be totally convinced by each interpretation.

There are any number of ways to approach the phenomenon of "song." The one here pursued makes no claim to supplant others, but it does claim equal validity. Since the middle of the eighteenth century, song composers almost without exception have regarded the poems they used as the real nucleus of their songs, and have made a conscious effort to interpret those poems faithfully and fully in musical terms. Viewing the song as a potential synthesis of word and tone, I examine the problems inherent in the form and the ways in which the major composers have dealt with them. The greatest songs of the eighteenth and nineteenth century, thus analyzed, yield new insights into the critical relationship between text and setting in the art song.

Chapter I Problems of Combining Poem and Music

Since the time of Lessing's *Laokoon*, the basic differences between music and poetry as media of expression have been repeatedly analyzed. The most esoteric problem—one which has long since occupied music psychologists and theorists—is the exact nature of musical communication and the precise way it conditions the listener's reaction, without the conceptual assistance of words.[1] My concern is with a somewhat different question, that of how (or whether) the integrity of the poem can be preserved when music is added. The juxtaposition of lyric poem and music in the lied is full of problems. It is in fact fortunate that composers have not been inhibited by the critical factors involved in this relationship. Although the magnificent repertoire of songs presently in existence suggests that the difficulties must not be made too much of,[2] problems do exist, and a better understanding of them should contribute to a fuller comprehension of the song as an art form.

Meter and Rhythm

In the early seventeenth century, German poets first began to match metrical stress with natural accentuation. Martin Opitz' *Buch von der deutschen Poeterey* (1624) was the first poetics to point out that coincidence of natural accent with metrical stress was more logical in German, a language based on accentuation, than the counting of syllables, as in French verse, or the calculation of quantity (long or short syllables) as in Latin verse. Since that time, metrical stress based on natural accent has remained the operative principle in German versification: on an underlying regular metrical alternation of stresses—iambic, trochaic, dactylic, or other—based on accentuation, is superimposed the more flexible rhythm of the individual line.

At about the same time, in the late sixteenth century, monody or the homophonic style—a single melodic line above a figured bass with at first rudimentary harmony—was developed in Italy. With monody came the subdivision into the measure, a metrical unit with a recurrent underlying pattern of regular accentuation, upon which is superimposed the individual rhythm of the melodic line. This has remained the basic structural unit of music until the present, except in the more radical experimentation of the twentieth century, as in electronic music.

The similarity between meter and rhythm in poetry and music during the entire period from Gluck to Hugo Wolf is evident. What is not so often noticed are the differences, which have important implications for the lied. They can perhaps best be illustrated by an example where poetic and musical meter and rhythm seem to blend perfectly, where the composer has evidently made a conscious attempt to match the two with precision, as in the first line of the last song in Schumann's "Frauenliebe und —leben" cycle, "Nun hast du mir den ersten Schmerz getan":

Underlying the musical rhythm is a basic regularity, governed by the bar-line and the time signature, which is considerably more assertive than the metrical pattern underlying the verse. In spite of all manner of possible intricacies in the melodic and harmonic structure which can introduce crosscurrents and irregularities, the fundamental beat, the so-called "tyranny of the bar-line," is a major factor.

The beat that underlies the music in this example is the normal one for 4/4 time, with a primary accent (/) on the first beat of the measure, and a secondary accent (\) on the third:

╱ ∪ ╲ ∪ │ ╱ ∪ ╲ ∪ │ ╱ ∪ ╲ ∪ │ ╱

The metrical beat underlying the rhythm of the two lines of poetry:

Nun hast du mir den ersten Schmerz getan.
Der aber traf.

is iambic and can be diagramed as follows:

∪ — ∪ — ∪ — ∪ — ∪ —
∪ — ∪ —

Now, the precise rhythmic pattern of the melodic line can be pictured thus:

However, it is not possible to present a diagram of the rhythm of the poetic lines to parallel this, for poetic rhythm is by no means so precisely fixed as musical rhythm. Deviations from the metrical beat are introduced by the poet in any line of poetry. In the two lines under consideration, the accentuation of the first two words is very nearly the reverse of an iamb, with "nun" receiving a stress (though probably not a full one), and "hast" following as the first of two unaccented syllables (or perhaps as the first of four unaccented syllables, since the rendition of "hast du mir den" would give only a slight accent, if any, to "mir"). In the second line, the "der" must have a strong stress. The following syllable, "a-" of "aber," would also have a stress, somewhat slighter than the "der" but nonetheless more than the unaccented end-syllable of the word "aber." The "traf" would be accented.

Thus, any line of poetry is a composite of lesser or greater deviations from the basic metrical pattern, and the dynamics of the interplay between the two contributes to the beauty of the lyric. Although in music, too, the contrast between the underlying beat and the individual rhythm of the melody is a major source of beauty in the line, the individual note values must be observed with care by the performer. The assertiveness of these fixed elements in the music is psychologically greater than the corresponding values in the rhythmically more flexible poetic line. Even in the songs of Hugo Wolf, who often went to great lengths to adjust his vocal line to subtle nuances of the verse, it is the musical rhythm that is heard, not the poetic one, as in the unusual 5/4 measures:

Zierlich ist des Vogels Tritt im Schnee, wenn er wandelt auf des Berges Höh':

Even if a satisfactory coding system could be devised to indicate all the nuances of a poetic line, it would not only have to be much more complex than one for a melodic line, but it would still be only partially valid—for a line of poetry always has more than a single possible reading, and its essential nature includes the multiplicity of possible rhythmic variations as part of its effect. There is a very real sense in which most poetry written since the Renaissance communicates most fully only from the printed page; it is poetry for the eye. Any musical setting, like any recitation of the poem, places limitations on its scope.[3] Thus, when the composer chooses one of the numerous possibilities, even if he were able to match this perfectly with his musical rhythm (which he cannot do), he would be suppressing certain essential lyric qualities of the poetry.

Intonation and Musical Pitch

There is another element in the melodic line that adds to the domination of the music over the poetry: the configuration of the pitch variations. These also are exactly prescribed and must be observed with even greater precision by the performer than the rhythmic intervals.[4] In the same Schumann line they can be schematized thus:

(Nun hast du mir den er - sten Schmerz ge - tan. Der a - ber traf)

In their succession and progression, they form a cohesive unit which has a beginning, middle, and end. Whatever intonation and inflectional patterns would be exhibited by the poetry, whether in recitation or implicitly from the printed page, it is obvious that these are totally replaced by the sequence of musical pitches in the lied. In addition, the supporting harmony of the accompaniment (as well as any complementary melodic line and rhythmic patterns for the piano) adds substantially to the musical weight.

Duration

In the struggle—for it is a kind of struggle—for the listener's attention, duration of time is another factor that tends to emphasize the musical as against the poetic values. A musical note is almost always of longer duration, sometimes very much longer, than the syllable of a word. Any song, therefore, simply lasts longer than the poem alone. The extent to which poems can tolerate such expansion without serious loss to the poetic sense or the aesthetic effect varies greatly. Some poems experience little or no loss when slowed down by a sustained musical line. Such a lyric is Goethe's famous "Wanderers Nachtlied" ("Über allen Gipfeln ist Ruh"). But the opposite is more often true. Goethe's "Prometheus" or "Ganymed," to choose only two examples from among hundreds, achieve part of their effect by the pace with which the sounds, ideas, and images succeed one another. Much of the force of these poems is neutralized in the settings by Schubert, in part at least because the music dilates the poem. The same is true of Mörike's "Im Frühling" in the setting by Hugo Wolf, as of many others.

Conceptual and Emotional Values

A lyric poem is a marvelous combination of conceptual and emotional values, with the ability to blend the two into a single unit being not the least part of the genius of a poet. Music can readily reinforce the emotional implications of the poetry, and even to some extent the conceptual values, by such devices as melodic and harmonic configuration, accentuation, or syncopation. But the language of music is an abstract, emotional one, which raises serious problems when it is juxtaposed with the conceptual aspects of poetic language. In the opening of Beethoven's song to

Goethe's "Mailied," for instance, the musical phrase splendidly supports the emotional tone of the lines:

Wie herrlich leuchtet
Mir die Natur!
Wie glänzt die Sonne!
Wie lacht die Flur!

It also underlines the meaning of the two colorful words "herrlich" and "lacht." But the equally important meanings of "leuchtet" and "glänzt" are slighted because these two words fall on less prominent notes of the musical phrase:

In the lines:

Oft bin ich mir kaum bewusst,
Und die helle Freude zücket
Durch die Schwere, so mich drücket
Wonniglich in meine Brust.

from Mörike's "Verborgenheit," the contrast between the second and the third lines is subtly expressed in the conceptual meanings of the two rhyming words. The impact of the juxtaposition of "drücket" with the next word "wonniglich" is also largely conceptual. Such interplays of meaning cannot be paralleled by a musical line, at least not in the musical idiom of the late eighteenth and nineteenth centuries, and are therefore largely if not entirely lost in a musical setting of a poem.

Sound Values

Sound values are of the essence in any lyric poem, even when it is read silently from the printed page.[5] The degree to which they contribute to the total effect varies greatly, but in such lines as Mörike's "O flaumenleichte Zeit der ersten Frühe," or Uhland's "Die linden Lüfte sind erwacht," the sound values are very prominent. When a poem is set to music, there is a great likelihood that such delicate effects cannot compete with the more assertive musical values of the setting. When the composer selects a poem in which the sound values dominate even over the conceptual, as with the symbolist poets or their predecessors in the nineteenth century, an acute problem presents itself. This can be observed in Wolf's settings of some of Mörike's more advanced poems, such as "Im Frühling" or "An eine Äolsharfe."

Pictorial Effects

Often the musical setting renders pictorial effects that the poem has already expressed through words. In this case, too, the music always dominates. In Goethe's "Erlkönig," for instance, the rapid rhythm coupled with the meaning of the first line, "Wer reitet so spät durch Nacht und Wind?" readily suggests the galloping of a horse. But the "galloping" accompaniment for Schubert's setting of the song is so much bolder and more prominent that it overwhelms the less assertive poetic effect.[6]

Poetic and Musical Form

With regard to form, songs can be divided into four major categories: strophic, varied strophic, cyclic, and through-composed. In a strophic setting, such as was most common in the eighteenth century, a melodic line and its accompaniment are composed to one of the stanzas of a poem (not always the first[7]), and the identical music is performed to each of the other strophes. There are obvious limitations to this method, though in the happiest instances the flexibility of the setting allows for sufficient variation in speed, dynamics, or emphasis to adapt itself to the varying moods of the poem's successive stanzas. It is then up to the singer to introduce these variations. In 1824 the singer Eduard Genast found this out from no less a person than Goethe. According to Genast's report, he was singing Reichardt's setting of "Jägers Abendlied" for the poet one evening, when Goethe interrupted him:

Goethe sat in his armchair and covered his eyes with his hands. Toward the end of the song he leaped up and cried, "You sing the song badly!" He paced up and down in the room for a while humming the song to himself. Then he stepped up to me...and said, "The first stanza and the third must be delivered pithily [markig], with a kind of savagery, the second and the fourth more gently, for in them there is a different feeling. See, this way (with strong emphasis) 'Da ramm! Da ramm! Da ramm! Da ramm!" At the same time he beat the tempo with both arms and sang the "Da ramm" on a deep note. I knew then what he wanted and at his request sang the song again. He was satisfied and said, "That's better. In time you will learn how such strophic songs should be sung."[8]

Some composers of strophic songs took pains to indicate the desired variations by explicit printed directions. Heinrich Schwab cites the following example from Reichardt: "The first five stanzas are to be sung animatedly and in a naively narrative style, almost spoken; the sixth stanza somewhat more slowly and gravely; the final one swiftly and lightly."[9] Yet in the final analysis the exact repetition of the music, however subtly varied by the performer, creates a fundamentally different aesthetic effect from a strophic poem, whose form is repeated, but with a totally different set of concepts, sounds, or images in each stanza.

In the varied strophic song, there is a noticeable repetition of the melody and accompaniment for the successive stanzas of the poem, but changes occur in melodic line, rhythm, tempo, dynamics, harmony, or some other aspect, so as to adjust to the course of the poem. Many more songs of the eighteenth century than is commonly supposed made use of this device in order to achieve greater flexibility. It was even more widely used in the nineteenth century, being Schubert's favorite form. The possibility of a close parallel between musical and poetic form would seem greater in the varied strophic form than with the strict strophic repetitions.

The cyclical form, much favored by Brahms, is basically an A-B-A pattern: an extended melodic unit, followed by a totally different one, with a return to the original unit at the end. This basic pattern can be elaborated into highly intricate designs.[10] It is rare that a cyclical song parallels closely the form of the poem it sets, and the more elaborate the musical design, the farther it is likely to move away from the poem.

The through-composed song was introduced late in the eighteenth century by the Second Berlin School of composers, although used sparingly until the days of Schubert. It adheres to no formal pattern, and treats each successive poetic idea, even single words, in a relatively independent way. The technique allows much greater flexibility in musical delineation of the details contained in the poem. This was the form most favored by Hugo Wolf. But when used with strophic poems, as it often is, and not only by Wolf, it undermines the formal pattern of the lyric (Schubert's "Erlkönig" is an example). The through-composed form is essential for a song composed to a poem in free verse, but here there is the danger of emphasizing details to the extent that the over-all effect is fragmented.

It would be foolish to contend that composers have been inhibited by, or in most cases even consistently aware of, these word-tone problems. But the analyses will show that they did contend with them in one way or another. In this matter there is a great gulf between pre- and post-Schubertian song, for the late eighteenth century in general looked on the melody and harmony of a song as a modest embellishment to a lyric poem which did not cease to remain the chief element in the combination. Once Beethoven's influence came to be felt in music, and the musical genius of Schubert transformed the song form into a vehicle for unprecedented musical expressivity, the relationship between word and tone became more critical. The poem became, in a sense, embattled, by virtue of the fact that music had developed more precise and also more powerful means of extending poetic ideas into its own more abstract sphere.

These differences can be illustrated by the juxtaposition of Zelter's and Schubert's settings of Goethe's celebrated poem "An den Mond." Zelter's composition of 1812, written when he was fifty-six years old, is one of his most successful songs, and Schubert's version of 1815, composed when he was 18, has been called "in every respect the most significant composition of the poem, of which about forty have appeared in print."[11]

Goethe wrote the poem in 1778 and sent it to Frau von Stein with a musical setting by his friend Freiherr von Seckendorff. It first appeared in print, without music, in a revised form in *Goethes Schriften, 1787–1790*. Both Zelter and Schubert used this revised form:

(1) Füllest wieder Busch und Tal
    Still mit Nebelglanz,
    Lösest endlich auch einmal
    Meine Seele ganz;

(2) Breitest über mein Gefild
    Lindernd deinen Blick,
    Wie des Freundes Auge mild
    Über mein Geschick.

(3) Jeden Nachklang fühlt mein Herz
    Froh- und trüber Zeit,
    Wandle zwischen Freud und Schmerz
    In der Einsamkeit.

(4) Fliesse, fliesse, lieber Fluss!
    Nimmer werd ich froh,
    So verrauschte Scherz und Kuss,
    Und die Treue so.

(5) Ich besass es doch einmal,
    Was so köstlich ist!
    Das man doch zu seiner Qual
    Nimmer es vergisst!

(6) Rausche, Fluss, das Tal entlang,
    Ohne Rast und Ruh,
    Rausche, flüstre meinem Sang
    Melodien zu,

(7) Wenn du in der Winternacht
    Wütend überschwillst,
    Oder um die Frühlingspracht
    Junger Knospen quillst.

(8) Selig, wer sich vor der Welt
Ohne Hass verschliesst,
Einen Freund am Busen hält
Und mit dem geniesst,

(9) Was, von Menschen nicht gewusst
Oder nicht bedacht,
Durch das Labyrinth der Brust
Wandelt in der Nacht.

Zelter's placid strophic setting is simplicity itself, but beautifully supports the moonlit scene of the opening stanza:

The rhythm of the melody is not by any means identical with that of the poem, yet it is unassertive and scrupulously observes the trochaic meter. The melodic phrases divide exactly as do the separate lines of the poem, so that there is little sense of forcing the rhythm of the poem to that of the music. The accompaniment provides a graceful harmonious background, against which the sense as well as the beauty of the poem can be easily communicated. It is quite clear in this setting that the composer desires the poem to be the chief element in the song. He provides a gentle, unassuming, but lovely enhancement.

The second line of the melody (from "lösest endlich") expands to a modest climax, as does the verse. The melodic configuration on "meine Seele" is obviously not called for by the words, but this makes relatively little difference, since in the entire song there is no attempt to match declamation exactly or to bring out individual details of the poem. The rise to a climax with the lovely arpeggio flourish expresses the feeling and the sense of the two lines so admirably that the faulty declamation is scarcely noticed, if at all.

A fundamental and extremely important difference between poetry and music is well illustrated by this phrase. Note that, in the poem, the first word of the line, "lösest," has the immediate effect of intensifying the emotional tone. The expressive verb with its object "Seele" in the next line are the pivots of the thought. Thus, the direction in which the poem moves in these two lines is signaled by the first word. Music cannot normally parallel this device or ordinarily bring out emphasis so early. Music must build to its climax, which in this case is not reached until the middle of the phrase. The word "lösest" is engulfed, so to speak, by the forward-striving of the musical phrase, which crests on "meine Seele." This basic difference between the way poetry and music can build to a climax is one of the most pervasive problems in any musical setting of a lyric poem.

The strophic setting parallels the stanzaic pattern of a poem, but rarely can a strophic composition reflect the dynamic progress achieved by the successive stanzas of a poem. Goethe showed us that to some extent the singer can adjust his delivery to the changes in the lyric. The first five stanzas of this poem offer no major difficulty to the perceptive singer. By a sensitive differentiation of the phrases, for example, he can accommodate the differing qualities of the words "mild," "Schmerz," "Kuss," and "Qual," all of which fall on the climactic portion of the musical phrase. But the setting is unequal to the demands of the sixth strophe and even more so of the animated seventh. There is nothing in this gentle melody and accompaniment to match the force of such expressions as "ohne Rast und Ruh" or "wütend überschwillst." The music recovers again, to a degree, in the final two strophes. However, Zelter's melodic line is by no means an ideal extension of the philosophizing generalizations that make up the last two stanzas of the poem. The complete separation of stanzas required by the melody also runs counter to the striking enjambment that links the last two stanzas. An even greater deficiency in the setting becomes evident as the song progresses. Though it matched the mood and effect of the words of the opening stanzas, it is not equal to the increasing tension and enigmatic psychological implications that are in fact the essence of the poem.

The sheer repetitiveness of the strophic setting is an additional weakness. In a strophic poem, since each stanza has something different to say, the repetition of the strophic pattern can be relatively unobtrusive, while it provides a symmetrical framework of rhythm and rhyme that contributes a sense of unity. The effect of the strophic musical setting is much more prominent, and the ninefold repetition of the same melody and harmony, not benefiting from anything comparable to the completely new text in each strophe, can, and here does, become in the end monotonously repetitious

Schubert's setting is quite different:[12]

It can be seen at once that Schubert composed a longer melody, which bridges two full stanzas of the poem. This linking obscures the strophic pattern, creating a new scheme of its own exactly

twice as long. Schubert's treatment adds to the musical interest, because he can arch the melodic structure over a longer period and, in the second half, develop a considerably more animated phrase. But the pairing of the stanzas does not function very well. Above all, the third and fourth stanzas are two separate units, which do not combine easily into a single larger entity.

The rhythm of the Schubert setting is not as placid as that of Zelter's. It foreshadows better the developing mood of the poem, but it certainly does not capture the incomparable moonlit calm of the first two strophes. A tension between the words and their musical setting is created by the unnatural patterns into which the unusual rhythm forces the words. "Füllest" falls on an upbeat, with the main stress and the downbeat falling awkwardly on "wieder." "Busch und Tal" also occur on passing notes of the melody. As a result, the word that in a recitation of the poem would get the least stress ("wieder") bears the chief accent in the musical setting, and the three words that would be most heavily accented ("füllest," "Busch," and "Tal") are passed over in the musical line. Altogether, the 3/4 time signature forces the smooth trochaic meter of the poem into a succession of unnatural positions.

The unusual foreshortening of the second half of each melodic phrase strains the metrical pattern of the poem even more. In the verse, though the odd-numbered lines have four stresses and the even-numbered three, there is a pause after each second line which fills it out to a length equal or nearly equal to the first:

$$- \cup - \cup - \quad \cup - (\cup)$$
(Füllest wieder Busch und Tal)
$$- \quad \cup - \cup - (\cup -)$$
(Still mit Nebelglanz,)

Schubert clips this second line very short indeed.

It is not necessary to give the setting of the fifth strophe, as it is exactly the same as strophes one and three. The accompaniment through strophe five doubles the vocal melody, sometimes in octaves, over an unobtrusive harmonization. Schubert solves the problem of the marked difference in expression of the sixth and seventh strophes in a characteristic way:

(Strophe 6) Rau - sche, Fluss, das Tal ent -

lang, ___ oh - ne Rast und oh - ne Ruh, rau-sche,

flü - stre mei - nem Sang ___ Me - lo - di - en

zu! Wenn du in der Win-ternacht wü-tend ü-berschwillst, o-der
(Strophe 7)

um die Frühlings - pracht jun-ger Knos-pen quillst.

Instead of continuing as before, Schubert alters the melodic line and harmonic structure of stanza six. For the seventh strophe the accompaniment no longer parallels the melody but features prominent sixteenth-note broken chords in crescendo to portray the movement of the water. The melodic line reaches a peak of agitation appropriately at the words "wütend überschwillst." By joining this very different treatment of strophes six and seven to the first half of his original melody, which he repeated for strophe five, Schubert creates a longer unit and thereby solves the problem of the uneven number of strophes.[13] But here it is as evident as in Zelter's setting, if for the opposite reason, that music cannot do what poetry can; change the mood strikingly without altering the strophic form.

Schubert returns in stanzas eight and nine to a melodic line and accompaniment reminiscent of the original strophic pattern:

(Strophe 8) Se-lig wer sich vor der Welt— oh-ne Hass ver-schliesst, ei-nen

Freund am Bu - sen hält und mit dem ge - niesst,— was, von
(Strophe 9)

Men-schen nicht ge - wusst, o - der nicht be-dacht, durch das

La - by - rinth der Brust wan - - delt in der

Nacht, wan - - delt in der Nacht.

As in Zelter's setting, the vocal line is pointless as a musical rendering of the philosophic comments. Because Schubert has done so
much more tone painting than would ever have occurred to Zelter,
particularly in stanzas six and seven, this last rather barren repetition
becomes the more noticeable. The enjambment between the eighth
and ninth stanzas offers no problems in this rendering. In general,
the Schubert setting achieves a greater sense of the unrest that is
increasingly evident as an undercurrent in the poem, but in a far
less subtle manner than in the poem itself.

Schubert's setting is lacking in other ways. The transition in the
poem from a placid opening to the existential questions at its close
is gradual but inexorable. A careful reading of even the first two
stanzas reveals implicit agitation (the third line, especially "auch
einmal"; "ganz" at the end of the stanza; and "lindernd" in stanza
two). The third strophe is more explicit ("zwischen Freud und

Schmerz," "Einsamkeit"). Stanzas four and five belong together as a unit, with five expressing the peak of agitation in its last two lines. The more animated stanzas six and seven are an answering unit, less agitated despite the increase in movement. The stream and its melodies offer a kind of consolation to the poet in his loneliness. There follow the reflective, poised, enigmatical final stanzas, which return from the image of the brook to the moonlight of the opening lines. Schubert's setting in no way mirrors this development.

It may be objected that Zelter's composition would stand up far less well than Schubert's if it were subjected to so detailed a word-tone analysis. But the fact is that the degree of interpretation in which Schubert and other nineteenth-century composers indulged calls forth exactly this kind of examination, whereas the earlier composers restricted themselves to a more modest, generalized role, allowing the poem more freedom to communicate its own nuances.

Schubert's setting illustrates still another word-tone problem. It often happens that the lied composer, in working out the inner logic of the musical lines, needs more syllables than the poet provides. When this happens, the composer must repeat words and phrases, sometimes whole stanzas. Schubert was especially given to this technique, particularly at the close of his songs. In the present instance, he repeats the last line "wandelt in der Nacht" for the benefit of the closing cadence. This is not difficult to accept. But in the sixth strophe he eliminates the foreshortening of the second and fourth lines by adding an extra measure to each, in order to get a more expansive phrase. In order to do this, he changes the words in the second line from "Ohne Rast und Ruh" to "Ohne Rast und ohne Ruh." The second "ohne" even receives a marked stress. Schubert was by no means alone among composers in taking liberties with the poems he set to music. The practice appeared occasionally in the eighteenth and more frequently in the nineteenth century. Once the relationship between poem and music had reached a point where the composer's share of the total work was more prominent than the poet's, the temptation to adjust the words to suit the musical development became strong indeed. Sometimes the composer would even "improve" on the poem by altering words and expressions, and not always because of the exigencies of the musical development.

A total fusion of lyric poetry and music in the lied is a virtual impossibility. The achievement of Richard Wagner in his massive syntheses proves impracticable in the modest chamber form, largely because of the prior existence of the lyric poem as a complete artistic unit. But the degree of rapport between word and tone in the lied varies greatly, and in memorable instances a singleness of expression is achieved which overcomes many of the obstacles imposed by the differences in the two arts.

One major characteristic of both poetry and music in the later eighteenth and nineteenth centuries made this fusion uniquely possible. At about the middle of the eighteenth century, a new kind of lyric poetry made its appearance. Often called "Bekenntnislyrik" or "confessional lyric," this verse is a persuasive personal statement, whose form does not reduce the directness and subjective force of its message, although in fact the poet has made use of the mechanics of lyric expression to achieve this effect. Goethe particularly, who was a master of this kind of lyric expression, succeeded in using the mechanics of poetry (meter, rhyme, rhythm, strophe) to create a sense of transcending them in an intensely personal statement, and his influence on the nineteenth century was enormous. Toward the close of the eighteenth century, music had developed a similar capacity to surmount the technical aspects of musical expression in a powerful subjective communication. A musical language developed whose very virtuosity in using the techniques of musical expression created the impression of an overwhelmingly subjective, personal, "confessional" statement. When this kind of musical communication is blended with a lyric poem of a similar nature, and when the musical setting strengthens in its unique way the statement of the poem, an aesthetic peak in song has been reached. Such instances are rare, but when they occur, they represent the pinnacle of the art song.

Although there has not been wide recognition by composers of the many problems involved in combining word and tone, most lied composers have had something to say about the process of setting lyric poetry to music. Comment on the lied began in earnest in the last quarter of the eighteenth century with J. A. P. Schulz (1747–1800), whom Joseph Müller–Blattau calls "the first theoretician of the lied."[1] Schulz was fortunate in living at a time when, after a long bleak period for poetry in Germany, the earliest figures of the classic era were beginning to appear, and he proudly stresses his use of texts from the best poets. Such names as Stolberg, Bürger, Voss, Hölty, Gleim, Claudius, and Klopstock occur frequently in his song collections. In the preface to his *Lieder im Volkston*, published in Berlin in 1782, Schulz discusses his conception of the relation of text to music.

> Only by a striking similarity between the musical and poetic tone of the song; by a melody whose progress never deviates from the text, a melody which molds itself to the declamation and the meter of the words as a dress shapes itself to the body . . . does the song present an unforced, artless, familiar appearance, in a word, that of the folk song. And this must be the goal of the song composer if he wants to remain true to the only legitimate intention of making fine texts generally well known by means of this form of composition. Not the melodies, but by means of the melodies, the words of the good poet should receive increased attention through the agency of the song . . . Therefore all useless ornamentation in the melody or in the accompaniment, all padding by means of ritornellos and interludes, which draw attention away from the essentials to secondary matters, from the words to the music . . . are to be rejected as superfluities damaging to the song, indeed running directly counter to its proper intention.

Schulz's own compositions are far too spare and barren to hold any interest, but the relation between text and music that he argues was the dominant view taken by poet and composer alike in the second half of the eighteenth century. It was in the 1750's that the so-called First Berlin School reacted against the florid Italianate musical style then popular. Schulz's references to "useless ornamentation" and "padding by means of ritornellos and interludes" were directed at this style of composing.[2] The new school demanded and produced songs in which the music was reduced to an unadorned vocal line, often without accompaniment. With these works began a period when it was commonly agreed that the poem should play a dominant, not a subordinate role. The song composers cultivated an appropriate musical style of extreme modesty. They saw their compositions as resembling folk songs, though their products were far more rational, stilted, and dull than true folk songs, which in point of fact these composers knew little about. They were long on conviction, but short on expertise and talent. Both songs and theory were amateurish, superficial, and inept. Yet this Berlin school deserves credit for pointing the compass in the direction that led ultimately to Schubert, Brahms, and Wolf, which gives them a formidable claim to recognition.

Closely associated with the composers in Berlin was Carl Philipp Emanuel Bach (1714–1788), whose *Geistliche Oden und Lieder* can in fact be called transitional. It clearly reveals the contrapuntal, ornamental, figured-bass style of an earlier era, though on a reduced scale. Not surprisingly for the author of the celebrated treatise *Versuch über die wahre Art das Klavier zu spielen*, the piano parts are far more interesting and prominent than in any of the doctrinaire products of the First Berlin School. But C.P.E. Bach's musicality expressed itself more forcefully elsewhere. There is little likelihood of a revival of interest in his forgotten songs.

Gluck

Christoph Willibald Gluck (1714–1787) came to the lied from the far different world of opera and ballet, but he produced several of the finest examples of the new kind of song. Only eleven songs by Gluck are on record—ten to odes by Klopstock and one to a poem by Friedrich von Matthison.[3] The Klopstock odes were composed over a period of years between 1770 and 1792. Seven of them were collected and published in 1785 as *Klopstocks Oden und Lieder beim Klavier zu singen, in Musik gesetzt von Herrn Ritter Gluck.*[4]

The famous preface to *Alceste*, in which Gluck's operatic reforms become explicit, appeared in 1769. This was over a decade before Schulz's *Lieder im Volkston*, but the arguments are so similar that the one may have served as a model for the other. In any case, both prefaces are thoroughgoing products of the Age of Rationalism. "I sought to bring music back to its true function," writes Gluck, "that is, to support the poetry...without...a useless excess of ornaments... In short, I have tried to do away with all the abuses against which good sense and reason have long cried out in vain... I sought a beautiful simplicity, and I have avoided making displays of difficulty at the expense of clarity."

Gluck's songs, too, are composed in this spirit. Three of them—"Wir und Sie," "Vaterlandslied," and "Die frühen Gräber"—are so simple and spare as to provide splendid examples of precisely what Schulz was describing. Of these three, the poems of the first two are in regular iambic meter, but "Die frühen Gräber" is patterned after one of Klopstock's own strophic inventions:

(1) ∪ – ∪ ∪ – ∪ ∪ – ,
(2) – ∪ – ∪ ∪ – ∪ – ,
(3) ∪ ∪ – ,– ∪ – ,– ∪ – ∪ ,
(4) – ∪ ∪ – ∪ ∪ – ,– ∪ ∪ – .

Gluck manages these complicated rhythms expertly within his self-imposed melodic limitations:

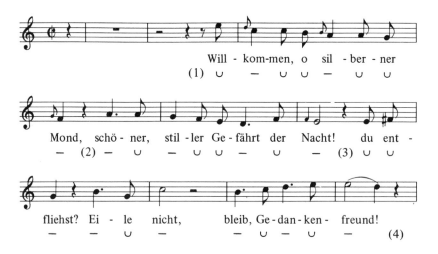

Se - het, er bleibt, ___ das Ge-wölk' wall - te nur hin,

Three other songs are strongly influenced by operatic recitative: "Der Jüngling," "Die Neigung," and "Der Tod." Two are as beautiful as any songs the eighteenth century ever produced: "Die Sommernacht" and "Schlachtgesang." Both poems follow strophic patterns constructed by Klopstock. Here, for example, is Klopstock's own metrical scheme for "Schlachtgesang":

(1) ∪ ∪ – ∪ – ∪ – ∪ –,
(2) ∪ ∪ ∪ – ∪ ∪ – ∪ –,
(3) ∪ ∪ ∪ – – –, ∪ ∪ – – ∪ – ∪,
(4) ∪ ∪ ∪ – ∪ ∪ – ∪ ∪ – ∪ ∪ ∪ – –

Gluck parallels this with precision in his marchlike composition:[5]

Maestoso

Wie er - scholl der Gang des lau - ten Heers von dem Ge -
(1)∪ ∪   –   ∪ –   ∪   – ∪ – (2) ∪ ∪ ∪

birg' in das Tal her - ab,   da zu dem An - griff bei dem
– ∪ ∪ –   ∪   – (3) ∪ ∪ ∪   –   – ∪ ∪

Wald - strom   das Kriegs - lied zu der ver - tilgenden Schlacht und dem
–   –   ∪   –   ∪ (4)∪ ∪ ∪   – ∪ ∪ –   ∪ ∪

Sie - ge den Be - fehl rief!

Only a small number of the songs of Reichardt and Zelter even approach these splendid creations, which clearly deserve to be revived. There are indications that Gluck composed more Klopstock songs, but no others have come to light.

Johann Friedrich Reichardt

None of the songs of Johann Friedrich Reichardt (1752–1814) reaches the heights of the best of Gluck's Klopstock compositions, but this standard is a severe one by which to judge any minor composer. Although he cannot be ranked among the greatest song writers, Reichardt was a key figure in the development of the form. He was experimental, expanding the scope of the song form considerably. He was also more sensitive to literary values than any song composer before him, and many later, though his prolific output of almost fifteen hundred songs necessarily includes many mediocre texts. He was the first prominent musician to devote himself extensively to Goethe poems. No less than 116 of his songs are settings of Goethe lyrics. There are also a large number of Schiller songs and many by other good poets.[6]

A large number of Reichardt's songs exhibit a simplicity of line and spareness of accompaniment that often descend to the banal, though the best of them are excellent specimens of the easily performed Hausmusik that he intended them to be. In his more important songs, however, he developed vocal lines, harmonic effects, and piano accompaniments that released the song form from the limitations imposed on it by the First Berlin School and moved it into areas closer to Schubert. This was an influential act, for which Reichardt receives insufficient credit. In settings like his "Rastlose Liebe," the music is beginning to perform a nearly Schubertian role:

Reichardt was most original in his "Deklamationsstücke," in which he created a declamatory musical line that did not, like most of those in his day, derive from the recitative of Italian opera, but was the result of serious preoccupation with the problem of word-tone combination and the adjustment of musical speech to the patterns of the German language. The best example, and one of his most lasting achievements, is his "Prometheus," which bears comparison with both Schubert's and Wolf's settings:

Kräftig deklamiert

Hast du nicht al - les selbst voll - en-det, hei-lig glü - hend

Herz? Und glühtest jung und gut, — be - tro - gen, Rettungsdank dem

Schla - fen-den da dro - ben?

Reichardt became a close friend of Klopstock and composed music to some of his odes, though he withheld the compositions from publication and they have unfortunately been lost. One day Reichardt heard the poet's wife sing Gluck's setting of "Willkommen, o silberner Mond," was dissatisfied with it, and returned later with his own setting, which soon became the poet's favorite.

That Reichardt was sensitive to lyric values and seriously concerned with the role of the poetic text in his songs is eloquently expressed in his comment:

I have noticed that, no matter how attractively my songs were performed, the singer almost never quite sang them correctly. When I investigated, I found that all those who failed to do so had first played the notes as a melodious instrumental piece and only later coupled the words to them. This is the exact reverse of the way I composed them! My melodies take shape automatically in every case from repeated reading of the poem without my having to search for them. And the only thing else that I do is this: I repeat them with slight changes, and do not write them down until I feel that the grammatical, logical, emotional, and musical accents are so closely interwoven that the melody speaks properly and sings pleasantly, and not just for one stanza, but for all of them. If the singer is to feel this when he performs them, he must first read the words in their entirety and keep reading them until he feels that he can read them with the correct expression. Only then should he sing them.[7]

When Goethe's celebrated *Wilhelm Meisters Lehrjahre* first appeared in 1795, it contained melodies by Reichardt to eight of the lyrics embedded in the work. These were printed on special oversized paper, which was folded into the edition at the appropriate place in the text.[8] Reichardt was thus the first of many musicians to try his hand at providing musical settings for these poems. Willi Schuh's *Goethe-Vertonungen: Ein Verzeichnis* lists no less than eighty-four settings of "Kennst du das Land;" fifty-six of "Nur wer die Sehnsucht kennt;" forty of "Wer nie sein Brot mit Tränen ass." All the other lyrics have fifteen settings or more.[9] Together they present a challenge that has often been too much for even the best of composers.

The songs in *Wilhelm Meister* are an integral part of the novel. They are actually sung, not recited, by the chief characters, under circumstances and in situations that are precisely, sometimes elaborately, described. Author and composer were in complete agreement that the melodies provided were to be suited to the characters and the situations.[10]

For example, the novel tells that "Nur wer die Sehnsucht kennt" was performed as a duet by Mignon and the harpist, and Reichardt's setting is a duet. It is, in fact, the only duet among the important settings of this poem, with the exception of one of Schubert's lesser known settings. All the others are solos for Mignon. For another, at his first appearance in the novel, the harpist sings a number of pieces to entertain Wilhelm's group. Goethe first presents him as performing two songs, although the texts are not given. Everyone is impressed and delighted, Wilhelm most of all. Then he sings the ballad "Was hör' ich draussen vor dem Tor" in six identical stanzas, the complete text of which is given in the novel. "When the singer, after finishing the song, took up a glass of wine that had been poured for him and drank it, turning with a friendly gesture to his benefactors, there was general delight in the group. They applauded and wished him good health from the wine and strength to his old limbs. He sang a few more ballads to the ever-increasing joy of the listeners." Reichardt's simple setting of the ballad, a strophic melody to be repeated for each of the six stanzas, complements both poem and situation excellently:

Lebhaft doch nicht zu geschwinde

Later composers were lured into a very different kind of treatment.

Most of Reichardt's *Wilhelm Meister* songs are not particularly distinguished or imaginative, by no means representing his best work. But at least they provide a musical supplement fully in accord with the situation and growing out of the circumstances in which the songs are presumably performed in the novel. In a few instances they are of much more than routine interest. His version of "Wer nie sein Brot mit Tränen ass" is perhaps the only one among the forty or more settings, including those by Schubert, Schumann, and Wolf, which extends the real mood of the poem into the music:

Wer nie sein Brot mit Trä-nen ass, wer nie die
Ihr führt ins Le-ben uns hin-ein, ihr lasst den

kum-mer-vol-len Näch-te auf sei-nem Bet-te wei-nend
Ar-men schul-dig wer-den,dann u-ber-lasst ihr ihn der

sass, der kennt euch nicht, ihr himm-li-schen Mäch-te.
Pein, denn al-le Schuld rächt sich auf Er-den.

The directions to the singer are "In sich verloren klagend," which the melodic line does indeed express. The descriptive words of the poem are reinforced in a variety of ways. A few examples are: the intensification of "Tränen" by a rise in pitch; the expressive convolutions of the melody at "kummervollen" supported by a diminished seventh chord; the steady descent of the melody to "auf seinem Bette weinend sass"; and the sturdy assurance expressed by the decisiveness of the rhythm and melody of the last line. The musical declamation does not always coincide with the word accent, as on "kummer*voll*en," "auf *sein*em Bette." This is quite common in eighteenth century song and is by no means as noticeable a factor as it becomes with the richer and fuller settings of the nineteenth century.

The setting of "Nur wer die Sehnsucht kennt" for duet that appeared with the novel is undistinguished, but for his later collection of songs Reichardt composed another setting, this one for solo, which is his greatest accomplishment among the *Wilhelm Meister* songs. There are some awkward spots, the worst being a full stop cadence at the end of the line "Seh ich ans Firmament/ Nach jener Seite," followed by a half-note rest, which brings the song to an abrupt halt at a point that should rather be joined to the next idea, "Ach, der mich liebt und kennt." However, from then on the song builds to a masterly climax on the word "Sehnsucht" in the final line:

This song achieves an expressiveness not usually associated with the pre-Schubertian era, and indicates that one needs to be careful about accepting the derogatory stereotypes so often attached to the eighteenth century style of song writing. The abrupt modulation from D minor to E-flat major for the words "Es schwindelt mir" is a striking parallel to the intensification in the text. The melodic line rises impressively through this phrase by sustained half-notes to reach the high E-flat at the beginning of the still more expressive "es brennt mein Eingeweide." Note the intensifying effect of the repeated and surely heavily stressed high E-flat notes, and the strongly chromatic quality of this phrase, ending with the somewhat sinuous C-sharp. This important C-sharp does several things at once: it holds the expressive level of the phrase high at the very spot where it might be expected to fall off; it provides a firm bridge leading to the musical and poetic climax in the final phrase; and it highlights the leading tone of the necessary modulation back into D minor. The accompaniment, which up to the beginning of this segment of the song had been relatively bland, changes at "Es schwindelt mir" to a steady succession of insistent quarter-note chords on each beat through five full measures. This treatment adds to the accumulation of tension. For the final climactic phrase, Reichardt reserves a downward-sweeping melodic line with another chromatic C-sharp at the climax on "Sehnsucht," and an electrifying change in the accompaniment from quarter-note chords to open octaves in both hands in unison with the melody.

Although Reichardt's setting of "Heiss mich nicht reden" is not distinguished, it provides another example to counteract the eighteenth century stereotype. It is through-composed, with each of the three stanzas set off from the others as a distinct subdivision, with totally different melodic lines, accompanying figures, and even a change of key. The first stanza is in A-flat major; the second in C minor; and the third in its relative major E-flat. Although this was, for its time, a drastic solution to the problem inherent in the poem, a glance at the words shows why a strophic repetition of the same melody and accompaniment for each stanza could hardly be satisfactory:

Heiss mich nicht reden, heiss mich schweigen,
Denn mein Geheimnis ist mir Pflicht;
Ich möchte dir mein ganzes Innre zeigen,
Allein das Schicksal will es nicht.

Zur rechten Zeit vertreibt der Sonne Lauf
Die finstre Nacht, und sie muss sich erhellen;
Der harte Fels schliesst seinen Busen auf,
Missgönnt der Erde nicht die tiefverborgnen Quellen.

Ein jeder sucht im Arm des Freundes Ruh,
Dort kann die Brust in Klagen sich ergiessen;
Allein ein Schwur drückt mir die Lippen zu,
Und nur ein Gott vermag sie aufzuschliessen.

Although this lyric, like other *Wilhelm Meister* poems, presents problems none of its composers can be said to have entirely overcome, Reichardt shows he was well aware of the difficulties. He provides a succession of explicit guides to expression, which bear out his intention of getting from the performers the differentiation and progression of moods he had tried to build into his through-composed song. The directions read, "langsam and zärtlich," "ernst und mit zunehmender Lebhaftigkeit," "leise, tief gerührt, nach und nach angehalten," "mit zunehmender Stärke," and "immer stärker und lebhafter."

Only three major composers have been attracted to Philine's charming and somewhat racy "Singet nicht in Trauertönen." Reichardt's melody and simple accompaniment has charm and an airy quality that carries the words lightly and easily:

Sin - get nicht   in Trau - er - tö - - nen   von der

Karl Friedrich Zelter

Karl Friedrich Zelter (1758–1832), master mason, choral director, and leader of musical life in Berlin in the late years of the eighteenth and early nineteenth centuries, wrote close to four hundred songs (about two hundred of which were published), even though he had not turned to song composing until he was thirty-eight. There are seventy-five songs to lyrics of Goethe, with whom he formed an enduring friendship and maintained a voluminous correspondence. Goethe's letters give ample evidence of the poet's high regard for Zelter's compositions. On May 11, 1820, he wrote: "I feel that your compositions are identical with my poems: the music simply takes the poem aloft, as gas does a balloon. With other composers I must first determine how they have understood the poem, and what they have made out of it."[11]

Even more detailed is the following statement by Goethe from a letter of May 2, 1820: "The purest and most exalted painting in music is that which you accomplish; the important thing is to put the listener into the mood that the poem establishes; the imagination can then conjure up the figures according to the text, without really being aware of how it does it . . . To paint tones by tones: to thunder, to crash, to splash, to smack is detestable."[12] This is not generalized praise, but a precise analytical characterization. The poet argues that Zelter's settings help the listener to understand the essential spirit of the poem.   In a letter to August Wilhelm Schlegel, Goethe calls Zelter's songs a "total reproduction of the poetic intentions." Nor was Goethe alone among poets in his praise of Zelter. Schiller, Klopstock, Tieck, and Voss, among numerous others, had words of approval for his settings of their poems.

Most of Zelter's own public and private statements brand him an arch-conservative, though in his compositions he was often enough the reverse. Nevertheless, he took pride in being the head of the dominant conservative Berlin group and was impelled to resist the innovations of the newer generation, sometimes with humor, sometimes with vitriol. When the admiring young Hector Berlioz sent Goethe his *Eight Songs from Faust*, the poet sent them on to Zelter for his reaction. Zelter sent the following reply:

> Certain people can show their presence of mind and their interest only by coughing, snorting, croaking and spitting. Mr. Hector Berlioz seems to be one of these. The sulphurous smell of Mephisto attracts him and so he has to sneeze and spit like a cat, so that all the instruments in the orchestra get into action and haunt us—only he never comes near Faust. Thank you for sending them to me. Perhaps in a lecture I will be able to make use of an abcess, a monstrous birth which is the result of ghastly incest.[13]

Eckermann has recorded Zelter as saying: "When I decide to compose a poem, I try first of all to penetrate to the meaning and realize the situations depicted as vividly as possible. I read it aloud until I have it by heart, and then while I keep reciting it the melody comes of its own accord."[14]   The humility before the poet that these words imply is not at all typical of Zelter's peppery temperament. More characteristic is his testy reaction to an objection raised by Voss against a word change he made in one of Voss's poems: "What do I care about the poet! His word is a stone which he has thrown and I have picked up. How I pick it up, and how I regard it and interpret it is *my* business."[15]

Zelter's "An den Mond," analyzed earlier, is fully in the eighteenth century tradition. However, for a man who underrated Berlioz so abysmally, his songs contain occasional surprises. His setting of Goethe's "Rastlose Liebe," for example, is robust and daring in its vocal line, has an elaborate accompaniment with an eight-measure introduction, and is through-composed. This is an impressive accomplishment, even though the witty composer expressed doubts to Goethe "whether a man fifty-four years old can still portray restless love":[16]

Gertraud Wittmann has counted 178 strophic, 20 varied strophic, and 16 through-composed songs in Zelter's output. The strophic songs reflect most fully the eighteenth century tradition, but even in these Zelter was capable of striking effects. A magnificent example of the kind of balance between word and tone that was sought in the eighteenth century and forgotten in the nineteenth is his celebrated modal setting of Goethe's "König in Thule":

Grab,   dem ster - bend sei - ne Buh - le   ei - nen
Schmaus,   die Au - gen gin - gen ihm ü - ber, so
Reich,   gönnt' al - les sei - nen Er - ben, den

gold - nen Be - cher gab.
oft   er   trank da - raus.
Be - cher nicht zu - gleich.

The poem occurs in *Faust*. It is sung by Gretchen in her room as
she prepares for bed, on the same night that Faust had accosted
her on the street. Moments before, Faust and Mephistopheles
were in the room in her absence, and although she does not know
this, her intuition warns her that all is not as it should be.
Frightened by something inexplicable to her, she sings this song
to bolster her courage while she undresses. It is a folk song she has
long known and often sung, which she sings negligently and somewhat mechanically. In one sense it is not related to the action, but
in a deeper, vaguer sense her choice of a song about faithfulness
till death shows her preoccupation with the handsome stranger.

In Zelter's setting, there is an archaic quality to the melody,
which parallels the legendary vein in the text.[17] The general
atmosphere of the song is both simple and somber, in perfect
accord with Gretchen's mood of apprehension and underscoring

the ominous implications of this critical point in the drama. Zelter's melody, unaccompanied, has become the standard one for use in performances of *Faust*, and rightly so. The interesting fact that Zelter's bass line doubles the melody indicates the possibility that he planned the song to be performed as an unaccompanied solo line. Surely this setting is a "radical reproduction of the poetic intention."

Zelter was readily inspired by *Wilhelm Meister* and set five of the poems in the very year that the novel appeared (1795). He was thirty-nine at the time and had only begun song composing the year before. The pieces appeared in 1796 in his first collection of songs, *Zwölf Lieder am Clavier zu singen componiert von Karl Friedrich Zelter*. The composer, who was not yet acquainted with Goethe, sent two copies of this publication to the wife of Friedrich Unger, the publisher of *Wilhelm Meister*, with the request that she send one on "to the most excellent writer of *Wilhelm Meister*." "I would like my songs," his letter continues, "to be not as unfamiliar to him as my name must be. I have not composed his verse superficially . . . Herr von Goethe will know best whether I have caught the sense of them." The sequel provides a splendid insight into the relationship between poet and composer in the pre-Schubertian era. After the songs reached Goethe, he replied to Frau Unger not only that he was delighted with them, but that he had already been attracted to Zelter's setting of a poem, "Ich denke dein" by Friederike Brun, which had appeared a year before in a collection edited by Reichardt, *Vierter musikalischer Blumenstrauss: Musikalische Blumenlese für das Jahr 1795*. In fact, Zelter's melody had already inspired Goethe to write his own "Ich denke dein" to fit the tune. The poem was published in Schiller's *Musenalmanach* for 1796 under the title "Nähe des Geliebten." Twelve years later, Zelter composed a setting for duet of this poem as well.

Ultimately Zelter composed all but two of the *Wilhelm Meister* songs. Of "Kennst du das Land" he wrote no less than six versions, the first in 1795, the last in 1818. "Wer sich der Einsamkeit ergibt," one of the first composed, is the only one with exceptional qualities. The song begins with an arresting rising sequence of four notes sung without accompaniment. When the piano enters, it provides an imitative contrapuntal line quite different from the simple harmonic accompaniment usual at the time. With its slow pace, the song, in B minor, thus begins on a note of tension. The strain is heightened in the second phrase by a tortuous melodic line, expressing not what is said, "Ein jeder liebt, ein jeder liebt," but the awful loneliness of the man who says it. This leads to a climax in a high register on "lässt ihn seiner Pein":

The isolation and lengthening of the "Ja!" that follows, reinforced by the dynamic mark $<>$, is a stunning preview of the grim resolution expressed in the next line. The rest of the song sustains this intensity and closes impressively with a downward-sweeping melody and an expressive trill on the cadence:

It is perhaps difficult to plead for Zelter's and Reichardt's songs in the light of the hundreds of Romantic lieder that have superseded them in the modern taste. Nevertheless, in the total output of all the song writers of the eighteenth and nineteenth centuries, the compositions of these two men represent, as a consistent accomplishment, a more ideal blending of text and music than was achieved by any other composer before or since. If one is careful to distinguish between "successful songs," that is, songs the recital public likes to hear, and songs which are a balanced combination of poem and music, there is little question that more of the latter were produced by Reichardt and Zelter than by anyone else. Though the purely musical interest of their songs is much less, the fact that they are literally never performed is a real loss, at least to that part of the musical public which is most aware of poetic values.

Haydn and Mozart

Haydn (1732–1809) wrote about forty songs; the number is uncertain, because the authenticity of some is doubtful. The interest and quality of the music is varied, but the quality of the verse he used is uniformly low. The one exception is "She never told her love," Viola's poignant lines from *Twelfth Night*. But Haydn's setting of this lyric shows no glimmer of understanding of what the words are about. The composer tried to make something dramatic out of what is the essence of pure lyricism.[18]

Mozart (1756–1791) is the only eighteenth century composer whose songs are performed much in recitals today. Most of the texts of his songs are puerile. His choice of Goethe's "Veilchen" for his most celebrated song is the one exception. Though the song is eminently enjoyable, its faithfulness as a setting for Goethe's poem is another matter. The poem, from the Singspiel *Erwin und Elmire*, is a charming ballad in fragile rococo style. Its sad tale, if slight, is nonetheless seriously conveyed, and not a small part of the effect of the poem is derived from the elegance and grace with which the tiny tragedy unfolds. It consists of three six-line strophes.

Mozart set it as a miniature aria, through-composed. Each detail of the narrative is pictorialized in the musical line and accompaniment. These pictorializations contribute greatly to the charm of the work: the grace notes on "gebückt in sich"; the strongly diatonic line of "Es war ein herzig's Veilchen"; the staccato notes of "mit leichtem Schritt"; the little piano interlude after "und sang," standing for the song the carefree girl sings as she strolls along; the "longing" intervals at "ach nur"; the climax at "ertrat das arme Veilchen"; the sinking line at "es sank und starb"; the sudden quickening at "und freut sich doch," with the joyful flourish of "durch sie." At the end, Mozart adds an extra line, "Das arme Veilchen! Es war ein herzig's Veilchen," as a kind of coda, which he derives from parts of two different lines in the first strophe of the poem. All these devices remove the strophic feeling and center attention on the narrative alone. But the pictorializations in their cumulative effect add such weight and seeming earnestness to each small detail that the dramatic fate of the violet grows ludicrous. The song becomes a tongue-in-cheek parody, in spirit far from the delicate seriousness of the poem. Mozart may not have consciously intended the parodic effect, though his ironic coda, with its extra line of poetry, is a pretty good indication that the effect was deliberate. At any rate, it is impossible to perform the song without conveying a sense of parody. It clearly derives from operatic style, where pictorialization of detail was very much in the baroque-rococo tradition. It stands outside the mainstream of the art song in the later eighteenth century.

Beethoven

In the lied, as in other musical forms, Beethoven (1770–1827) is the great bridge between the eighteenth and nineteenth centuries. His songs, about sixty-seven of them, are a minor part of his total output and are, in general, not as experimental or nearly as influential as the rest of his work. Yet since in them the musician's attitude toward the poet has changed, they clearly show Beethoven taking leave of the eighteenth century and ushering in the nineteenth. Though there is good evidence that he knew quality in lyric poetry (he claimed Homer, Ossian, Klopstock, Schiller, and Goethe as his favorite poets), he was more often than not attracted to a poem because of its compatibility with his personal views and convictions. The intrinsic caliber of the verse was a secondary consideration. These ideals he then sought to express in the musical setting of the poem. Accordingly, in a number of his songs the lyric atmosphere is required to convey an ethical message.[19]   Lines like the following offer little opportunity for musical embellishment:

So jemand spricht: ich liebe Gott!
Und hasst doch seine Brüder,
Der treibt mit Gottes Wahrheit Spott
Und reisst sie ganz darnieder.
Gott ist die Lieb' and will dass ich
Den Nächsten liebe gleich als mich.

This is one of six religious poems of Christian Fürchtegott Gellert, which Beethoven set in 1803. Five of the six settings are of utmost brevity. No. 1, "Bitten" ("Gott, deine Güte reicht so weit"), contains in the lines "Herr, meine Burg, mein Fels, mein Hort,/ vernimm mein Flehn, merk auf mein Wort" a simple but powerful climax, which overshadows anything of Zelter and Reichardt and indicates the wellsprings of expressivity that are to open up in the new century:[20]

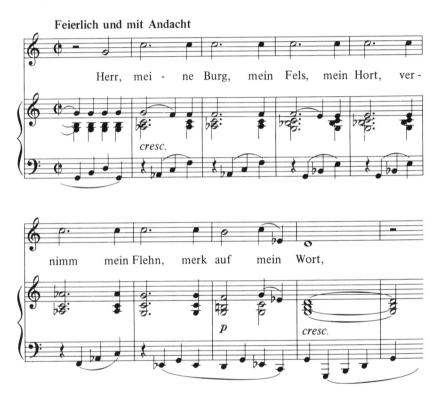

The song is in C major. The steady C in the melody of this passage seems to characterize God as the sure refuge, while the rich chordal progression through F minor to C minor, above a bass line with motivic interest, conveys the fervency of the plea to God for support. With its return to C major after the dominant on "Wort," the melodic line that closes the song is remarkably evocative of the prayerful piety contained in the verse:

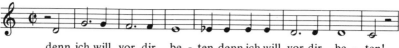

denn ich will vor dir be - ten, denn ich will vor dir be - ten!

No. 2, "So jemand spricht," set to the words quoted above, is not surprisingly the weakest of the six. No. 3, "Vom Tode," in contrast, is an intense song, foreshadowing in one passage the tone color and intensity of Brahms's "Vier ernste Gesänge":

Nos. 2 and 3 are provided with *dal segno* signs, which seem to indicate the composer's willingness to have them sung to successive stanzas of the respective poems. This is never done, and should not be. As the musical examples make clear, in every case except No. 6 Beethoven set to music only the first stanza of Gellert's poems, which run to as many as fifteen stanzas. The individuality and forcefulness with which the music expresses the import of those words is so great that to repeat the music for additional stanzas would be a mistake. The songs are in truth not strophic. Each is a complete miniature, whose unity would be destroyed by repetition.[21]

No. 4 is the well-known "Die Ehre Gottes aus der Natur" ("Die Himmel rühmen die Ehre Gottes"), a somewhat stiff, cantatalike treatment, which is actually more satisfactory as an anthem for four-part chorus with organ accompaniment, as it is often performed in church services, than as a solo. No. 5, "Gottes Macht und Vorsehung," is the briefest of these songs, eighteen measures in total length, and the most powerful. The simple text offered Beethoven a splendid opportunity:

Gott ist mein Lied!
Er ist der Gott der Stärke;
Hehr ist sein Nam', und gross sind seine Werke,
Und alle Himmel sein Gebiet.

Sung according to the marking "mit Kraft und Feuer," the
vigorous melody provides a magnificent musical counterpart to
the words:

Gellert's poem goes on for fourteen additional stanzas. It is
unthinkable, however, that the song should be one note longer.
The last song, "Busslied," has a totally different character.
Beethoven through-composed all seven stanzas of this Gellert
poem to create a kind of aria, which provides an uncharacteristic
close to the series.

Beethoven set nine poems of Goethe to music, among which
are the finest examples of his more lyric vein. Three of them in
particular are brilliant syntheses: "Mit einem gemalten Band,"
"Neue Liebe, neues Leben," and "Mailied." The dazzling rococo
musical setting of Goethe's equally rococo poem "Mit einem
gemalten Band" is a perfect musical complement to the slight but
elegant verses. Here, in fact, rather than in Mozart's "Veilchen,"
is the ultimate synthesis of rococo verse and rococo music.

The song "Neue Liebe, neues Leben" ("Herz, mein Herz, was
soll das geben?") is a daring and isolated experiment in song
structure. Ernst Bücken has shown that the music is in sonata
form. The main theme, in A major, is stated in the vocal line to

the first seven verses. The last verse of the first stanza provides a modulation to the key of the dominant E major, and the second theme is then stated with the first four lines of the second stanza. To the remainder of this stanza is set a third theme, also of course in E major. On a repetition of the first line of the poem, there is a delightful brief development section of only five measures, leading into a complete recapitulation of music and words of both stanzas, this time entirely in A major. A coda provides the musical material for the entire third stanza. The piano provides for the most part only rhythmic accompanying figures and harmonic support. All the thematic material is in the vocal line. Under the circumstances, one would scarcely expect a close rapport between word and tone, but the remarkable fact is that in a very real sense they are in accord. The swiftness, exuberance, vitality, and directness of the music is in the words too, and Beethoven follows extremely well the nuances of the verse. There is a certain rigidity of rhythm occasioned by the formal musical patterns, but this is not disturbing in view of the surprising identity of verse and music.

Perhaps the finest fusion of poem and music is his setting of Goethe's "Mailied" ("Wie herrlich leuchtet/Mir die Natur"), a poem which, in its concentrated energy and enthusiasm, had eluded the best efforts of many eighteenth century composers, including Reichardt and Zelter. The declamation in Beethoven's setting is not faultless, but the melodic line is magnificently constructed so as to permit the words to get across effortlessly and to support the many emphases in the poem. There is a joyful buoyant quality to the vocal line of the first words. This is followed by an ascending line on "Wie glänzt die Sonne,/Wie lacht die Flur," with the climax on "lacht" in both poem and setting. There is added melodic emphasis on the next line, "Es dringen Blüten /Aus jedem Zweig":[22]

Es   drin - gen   Blü - ten aus   je - dem   Zweig __

The final phrase of the musical line, to the words "O Erd, O Sonne!/ O Glück, O Lust!" readily divides up into four brief subdivisions, at the same time combining these into a unit, as does the poem. Beethoven joins three of Goethe's brief stanzas into a single unit, but the subdivisions convey the strophic feeling of the poem admirably, particularly in view of the fact that the second and third subdivisions are identical except for the cadence. At the end of the song there is a codalike extension set to a threefold repetition of the closing words, "Sei ewig glücklich,/ Wie du mich liebst," providing a final exuberant flourish for this fresh, breezy song.

Beethoven composed two *Wilhelm Meister* songs, "Nur wer die Sehnsucht kennt" in 1808, and "Kennst du das Land" two years later. For the former he wrote no fewer than four separate settings and published them together as *Die Sehnsucht von Goethe mit vier Melodien nebst Klavierbegleitung* in 1810. This was an unusual move, and Beethoven's intention in doing so is somewhat obscure. Ernst Bücken and others claim that the four settings show that Beethoven "struggled with this text . . . and clearly in order to achieve a melodic figuration in which to the maximum degree each word got the emphasis he thought proper."[23] But a close analysis of the four versions does not reveal much of a "struggle." The settings are not particularly noteworthy. They are all extreme- ly simple and brief, strongly in the eighteenth century tradition. The first three even treat the poem as though it were in two four- line stanzas, so that in each case the entire brief song is repeated. The fourth is through-composed, with more of the Beethoven characteristics in evidence, but still on a very modest scale indeed. It is startling to reflect that 1808 was the year of the *Pastoral* Symphony, two years after the *Leonore* Overture no. 3, one year before the E-flat String Quartet op. 74. Clearly Beethoven was not the great innovator in song that he was in virtually all other musical forms.

His "Kennst du das Land" is a quite different matter. Schumann is on record as having said, "Except for Beethoven's composition, I do not know a single one which achieves an effect in any way comparable to that of the poem without music."[24] This was in 1836, thirteen years before his own setting, but the comment can still be defended today, after Schumann, Hugo Wolf, and a host of lesser composers have tried their hand at the verse. Goethe himself, however, was displeased with Beethoven's setting. "I cannot understand," Wenzel Tomaschek, the Czech composer, quotes him as saying in 1822, "how Beethoven and Spohr so thoroughly misunderstood the poem as to through-compose it. I should have thought that the divisions occurring in each stanza at the same spot would be sufficient to show the composer that I expected a simple song from him. Mignon is a person who can sing a song, but not an aria."[25] If he really did think this about Beethoven's song, one can well imagine how much Schubert's, Schumann's, and Wolf's settings would have displeased him.

Goethe's error about Beethoven's composition, which is in fact not through-composed but strophic, signals an important shift in balance between word and tone in the lied, which was an inevitable result of the far-reaching changes in the nature of music occurring at the beginning of the nineteenth century, largely through the influence of Beethoven himself. His "Kennst du das Land" is transitional: its ties with what preceded are still clear, but equally prominent is the move toward musical richness, which became the accepted norm from Schubert on.

A close examination of the melodic line to the first four verses in each of the three strophes of the poem reveals little that could set off this song in any significant way from the normal practice in the eighteenth century:

still	und	hoch	der	Lor -	- beer__	steht?
dir,	du	ar -	mes	Kind_____	ge -	tan?
Fels	und	ü -	ber	ihn _____	die __	Flut.

The melody follows the sense of the first two verses very closely indeed. There is a strong parallelism in the opening line of each strophe of the poem, with identical initial words and a distinct pause after the fourth word in each instance. This is not true of the respective second lines, and though here Beethoven repeats essentially the melody he had used for the first line, he accommodates it to the different sentence structure by an ingenious foreshortening, so that its duration is only three measures instead of the four required for the first line. This eliminates the pause in the middle and adds an intriguing asymmetry. There is in this succession of phrases a forcefulness and dynamic quality that is typical of Beethoven. In the build-up to a climax on the D-flat in the last phrase there is a tendency for the music to dominate the words. Yet similar instances can readily be found in eighteenth century songs. Nor is there much in the piano accompaniment that differs from earlier practice (with the exception of the accompaniment to lines three and four of the third strophe, of which more later). The top line of the accompaniment doubles the vocal melody, as in many songs of the eighteenth century. The chords that fill in beneath this are standard. Beethoven increased the movement in the second half by breaking up the intervals of the chords into triplet figures. The lowered third (A-flat) in the melody at the beginning of this section alters the key from major to minor, and at the beginning of the final line a lowered third of the dominant chord in the accompaniment introduces a modulation to A-flat. Equally striking modulation was used by Reichardt.

It is in what follows that the new era of nineteenth century song is heralded. The piano accompaniment prepares for the change in a way that would not have been found in the preceding century. In the last line preceding the refrain, there is a dynamic build-up in the accompaniment. To the triplet figure and the modulation is added a decided crescendo, which reaches a fortissimo on "Lorbeer."

From here on Beethoven's song departs markedly from eighteenth century practice. A two-measure interlude for piano alone follows, which in effect keeps the tension high while modulating back to F minor, and in its contour strikingly anticipates the melodic line of the following "Kennst du es wohl?" The rising pitch on this question and a fermata on the last word create the effect of being poised for a fresh start. And the listener is not disappointed, for with a change to 6/8 and an abrupt tempo increase Beethoven literally sails into his "Dahin, dahin" refrain:

The end of the stanza has been reached at this point, but the musical fervor of the passage is so great that it demands continuation and elaboration. The composer uses the whole last line over again to complete the section. Once again he foreshortens the repetition, this time from six to five measures. Given the swifter 6/8 rhythm and the power that has accumulated, this foreshortening increases the sense of breathlessness, and indisputably results in a musically dominated word-tone relationship. With the repetition, a satisfactory end point has been reached. Two more "dahin's," separated by brief piano phrases, cool off the superheated atmosphere and provide a satisfying transition back to a suitable mood for the start of the next stanza.

Two additional features shift the balance even more toward the music. A favorite device Beethoven used throughout his music is the off-beat accent. In the 6/8 passage of this song he marks the dynamic accent > four times in the accompaniment on the third or sixth beat, the weakest in the 6/8 measure. This is a purely instrumental effect, not evoked by the text.

In the third stanza, Beethoven was moved by the powerful words:

In Höhlen wohnt der Drachen alte Brut,
Es stürzt der Fels und über ihn die Flut.

to thicken the texture of the accompaniment markedly, so that
this third and last repetition moves to a dynamic climax more
powerful than any that have preceded. Here the impetus for the
increased dynamics comes clearly from the words, but the musical
power has been so augmented that the balance shifts markedly
away from the lyrics. Of this Goethe must surely have dis-
approved.[26]

Beethoven's most celebrated and significant innovation in song
form is his cycle of six songs, "An die ferne Geliebte," the first
song cycle in musical history. But the poems are markedly
inferior to the music. The greatness of the song cycle is strictly a
musical achievement.

Though Beethoven's songs clearly represent a break with the
past, their individuality is so powerful as to separate them as much
from Schubert and his successors as from Zelter and his predecessors. There is a self-energizing quality in the melodic lines which
often gives the impression of spontaneous generation; whereas the
spirit of the poem provided the inspiration, the actual text was
not decisive. Beethoven's contributions to the literature of song
are greatest in those few instances where this quality is combined
with a sensitive interpretation of a fine poem.

Chapter *III* Franz Schubert

In the development of song, Schubert (1797–1828) is a classic case of the right man appearing at the right time. It is worth a moment to speculate on what might have happened had there been no Schubert. Before him, no major composer—Bach, Handel, Gluck, Haydn, Mozart, Beethoven—had been particularly serious about the form. No more than a handful of notable songs were in existence, though there were thousands of undistinguished ones, and hundreds of song composers. It was Schubert who elevated the song to a major form for the first time in musical history. His principal successors—Schumann, Brahms, and Wolf—were none of them innovators, but merely carried on the form. All the Spohrs, Mendelssohns, Franzes, Loewes, Corneliuses, or Jensens of the early nineteenth century could not have given to song the stature and prestige that Schubert imparted to it.

In his pitifully short life, spanning only thirty-one years, Schubert composed nearly six hundred songs, more than half, unfortunately, to inferior poems by third- and fourth-rate poets. Still, there are an impressive number set to fine poetry in Schubert's considerable oeuvre. Two hundred and fifty-one of his songs, excluding the multiple settings of some poems, were distributed as follows among the leading poets:[1]

66—Johann Wolfgang von Goethe
45—Wilhelm Müller
41—Friedrich Schiller
23—Ludwig Hölty
16—Friedrich Schlegel
13—Friedrich Klopstock
12—Matthias Claudius
10—August Wilhelm Schlegel
 6—Heinrich Heine
 6—Novalis
 5—Friedrich Rückert
 4—Daniel Schubart

2—August von Platen
1—Ludwig Uhland
1—Franz Grillparzer

Of course, not all of these two hundred and fifty-one poems are great, or even good. The poets do, however, represent the mainstream of German lyrics, and from this group come the highest quality word-tone compositions of Schubert.

Friedrich Schiller

Schubert's enthusiasm for Schiller (1759—1805) appeared early. More than two-thirds of his forty-one Schiller settings were written before he was twenty, eight of them before he had turned eighteen. His first song-writing tended toward massive through-composed settings of long ballads, very much in the style of Johann Zumsteeg (1760—1802), a highly regarded composer of ballads and other songs, the most celebrated of which was a through-composed setting of Gottfried Bürger's "Lenore," consisting of thirty-two eight-line stanzas! Schiller's "Bürgschaft," twenty stanzas, and his "Taucher," twenty-seven stanzas, are among Schubert's longest settings. Though it is hazardous to generalize about the kinds of poem suitable for musical setting, since so much depends on the originality and ingenuity of the composer in the individual instance, it seems safe to say that poems this long cannot be made into satisfactory lieder. The song becomes endless. In the early through-composed Schubert ballads, his tendency to pictorialize musically any and all dramatic elements emphasizes these individual features to a degree that becomes ludicrous. This is especially true of the Schiller ballads, because in many of them the melodrama and pathos approach the borderline of good taste. When the musical setting adds—as in Schubert's "Bürgschaft" —such descriptive devices as the interlude of wedding music when Damon is hurrying home to see his sister married; the musical depiction of the storm that delays his return; the raging river; the band of thieves; his terrible thirst, followed by the sudden appearance in the accompaniment of the rippling sound effect of water when he discovers the spring; and the exceedingly dramatic last-minute-rescue music—it drags a poem which has real aesthetic merit down into a morass of bathos. Fortunately, Schubert composed only a few Schiller ballads, though there are a good number of ballads by other writers. Johann Mayrhofer's "Einsamkeit," for example, a third-rate poem to begin with, becomes a fourth-rate song (14 pages long in the vocal score); and Schubert's popular setting of "Der Wanderer" by Schmidt von Lübeck is a cheap musicalization of a cheap poem.

If the early through-composed ballads are among Schubert's least happy word-tone combinations, his slightly later through-composed setting of Schiller's "Gruppe aus dem Tartarus" (1817) is one of his triumphs. This brilliant song transmits the high pathos of Schiller's poem faultlessly, and heightens the dramatic effect in ways that are possible only through music. The slow-moving chromatic ascent to the words "stöhnt dort dumpfig-tief," with the tortured climax on "qualerpresstes Ach," over dark hollow-sounding tremolo chords in the accompaniment, is frightening in its impact:

In similar fashion detail after detail in the poem is enhanced. The climax of Schiller's dramatic portrait of the anguish of the damned in hell is reached when the tormented souls express their desperate hope for the Last Judgment in the lines:

Fragen sich einander ängstlich leise,
Ob noch nicht Vollendung sei.

With a sure musical instinct Schubert expands this by repetition, so that the words of the song become:

Fragen sich einander ängstlich leise, ob noch nicht Vollendung sei,
fragen sich einander ängstlich leise, ob noch nicht Vollendung sei,
ob noch nicht Vollendung sei, ob noch nicht Vollendung sei.

Each phrase is set dramatically on a repetition of a single tone in a low register, with the successive phrases rising a half or whole step (middle C-sharp to G). This is an excellent example in which repetition, often detrimental to the poetic values, or at best a device to be tolerated because the composer needs it to work out his musical patterns, actually enhances the effect of the poem.[2]

After an extreme of tension has been built up in this way, the broadly diatonic "Ewigkeit" which follows (C major in the original) with thrilling arpeggios high in the piano is an electrifying contrast to the earlier chromaticism. This fusion of word and tone directly foreshadows the art syntheses of Richard Wagner and shows what heights can be reached by a work whose music has captured the essence, the spirit, and all the nuances of a fine poem.

Schiller wrote a companion piece, "Das Elysium," which Schubert composed along with "Gruppe aus dem Tartarus." Though there are wonderful touches to it, the second song does not sustain itself with anything near the concentration of the first. Hell lends itself to vivid pictorialization more readily than paradise, as the Divine Comedy shows.

Both Schiller and Schubert later had another try at depicting paradise, in "Sehnsucht," a fine poem from Schiller's maturity. Schubert composed it in 1819. The song, despite effective passages, does not reach the stature of the poem, chiefly because it is fragmented by naive pictorializations of individual details.

Among Schubert's Schiller songs are also a number of strophic and varied strophic settings, of which the finest are "Die Hoffnung" and "An den Frühling," two simple poems in straightforward settings. Especially pleasing in "Die Hoffnung" is the musical lift in the last line of each stanza, at the words "immer Verbesserung," "pflanzt er die Hoffnung," and "hoffende Seele":

A late varied strophic setting of "Der Pilgrim" (1823), one of the last Schiller songs of Schubert, beautifully portrays the spirit of optimism · expressed in the early stanzas of the poem. Here Schubert was not lured by words like "Berge," "Ströme," "Schlünde," and "wilden Fluss" into clichés of musical pictorialization that would have broken the prevailing mood, as he was inclined to do earlier. Werner Jelinek has shown that Schubert's development led him "in the course of his song composing from the representation of events to the portrayal of the purely spiritual, the abstract."[3] This setting is an admirable example of the spiritual, though it is slightly marred at the end by a somewhat heavily dramatic reversal into a pathetic mood at "Ach, kein Weg will dahin führen" and a fourfold repetition of the final phrase, "ist niemals hier."

One of Schubert's most delightful songs, unjustly neglected, is his gay strophic setting of Schiller's joyous "Dithyrambe" ("Nimmer, das glaubt mir, erscheinen die Götter, nimmer allein"; 1823). The poem is in full dactyls, and Schubert's melody in 6/8 is just right for them:

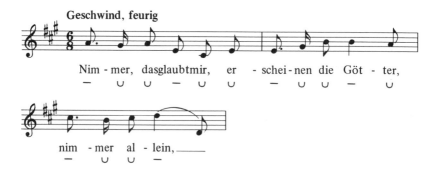

The last two lines of each of the three stanzas begin with an upbeat, and actually consist of amphibrachs (∪–∪) rather than dactyls (Sie nāhen, sie kōmmen, die Hīmmlischen ālle). This difference is charmingly paralleled in Schubert's setting:

Goethe

The ballads of Goethe (1749–1832) are a quite different matter. Schubert's settings of some—though not all—are masterpieces. For instance, the through-composed "Der Sänger" from *Wilhelm Meister* rambles. Against this can be set his through-composed "Erlkönig," a song with unprecedented power and force. The heavily dramatic interpretation, highly realistic in its rendering of the voices of the three persons (the child, the father, and the erlking) and the pounding of the horse's hooves, is overwhelmingly convincing. Even the listener with an eye for the poem is inclined to forgive Schubert for having through-composed a ballad that is in the simplest of folk song strophes:

Wer reitet so spät durch Nacht und Wind?
Es ist der Vater mit seinem Kind.
Er hat den Knaben wohl in dem Arm,
Er fasst ihn sicher, er hält ihn warm.

because the tense drama in the music appears in the poem as well, and Schubert's setting exploits it to the utmost.[4]

It is a fact that the Schubert setting was puzzling to Goethe, and this has often prompted unkind remarks about the poet's musical discrimination. His reaction is not surprising, however, in view of the way he himself used the poem. It occurs at the opening of the Singspiel "Die Fischerin", written in the year 1782. As the curtain rises, Dortchen, the heroine, is discovered mending nets and singing. She sings the "Erlkönig" from beginning to end. When she finishes, she says, "Now I have sung practically all my songs twice through out of impatience, and it looks as though I'll have to sing them a third time." (There is a similarity here to Gretchen's song "Der König in Thule," for which Zelter's setting is so appropriate.) For this purpose the extremely simple setting composed by the actress Corona Schröter, who played Dortchen in the first performance at Weimar, is admirably suited:

One must go even farther and say that it captures the folk song spirit of the poem better than Schubert's intensely gripping rendition. Carl Loewe's version, composed three years after Schubert's but with no knowledge of it, is about midway between the two extremes of Schröter and Schubert, preserving the folk atmosphere, while bringing out the demonic and the dramatic. It deserves to be much better known.

Goethe's "Prometheus" and "Ganymed" are more difficult poems to transfer into music, and Schubert was only partially successful in attempting to do so. For these two poems in free verse the through-composed form is the inevitable choice. However, as the language of both poems is highly concentrated, it is difficult to conceive how any musical setting could preserve this important quality. Certainly the intensity is missing in Schubert's composition. I have said before that the tolerance of different poems varies greatly toward the expansion inevitable in a musical setting. These two poems have a low tolerance.

Schubert's "Prometheus" begins forcefully with recitative:

Be - dek - ke dei-nen Himmel, Zeus,— mit Wol - ken - dunst

and engenders a good deal of power during the course of the first stanza and the first two lines of the second stanza. But at this point ("Ihr nähret kümmerlich") smoother melodic patterns break the mood of scorn which has been built up in the earlier part of the song and which is an essential feature of the entire poem:

Ihr nährt küm - mer - lich von Opfer - steuern

und Gebets - hauch eure Ma - je - stät,

At "Wer half mir/Wider der Titanen Übermut" the powerful recitative lines return, but as the midpoint of the song has not yet been reached, despite individual excellences the extended musical setting drags the verses out so long that one is relieved when it is over. Though Schubert is breaking new ground in attempting to adapt his musical style to such a difficult poem in free verse, and the work shows resourcefulness, inventiveness, and courage, it is far from a compelling musical portrayal of the great lyric poem.

He has difficulties with "Ganymed," too. Here the mood is the quite different one of quiet bliss, with a gradual transition to an ecstatic expectancy as Ganymed is borne up to Father Zeus on a cloud. Schubert has understandably refrained from the dramatic recitative-like patterns that made up a major portion of "Prometheus," favoring a more sustained melodic line. After a beautiful opening, however, he soon comes upon a phrase that causes trouble:

Mit tausendfacher Liebeswonne
Sich an mein Herz drängt
Deiner ewigen Wärme heilig Gefühl.

This gorgeously balanced periodic sentence is fragmented by Schubert into four separate musical phrases, with some of the most awkward declamation to be found in any Schubert song:

The setting never recovers. It stretches out too long in the ensuing sections (which include two brief piano interludes portraying rather too realistically the morning breeze and the nightingale). The final section, which relates the ascent into the clouds, engenders some excitement, but in its total effect is a pale imitation of the magnificent impact of the verse. The climax of the poem is reached in the striking phrase "umfangend umfangen," which Schubert's setting makes little of. The repetitions of the final phrases, which the composer needed in order to build to his musical climax, lengthen the song still further. Despite some fine points, this setting is a far from successful attempt to extend into musical expression one of Goethe's greatest Sturm und Drang poems.

Some strophic settings of Goethe ballads are better. There is the irresistible "Heidenröslein," which matches the folk song quality of the Goethe poem ideally. One wishes Schubert had composed a similar setting to Goethe's "Veilchen," to compare with the operatic Mozart composition. Schubert liked to seize on dramatic elements for musical portrayal, especially in his early period, and "Heidenröslein" is an early song (1815). But with a sure artistic sense he refrained from an "epic" setting of this ballad, so that expressions like "wehrte sich und stach" and "half ihm doch kein Weh und Ach" are sung to lilting musical phrases of great charm. This is as it should be, for in the ballad the mood, the melodiousness of the rhythmic patterns and the rhyme scheme, and the colorful refrain, "Röslein, Röslein, Röslein rot,/ Röslein auf der Heiden," dominate over the narrative. Schubert's indication "lieblich" is an apt one-word description of both the poem and its musical setting, conveying their extreme simplicity.[5] The work shows what can be produced by a first-rate musical genius in the style of Zelter and Reichardt.

Schubert's setting of "Der Fischer" is another admirable fusion of word and tone. It is a strophic setting, not quite so simple and direct as "Heidenröslein," with a gently undulating accompaniment that suggests the rippling of water. The lilting melodic line intensifies modestly during the fifth and sixth verses and reaches a measured climax at exactly the point where the peak of the poetic stanza is attained ("teilt sich die Flut empor"). The final musical phrase of each strophe levels out from this high point until the unexpected heightening of interest again in the last two measures, once more exactly corresponding to the thrust of the poetic lines ("ein feuchtes Weib hervor"). The declamation is by no means faultless if judged by the kind of accentuation and stress with which the poem would have to be recited. The rhythm of the poem is in fact surprisingly intricate. Ernst Bücken[6] points out that Schubert's basic rhythm:

Das Was-ser rauscht', das Was-ser schwoll, ein Fischer sass da - ran,

is like a folk song in its alternation of strong and light accent in 2/4 time, (∪–∪–∪–∪–), whereas the unusual accentuation of the poem is the reverse: light–strong:

∪ — ∪ —   ∪ — ∪ —
Das Wasser rauscht, das Wasser schwoll.

This is indeed true for the first stanza, but by no means uniformly thereafter. For instance, the first line of the second stanza is the reverse:

∪ — ∪ — ∪ — ∪ —
Sie sang zu ihm, sie sprach zu ihm

Some lines combine the two types of stress, as in the following from the last strophe:

— ∪ ∪ — ∪ —
Netzt ihm den nackten Fuss

If Schubert had chosen a more elaborate form, as in fact Loewe did, he would have had to contend with these intricacies. But his choice of the simple strophic setting, which splendidly renders the spirit of the poem, was a master stroke. It absolved him of the necessity to treat the nuances of the rhythm, and in this way avoided a real danger. For this poem could easily have deteriorated into a parody like Mozart's "Veilchen."[7] In any case, I cannot agree with Bücken's conclusion that Schubert fails to achieve a close rapport between text and music.

Schubert's strophic treatment of "Der König in Thule" is far overshadowed by Zelter's masterful setting. However, Schubert has captured the spirit of a number of Goethe's Sturm und Drang lyrics. He conveys the breathless quality of "Rastlose Liebe" in a swiftly moving setting of great charm. This song, because it is such a perfect union of word and tone, is an admirable illustration of the difference in pace between a fast-moving poem and a song on that text. The movement in the poem is indeed breathless:

Dem Schnee, dem Regen,
Dem Wind entgegen,
Im Dampf der Klüfte
Durch Nebeldüfte,
Immerzu, immerzu,
Ohne Rast und Ruh!

The pace of the song is swift, too, but the composer, to give the music expressive scope, must adjust the speed of the poem to the quite different headlong quality of the music. The effect is so similar, however, that the listener is not in the least disturbed by the fact that the song takes over twice as long to perform as the poem would require in recitation. This natural tendency of the music to expand is best illustrated in the brilliant close of the song:

Alles vergebens!
Krone des Lebens,
Glück ohne Ruh,
Liebe bist du.

By repetitions Schubert builds to a soaring climax, which is almost as long as the entire rest of the song (44 measures as compared with 48 for all that precedes). This treatment, however, is a faithful transference into musical form of the exuberant poem. The transcendence of spirit over letter is further proved by the fact that the song is through-composed, though the most dominant characteristic of the poem is its prominent couplet rhymes. Half the accents of the poem fall on the rhymes, because the lines are so short. But Schubert retains the feeling of the short lines, so that the essential form of the poem remains, especially the prominence of the rhymes.

The vigorous "An Schwager Kronos" ("Schwager" here meaning coachman, and "Kronos" standing for Chronos, the god of time), another of the Sturm und Drang lyrics, is transferred into a boisterously compelling song with an amazingly energetic accompaniment. The free rhythms and irregular accentuation of the rhapsodic poem are this time no problem. Schubert adjusts the melodic line in every instance, so that there is never any sense of unnaturalness in the declamation. Nor does his regard for the poem's irregular rhythms prevent him from producing a melodic line that asserts itself as a continuum:

The poem vividly recreates the details of a coach trip, which is simultaneously a metaphor for the stages in the poet's life. The song matches it with some brilliant individual effects. It moves with the poem up and down hill as the poet urges on the coachman ("Spute dich"—"Hurry up"). The musical evocation of the moment when the peak of the mountain (and of life) is reached, with its expansive panorama, both literal and figurative, is electrifying:

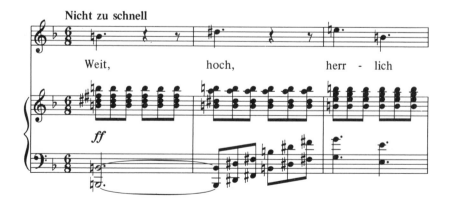

rings den Blick___ ins   Le - ben hin - ein,

The subsequent rapid descent to the plain (and to the gates of Hades) in order to beat out the setting sun (and old age) becomes even more insistent. The poet wants his life to end before his life force ebbs in old age. At "Töne, Schwager, ins Horn" in the last stanza, Schubert produces a fanfare in the piano part that wonderfully expresses the urgency, the confidence, the boldness, the impetuosity of the young poet. The cumulative impact of the poem is breathtaking, of the song even more so.

"Der Musensohn" is another of Schubert's splendid settings of a fine lyric. The poem has five regular stanzas; Schubert uses a simple cyclical form (ABABA), which adds variety without seriously interfering with the strophic feeling. The music is fully attuned to the mood of relaxed gaiety in the poem.

One of Schubert's most celebrated songs is his setting of another Sturm und Drang poem, "Gretchen am Spinnrade," composed when he was only seventeen.[8] The poem constitutes an entire scene in Goethe's *Faust*. As the curtain parts, Gretchen appears sitting at a spinning wheel, lost in memories; she speaks (not sings) the words of the poem as a monologue, and the curtain closes.[9] This is one of the most poignant scenes in all dramatic literature. Schubert makes a magnificent independent synthesis out of it. The ingenious "spinning wheel" piano part offers as rich a background as the galloping in "Erlkönig." The accompaniments to these two songs alone signalize the profound difference between song before and after Schubert. The vocal line fits the progress of the poem superbly; both express the bewilderment and forlornness of the innocent girl, whose erotic desires have been awakened by a lover who has forsaken her (Gretchen is still a virgin, and Faust has fled in order not to harm her). Structurally, the poem contains two intense emotional climaxes, each led up to by a succession of ever more insistent erotic memories. Both the poem and the music build in parallel from relatively quiet beginnings—but ones fraught with emotional potentialities—to shattering emotional heights (at the words "und ach, sein Kuss" and "an seinen Küssen vergehen sollt' ").

Schubert finds it necessary, in order to strengthen and expand the final climax, to repeat "an seinen Küssen vergehen sollt' " and then, in order to bring the emotions down from an almost unbearable pitch, to taper off with a repetition of the first words, "Meine Ruh ist hin, mein Herz ist schwer." This device illustrates another basic aesthetic difference between poetry and song: Goethe achieves a stunning effect by ending both poem and scene at the moment of highest intensity, on the words "an seinen Küssen vergehen sollt'." The theater audience is left limp with empathy as the curtain closes. But the song is so much more aggressive in impact that the effect of breaking it off at this climax would be brutal. Hence, the necessary tapering off. Nineteenth century song was frequently faced with this problem, and the solutions found by composers, even by Schubert himself in other songs, are not always so ideal as the one here.

Schubert composed the two famous "Wanderers Nachtlieder" ("Der du von dem Himmel bist" and "Über allen Gipfeln ist Ruh"). The first is early Schubert (1815) and, though a beautiful song, does not do the poem justice. There is complete unity of theme and expression in Goethe's brief prayer by the wanderer for an end to his tribulations:

Der du von dem Himmel bist,
Alles Leid und Schmerzen stillest,
Den, der doppelt elend ist,
Doppelt mit Erquickung[10] füllest,
Ach, ich bin des Treibens müde,
Was soll all der Schmerz und Lust?
Süsser Friede,
Komm, ach komm in meine Brust!

Schubert divides the poem into four pairs of lines and then tries
to express musically the individuality of each pair. The unity of
the poem is not reproduced in the song.

In contrast, "Über allen Gipfeln," composed considerably later
(1822), is one of Schubert's supreme word-tone achievements.
The celebrated poem is so perfect in itself as almost to defy musical treatment:

Über allen Gipfeln
Ist Ruh,
In allen Wipfeln
Spürest du
Kaum einen Hauch;
Die Vögelein schweigen im Walde.
Warte nur, balde
Ruhest du auch.

Yet the song, a magnificent word-tone counterpart of the poem, is
no less great. The poem progresses from inanimate nature
("Gipfel") to flora ("Wipfel"), then to fauna ("Vögelein").
Paralleling this sequence, the sentence rhythms become successive-
ly more lively, the full stop on "Ruh" in striking contrast to the
relative animation of "Die Vögelein schweigen im Walde." At the
same time the sounds pass from darker to brighter ("Ruh";
"Hauch"; "schweigen"). An ingenious parallel to these elements
is found in the music. The melodic line begins with measured
deliberateness and becomes gradually more animated. The chordal
accompaniment is at first dark, low, and sustained; but with the
word "Wipfeln" the chords are broken up into an eighth-note
rhythm, with the right-hand notes delayed a sixteenth; and on the
word "Vöglein" (Schubert omits the added "e" of "Vögelein"),
the accompaniment leaves the deep register, rising a full octave.
At the same time, the eighth-note alternation of the bass figure is
reversed, now going from upper to lower, adding an additional
element of animation. On "Warte nur," both poem and music
revert to a more deliberate rhythm commensurate with the import
of the words. In this song, if anywhere in song literature, appears
the ultimate refutation of the notion that great poems should not
be used as texts for art songs.

In 1819 Goethe's *West-östlicher Divan* appeared, when the poet was 70, and two years later Schubert, at age 24, composed four poems from this amazing collection. Two of the four he chose were actually by Marianne von Willemer, though the composer could not possibly have known this fact. That Goethe had at long last found a beloved who could answer his love poetry with verse of her own had been a secret between them that was not revealed until many years after the poet's death, when Marianne von Willemer let it be known that four of the poems in the *Divan* were hers. She was thirty-five years his junior and a married woman when the poems were written. There was pathos for both of them in the necessity to sublimate their mutual love into poetry, and the inimitable verses that fill the "Buch Suleika" are at once passionate and a bit intellectualized, with strong touches of wit, especially a playful irony. And for the initiate, there is an unspoken element of poignant renunciation. One of Marianne-Suleika's poems addresses the east wind ("Was bedeutet die Bewegung") and another the west or rain wind ("Ach, um deine feuchten Schwingen") as messengers of love. The charm of the poems lies in their unique blend of emotional sincerity with a considerable degree of stylization and playfulness. Schubert sensed this fascinating combination of moods and retained it in his two songs. Earnestness and gaiety are both found in such consummate lines as "Kosend spielt er mit dem Staube, / Jagt ihn auf in leichten Wölkchen" from "Was bedeutet die Bewegung":

At the climax of this song, the somewhat detached playfulness changes to eager anticipation of the approaching reunion ("dort find ich bald den Vielgeliebten"):

The reflective closing lines, thrice repeated by Schubert, seem to be a commentary on the poem itself, as well as a revelation of the true depth of her love:

Ach, die wahre Herzenskunde,
Liebeshauch, erfrischtes Leben,
Wird mir nur aus seinem Munde,
Kann mir nur sein Atem geben.

"Geheimes," the third of this group, written by Goethe, is a much more playful, tongue-in-cheek poem. Here, too, the mood of the music matches the poem magnificently. The rich accompaniments to all three songs have a great deal to do with their charm.

Schubert's choice of the fourth *Divan* poem is puzzling. The first three can easily be detached from the collection and stand independently. But there are many poems from the *West-östliche Divan* that need the atmosphere of the entire setting. Out of context they sound ludicrous. "Versunken" ("Voll Locken kraus ein

Haupt so rund") is one of them, as a second look at that first line shows. Schubert tries to make a love song out of it. Although it is a love poem, in a highly stylized, intellectual, ironic way, it does not yield to the emotionalizing attempts of Schubert. He left out one line, "Hier ist nicht Fleisch, hier ist nicht Haut," which would not have contributed to the atmosphere of a love song, and he would have done well to leave out its rhyming line, "Doch wie man auf dem Köpfchen kraut." There are other things wrong with the word-tone combination, but this is enough to show that the poem simply cannot become what Schubert tries to make it.

Schubert set all of Mignon's and the harpist's songs from *Wilhelm Meister*, most of them in two or more versions. Only the best-known settings, those published in the standard seven-volume Peters edition edited by Max Friedlaender, are treated here. It would be unfair to consider these settings in the same terms as the Reichardt melodies that appeared with the novel. Schubert's musical idiom being what it is, one cannot expect his songs to reflect closely the characters and situations in the novel. He in fact must have chosen the poems not directly from the novel, but from the section "Aus *Wilhelm Meister*" in Goethe's collected lyrics. Proof of this, aside from other minor differences, is found in the considerable changes Goethe made in "Was hör' ich draussen vor dem Tor" before putting the poem into his collected lyrics. Schubert's, Schumann's, and Wolf's settings (as well as Loewe's) all show these variants. The connection between the poems and the novel, then, must have been a loose one.

However, it is not easy to separate these particular poems from their context. In order to make sense, they have to be associated in varying degrees with the characters and situations of the novel. Mignon's "So lasst mich scheinen, bis ich werde" is the most striking case in point, but not the only one. This poem is scarcely intelligible unless one knows it is sung by the pathetic waif Mignon, who has worn boy's clothing all her life. (It often escapes notice that even her name is a masculine form). She has been dressed in flowing white robes to play the part of an angel in a little birthday ceremony. When it is over and she is expected to remove her costume, she picks up her zither and sings this song instead. It expresses her blissful delight at wearing flowing feminine robes for the first time in her life. At the same time it reveals a moving foreknowledge of her approaching early death. Most of the lines make little sense without this context. Otherwise one would have difficulty interpreting that very first line, the one that follows, "Zieht mir das weisse Kleid nicht aus," the line in the third stanza, "Sie fragen nicht nach Mann und Weib," or the third line of the final strophe, "Vor Kummer altert' ich zu frühe." A connection with the characters and situations in the novel is clearly necessary.

Most of the *Wilhelm Meister* poems are quite complex, and Schubert's songs offer considerable evidence that he did not fully understand them. For example, in the three harpist's songs of his op. 12—"Wer sich der Einsamkeit ergibt," "Wer nie sein Brot mit Tränen ass," and "An die Türen will ich schleichen"—the settings by no means interpret the poems. Schubert saw only the pathos in the words, with the result that his music is heavily emotional. But it is the combination of the pathos with other elements that gives the poems their striking individuality—their bitterness, for example ("Der kennt euch nicht, ihr himmlischen Mächte"), and their intellectual, epigrammatic quality ("Denn alle Schuld rächt sich auf Erden"). All three Schubert songs become almost maudlin at their most expressive points. The composer has simply misinterpreted, or at the least inadequately interpreted the poems.

His setting of the other harpist's song, the ballad "Was hör' ich draussen vor dem Tor," is deficient for a different reason. This is not a complex poem, but a straightforward narrative in six stanzas, each having seven lines with identical rhythm and rhyme scheme. It tells the story of a minstrel who performs before a king and his assembled court, is offered a rich reward for his singing, but refuses it, asking instead for a simple glass of wine. The song that the balladeer sings for the court is not part of the ballad, which dwells on what precedes and especially on what follows the performance of the minstrel. Schubert—and after him Loewe, Schumann, and Wolf—through-composed the poem in a kind of enhanced recitative. First of all, this treatment disregards the strict stanzaic form of the poem, but more important, it raises the expectation from the beginning that the recitative is preliminary to a more broadly melodic rendering of what the minstrel is to sing before the court. Since what he does sing is not part of the poem, which merely states, "Der Sänger drückt' die Augen ein / Und schlug in vollen Tönen," the through-composed recitative "introduction" leads nowhere[11] and in fact seems to give way to a whole series of further introductions, preparing for something that never arrives. By the time the main theme of the ballad is stated and the climax is reached, the song is over and everybody feels cheated.

The published Mignon songs—op. 62, no. 1, "Nur wer die Sehnsucht kennt" (a duet); no. 2, "Heiss mich nicht reden" (Schubert's second setting of this poem); no. 3, "So lasst mich scheinen, bis ich werde" (his second complete setting, there also being two incomplete ones); and no. 4, "Nur wer die Sehnsucht kennt" (a solo this time, the composer's sixth version of the song, another being a quintet)—are all disappointing. The settings are uninspired. In the poem "Heiss mich nicht reden" Schubert clearly did not know how to cope with the lines "Zur rechten Zeit vertreibt der Sonne Lauf / Die finstre Nacht und sie muss sich erhellen." The music here is downright pointless:

"So lasst mich scheinen, bis ich werde" does begin with simple charm:

But the 3/4 time Schubert uses fits the rhythm of the poem badly, and words must often be forced awkwardly into the musical pattern: "zieht *mir*" in the illustration, and later, "Dort ruh ich *ei*ne kleine Stille, dann öffnet *sich* das frische Blick.''

The solo version of "Nur wer die Sehnsucht kennt," which is far better known than the duet, is in part the most effective of the op. 62 songs. The opening line in a slow A minor shows a subdued tone:

A D-sharp added to the tonic chord at the word "Sehnsucht" adds a poignant dissonance, which highlights the key word of the poem. The mood thus established is sustained throughout, except for an abrupt and most uncomfortable change at the climactic words "Es schwindelt mir, es brennt mein Eingeweide." This passage tempted Schubert into an impassioned vocal line accompanied by an agitated figure in the piano, which lasts only to the end of a repeated "es brennt mein Eingeweide." Then the original mood as suddenly returns. This is surely a superficial reading of the poem, as contrasted to Reichardt's, for example.

"Kennst du das Land" was composed in 1815, but never published by Schubert. This early Schubert song was completed only five years after Beethoven's setting and gives inconclusive evidence of having been influenced by it. But Schubert has pushed the balance between poem and music considerably further in the direction of musical dominance than did Beethoven. This becomes clearest in the treatment of the refrainlike "Dahin! Dahin / Möcht' ich mit dir, O mein Geliebter, ziehn!" Schubert's song at this point is much more elaborate, particularly in the rapid accompanying figures, and is extended over a much longer stretch. The sequence of word repetitions that he must use in order to work out the full musical line is:

Dahin, dahin, dahin möcht' ich mit dir, O mein Geliebter, ziehn.
Dahin, dahin, dahin, dahin möcht' ich mit dir, O mein Geliebter,
Ziehn, dahin, dahin, dahin, dahin!

Heinrich Heine

The fact that Schubert composed six poems of Heine (1797–
1856) is significant. Goethe was almost fifty years his senior and
internationally celebrated long before Schubert's birth. By the
time he began writing music, it was certainly no novelty to compose Goethe. But Heine was a contemporary exactly his own age,
who had just published his first major collection. Schubert must
have been one of the first to set this new poet to music. Certainly
he was the first important song writer to do so. It shows that he
could recognize good poetry, even if it was not part of the canon.

The six songs are very late works, composed in 1828, the year
of Schubert's death, and appearing posthumously as nos. 8–13 of
his "Schwanengesang." The sixth, "Der Doppelgänger," is the
best known, but all of them are generally considered to be among
Schubert's greatest songs. A word-tone analysis shows them in a
quite different light.

Heine's *Buch der Lieder* appeared in 1827, less than a year
before Schubert's songs. The 236 poems of the collection are
mostly short love lyrics, constructed with great precision by a
virtuoso poet, and arranged skillfully into various subgroupings.
Schubert selected all of his texts from the section entitled
"Heimkehr," a group of 88 poems that forms the heart of the
collection. Here the poet strikes a pose hinted at earlier with
increasing frequency but revealed fully only now—that of a bitter,
disillusioned, self-mocking lover who has been made a fool by
the naïveté and sincerity of his love for a girl who was untrue to
him.

Heine's poems are not in the Goethean tradition of confessional
poems, drawn from life, each triggered by an individual experience.
They are brilliant exercises in permutation and variation on a
highly sophisticated theme. They abound in theatrical gesture,
paradox, word play, irony, destruction of illusion and atmosphere,
and surprise endings; they are in essence rational and epigrammatic.
Heine was by no means the naive poet he seemed to be in poems
like "Du bist wie eine Blume," and as all too many composers have
considered him; he was a brilliant inventor, a cynic, and with it
all, a poet of deep feeling. His genius was a puzzle to his own
generation and to later ones as well, and only recently has he come
into sharper focus, thanks to revealing studies by S. S. Prawer,

Barker Fairley, and others.[12]

The first of Schubert's songs is "Der Atlas" (all the titles have been added by Schubert):

Ich unglücksel'ger Atlas! eine Welt,
Die ganze Welt der Schmerzen, muss ich tragen.
Ich trage Unerträgliches, und brechen
Will mir das Herz im Leibe.

Du stolzes Herz, du hast es ja gewollt!
Du wolltest glücklich sein, unendlich glücklich,
Oder unendlich elend, stolzes Herz,
Und jetzo bist du elend.

Even before the voice begins, the opening measures of the accompaniment give a strong hint that Schubert is on the wrong tack, as the ponderous tremolo chords surely suggest a pathetic reading of the poem. The entrance of the voice immediately confirms this impression. Heine's preposterous image of himself as Atlas has been taken seriously by Schubert, as though the figure were another Prometheus. In fact, the Atlas image is a highly personal, self-ironizing hyperbole, not a grandiose generalization such as Schubert makes of it. Heine's Atlas is bearing his own world of pain on his shoulders, so that the pathos in the poem is narcissistic. That Schubert misses the point is clear not only in the mood of the musical setting, but also in his repetition of the second line. Because the musical idiom requires expansion, both of the first two lines are repeated. In the repetition, though, Schubert omits the words "der Schmerzen," and the line is sung "Die ganze Welt muss ich tragen." In the context of the poem this is absurd, though Schubert probably felt that it strengthened the Atlas image, or was at least consistent with it. The marvelous paradox in the next line, "Ich trage Unerträgliches," is the intellectual and emotional climax of the first stanza. It is followed, as so often in early Heine, with a trite line, "und brechen / Will mir das Herz im Leibe." Schubert passes over the paradox with little emphasis and builds his musical climax on the hackneyed image:

und brechen will mir das Herz im Lei - - - be.

The second stanza of Heine's poem contains a theatrical hyperbole with contrasting extremes: "unendlich glücklich . . . unendlich elend," which prepare for the abrupt epigrammatic finale "Und jetzo bist du elend." In typical Heine fashion, the last line explains in a flash the entire imagery of the poem. Schubert's setting has none of this. He puts heaviest emotional stress on the repetition of "unendlich" and makes little of the contrast between "glücklich" and "elend," though he does repeat "unendlich elend" for its extra pathos. This very repetition, however, reduces the force of the reappearance of "elend" in the final line. The main thrust of the poem is thus weakened in the song. The last "elend," too, is heavily dramatized by Schubert, with a full measure on the first syllable and fortissississimo tremolo accompaniment. In the poem it is a masterstroke of understatement, bald, brief and cold, yet with a wealth of implications.

After such a terse, epigrammatic, bitingly self-ironic line, there can be nothing more to say, and the poem is over. But not so Schubert's song. It goes on to a highly dramatic recapitulation of the first two lines of the poem, complete with repetitions (including once again "die ganze Welt muss ich tragen"), and closes with still another repetition of the second line. The climax on the word "Schmerzen," with fortissississimo tremolo chords and the vocal line at its highest pitch contains an almost maudlin pathos. The piano ends the song with more tremolo chords, a crescendo in the penultimate measure, and a final sforzando resolution.

Many of Heine's poems, including almost all the "Heimkehr" lyrics from *Buch der Lieder*, achieve their effect in large part from the rapidity with which image, paradox, pun, and epigram surprise the reader. To expand them, as Schubert does in his "Atlas" setting, is to cancel out an essential, innate characteristic. In this respect at least, Schumann's briefer settings in the "Dichterliebe" cycle come closer to the spirit of the poems. Some Heine poems are much more expandable. Brahms's setting of "Der Tod, das ist die kühle Nacht," for example, is a perfect complement to that poem, though the song is extremely deliberate.

"Ihr Bild" is Schubert's second Heine song:

Ich stand in dunkeln Träumen,
Und starrte ihr Bildnis an,
Und das geliebte Antlitz
Heimlich zu leben begann.

Um ihre Lippen zog sich
Ein Lächeln wunderbar,
Und wie von Wehmutstränen
Erglänzte ihr Augenpaar.

Auch meine Tränen flossen
Mir von den Wangen herab -
Und ach, ich kann es nicht glauben,
Dass ich dich verloren hab'!

This poem is less theatrical and hyperbolic than "Der Atlas," yet it is not without a degree of theatricality (the portrait coming to life), certain paradoxical opposites (the smiling lips and tear-filled eyes), or an epigrammatic, surprise ending, which in a flash gives a new dimension to the brief poem. The electrifying switch to the second-person "dich" in the last line alone alters the tone of the entire poem and adds a touch of self-irony.

"Ich stand in dunkeln Träumen," like many of the poet's highly sophisticated poems, is written in a deceptively innocent, stereotyped folk song rhythm:

```
U   —   U   —   U   —   U
U   —   U   —   U   —
U   —   U   —   U   —   U
U   —   U   —   U   —
```

into which the poet introduces sporadic irregularities, making the approximation to true folk song even closer. The contrast between this apparent naïveté and the worldly-wise intellectual quality of the poem is deliberate, with the paradoxical result that the very simplicity of structure contributes to the artful effect. This verse form could well have influenced Schubert's superficial reading of the poem. His unpretentious setting sentimentalizes the content and misses every one of its truly characteristic aspects. The form of the song is cyclical (ABA), so that the first and third stanzas are sung to the same music. It is a bland, sweet, and simple treatment of a poem that has none of these qualities.

The third Heine song is "Das Fischermädchen":

Du schönes Fischermädchen,
Treibe den Kahn ans Land;
Komm zu mir und setze dich nieder,
Wir kosen Hand in Hand.

Leg an mein Herz dein Köpfchen,
Und fürchte dich nicht zu sehr;
Vertraust du dich doch sorglos
Täglich dem wilden Meer.

Mein Herz gleicht ganz dem Meere,
Hat Sturm und Ebb' und Flut,
Und manche schöne Perle
In seiner Tiefe ruht.

There is more to this charming trifle than meets the casual eye. It is, to be sure, an unproblematical interlude in the profusion of urgent poems that surround it in the *Buch der Lieder*, but it is not nearly so guileless as it seems, and as Schubert assumes it to be. Typical Heine patterns are once again in evidence; in particular, the highly conscious description of the poet's heart in terms of the sea ("Sturm," "Ebb'," "Flut"), a personalization that lends far more significance to those qualities in the poet's heart than in the sea. This being the point to which the whole poem progresses, the invitation to the fisher maiden to lay her head on his heart and not to worry is less innocent than it appears. The implication of danger is strengthened by the significant adjective "wild" in the

second strophe. She would do well to think seriously before ex-
posing herself to the sea of the poet's emotions. This time the
point of the poem is reached not in the final line but at the beginning of the last stanza. The remaining two lines then add a
tantalizingly ambiguous dimension, still within the heart-sea
equation, but through its suggestive vagueness throwing into
sharper relief the real differences between the sea and the poet's
heart.

Schubert's treatment glosses over the true thrust of the poem.
He conceives of the work as a charming scherzo, provides a lilting
accompaniment, and constructs a gay insouciant melody that
carries no hidden implications whatsoever:

"Die Stadt" is the fourth song:

Am fernen Horizonte
Erscheint, wie ein Nebelbild,
Die Stadt mit ihren Türmen
In Abenddämmrung gehüllt.

Ein feuchter Windzug kräuselt
Die graue Wasserbahn;
Mit traurigem Takte rudert
Der Schiffer in meinem Kahn.

Die Sonne hebt sich noch einmal
Leuchtend vom Boden empor,
Und zeigt mir jene Stelle
Wo ich das Liebste verlor.

The note of melancholy is again struck in this poem, which once more shows familiar Heine patterns, in particular the revelatory last line that clarifies the mood of the entire piece. Yet it is the miracle of Heine's genius that each one of his hundreds of poems has individuality. The arresting quality of this one is its ostensible impersonality. Prawer calls the landscape in the poem a kind of objective correlative. The first stanza is purely descriptive, with the poet's psyche not seeming to enter the picture. The second stanza continues to describe the atmosphere, but in a restrained manner. Although the poet is strikingly introduced by the un-explained "meinem" of the last line, this hint only momentarily disturbs the apparent objectivity of the description. Only in the last two lines of the final stanza, with their implied pathos, is it revealed that the whole scene has been viewed far from dis-passionately by the poet, and only in retrospect does the reader discover that the poet's psyche has imbued the entire landscape with emotion.

Once again in Schubert's setting it is clear even before the voice part enters that the composer has not comprehended the subtleties of the verse. The piano begins with dark pianissimo tremolo octaves, followed by mysterious evanescent arpeggios in the treble. Clearly there is no objective correlative in this rendition. The emotional impact, the pathos, appears even before the words begin. The landscape is described by the singer in soft apprehen-sive tones as the arpeggios and tremolo continue. A very real suspense builds through the first two stanzas. With the third comes an abrupt change of mood, clearly not in the poem. The chromatics of the arpeggios give way suddenly to percussive diatonic chords; the vocal line likewise becomes sturdy and strong. In this in-congruous way the final two lines of the landscape description are delivered. The climax on the word "Liebste," fortissimo on the highest note of the voice line, is overstated, in sharp contrast to the steady understatement of the poem. There is no extramusical reason for this climax; its relation to the atmospheric description is unexplained. It is, in fact, pointless. The piano accompaniment ends in a return to the pianissimo arpeggios and tremolos with which it began.

The fifth song is "Am Meer":

Das Meer erglänzte weit hinaus
Im letzten Abendscheine;
Wir sassen am einsamen Fischerhaus,
Wir sassen stumm und alleine.

Der Nebel stieg, das Wasser schwoll,
Die Möwe flog hin und wieder;
Aus deinen Augen liebevoll
Fielen die Tränen nieder.

Ich sah sie fallen auf deine Hand,
Und ich bin aufs Knie gesunken;
Ich hab' von deiner weissen Hand
Die Tränen fortgetrunken.

Seit jener Stunde verzehrt sich mein Leib,
Die Seele stirbt vor Sehnen; -
Mich hat das unglücksel'ge Weib
Vergiftet mit ihren Tränen.

This is yet another poem whose effect depends on the apparent development of a sweetly sentimental atmosphere through three of its four stanzas, only to pull up short with a surprise ending in the last line, which casts a bitter tone back over the entire poem. So many of the hundreds of short poems in Heine's *Buch der Lieder* use this device that the reader soon learns to be wary in the early stanzas, so that when the almost inevitable jolt occurs at the end, he is not caught out in too naïve an acceptance of what has gone before. Thus, in the third strophe of this poem the overly pathetic gesture of the poet, on his knees drinking his beloved's tears from her hand, gives the discerning reader a premonitory warning that ultimately this sentimentality will be turned into self-mockery. Once again Heine strengthens the change in tone of the final lines by a shift in person. During the first three strophes the poet addresses his beloved directly: "Wir," "deine." In the last, this intimacy suddenly shifts to estrangement: "das unglücksel'ge Weib"; "ihren."

Schubert's approach to this poem is baffling. The song is in a slightly varied strophic form, each musical strophe incorporating two of the poem's stanzas, so that there is just one musical repetition. This scheme alone negates the main effect of the poem. The music to the first stanza is simple, bland, and colorless, even a bit trite. Then come pianissimo tremolo chords and an atmospheric crescendo, presumably evoked by the words "Der Nebel stieg, das Wasser schwoll." But these are ill-advised, because there is no real change in atmosphere. Proof of this is that they lead nowhere. The climax of the crescendo falls on "Möwe," followed by a rapid decrescendo to prepare for the final two lines of the second stanza, which are actually a continuation of the single mood present from the beginning of the poem. Schubert gives a pathetic emphasis to the final line of this stanza, which is the only moment in the song where text and musical setting are parallel:

Instead of developing the music from this first moment of pathos to the ultrasentimental gesture in the third stanza, Schubert begins his strophic repetition, so that the music to the third stanza, both voice and piano, is the identical bland, arrangement that began the song. The same tremolo chords and atmospheric vocal line follow for the beginning of the last stanza "Seit jener Stunde verzehrt sich mein Leib, die Seele stirbt vor Sehnen." This treatment would be an acceptable, though hardly inspired rendering of Heine's premonitory words, if it had not already been used before for the mists, water, and sea gull of the second stanza. Whereas the main thrust of the surprise ending in the poem is conveyed on the unexpected "vergiftet," this effect is lost by Schubert, since his music for this word is identical with "fielen" of stanza two. There is no bitterness, no mockery, not even much surprise in the song, which ends inappropriately with a sweetly sentimental turn on the cadence at the last word, "Tränen," a word which in the poem has been suddenly transformed into a cold hollow parody of its earlier tender self.

The last of the Heine songs, "Der Doppelgänger" is the most celebrated:

Still ist die Nacht, es ruhen die Gassen,
In diesem Hause wohnte mein Schatz;
Sie hat schon längst die Stadt verlassen,
Doch steht noch das Haus auf demselben Platz.

Da steht auch ein Mensch und starrt in die Höhe,
Und ringt die Hände vor Schmerzensgewalt;
Mir graust es, wenn ich sein Antlitz sehe—
Der Mond zeigt mir meine eigene Gestalt.

Du Doppeltgänger! du bleicher Geselle!
Was äffst du nach mein Liebesleid,
Das mich gequält auf dieser Stelle,
So manche Nacht in alter Zeit?

Schubert's setting is an intense, theatrical, musical dramatization
of the poem, which can be enjoyed by the listener only if he
suppresses Heine altogether, for it is painfully wrong in its interpretation of the poem. The first stanza, which Schubert sets in a
darkly atmospheric, highly charged recitative over somber chords
that form a basso ostinato throughout the song, is in reality the
innocuous opening typical of many Heine poems, revealing
absolutely nothing of the emotional fireworks to come. The
awkwardness and extreme banality of the last line of the stanza
are especially incongruous in the intense musical setting. The
pretentious turn on "auf demselben Platz" becomes downright
embarrassing, particularly in view of the jingly rhyme of "Platz"
with "Schatz":

The third stanza contains the climax of the poem in its last three words, "meine eigene Gestalt," which Schubert sets in a powerful, dramatic way. But poem and song are not parallel. The words "meine eigene Gestalt" of the poem are a surprise twist, a revelation that suddenly throws new light on everything that preceded. The climax of the song is the highly charged culmination of the oppressive atmosphere that has been building steadily from the beginning.

After the shock of the revelation, Heine's final stanza is full of complicated self-mockery. The poet calls the figure a "Doppeltgänger" (Schubert omits the "t"), adding a wryly humorous epithet, "du bleicher Geselle," and asks him why he is imitating the poet's former self as he used to stand there in the old days lamenting his unrequited love. This device would seem to remove the poet in the present from similar torture, especially since the girl has long since departed. But the poet is there nonetheless, and the fact that he encounters his own "Doppeltgänger" reveals, despite his words, that the pain of love "in alter Zeit" still plagues him. Of these complex layers there is nothing in Schubert's setting. The vocal line to "Was äffst du nach mein Liebesleid, das mich gequält auf dieser Stelle," could conceivably contain a touch of irony and mockery:

but if so, it is far less detached than in the poem. Schubert builds his climax on the wrong line, the final one, for the poem has reached its peak with the second and third lines.

It was surely no accident that Schubert began and ended his group of six Heine songs with the two most intensely dramatic settings. This was clearly his picture of the poems, a picture that one has to recognize as faulty. None of these songs is in any way a real synthesis of poetry and music.

Other Poets

Schubert composed thirteen poems by Friedrich Klopstock (1724–1803) in the years 1815–1816. Most of these early songs are lesser works. His developing song style apparently could not yet accommodate the unusual, often intricate rhythmic patterns of many of Klopstock's odes. However, the regular iambic rhythm of the lovely "Das Rosenband" ("Im Frühlingsschatten fand ich sie") gave Schubert a chance to compose a simple, unpretentious melodic line that gently enhances the beauty of the modest verse.

At the opposite end of both the poetic and musical spectrum is the powerful "Dem Unendlichen." This is one of Klopstock's overwhelming dithyrambic hymns in free rhythms, and Schubert conveys the unabashed emotion, the bold syntax, and the long sweep of the lines by the use of a modified recitative style. The music surges to big climaxes in accord with the verse, supported by highly rhetorical fortissimo and sforzando chords in the accompaniment:

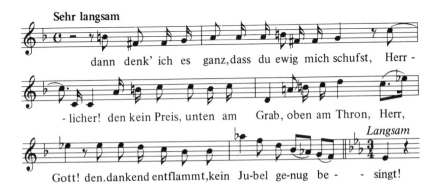

Later Schubert introduces a sonorous sustained melodic line with a rich arpeggio accompaniment. Toward the end he alters the poem a little, changing the word order slightly, even omitting one line, but he achieves an exultant close to match the full fervor of Klopstock's ending:[13]

Ludwig Hölty (1748–1776) was an inspiration for many eighteenth and nineteenth century composers, Brahms in particular, because of the poet's melancholy cast. Schubert set no less than twenty-three of his poems. The poet died at the age of twenty-seven, leaving behind only a relatively small amount of verse, about one quarter of which is in alcaic and asclepiadic strophes. Schubert composed one poem in each of these meters ("Die Apfelbäume"–alcaic; "Die Mainacht"–asclepiadic). But it is with Hölty's less characteristic joyful poems in simple iambic or trochaic rhythms that Schubert comes out best, especially in the naïve "Seligkeit," the playfully erotic "Der Traum," and the charming "Blumenlied."

"Der Tod und das Mädchen" is a recital favorite. The brief poem is by Matthias Claudius (1740–1815):

Das Mädchen
Vorüber! Ach, vorüber!
Geh, wilder Knochenmann!
Ich bin noch jung, geh, Lieber!
Und rühre mich nicht an.

   Der Tod
Gib deine Hand, du schön und zart Gebild!
Bin Freund und komme nicht zu strafen.
Sei gutes Muts! ich bin nicht wild,
Sollst sanft in meinen Armen schlafen!

Schubert intensifies the contrast between the two speakers by strikingly dissimilar vocal lines, the first portraying perhaps too drastically the girl's panic, the second the measured, comforting reply of death. This is all right as far as it goes, though it heavily underscores the obvious. But the poem is more than just a dramatic dialogue between a frightened girl and a benevolent death. It is also an extremely common folk motif, which has in it the implications of death as the lover. It is, or can be, a love poem with erotic overtones, both in the speech of death ("du schön und zart Gebild"; "Sollst sanft in meinen Armen schlafen") and in the frightened timidity of the girl ("rühre mich nicht an"). These nuances are omitted entirely in Schubert's naively dramatized setting. The song is in fact a superficial, one-dimensional reading of a poem that communicates various levels of meaning simultaneously.

Friedrich Rückert (1788–1866), a prolific but not a first-rate poet, was a contemporary of Schubert. Two of the four poems that the composer selected are among his very best, the gay "Lachen und Weinen" and the solemn "Du bist die Ruh." They were made into fine songs. August von Platen (1796–1835) was another contemporary whose deep melancholy, expressed in impeccable, sometimes complex verse, was later to inspire Brahms. Schubert used only two of his poems. "Mein Herz ist zerrissen" is a ghasel, a Persian verse form adapted to the German language with varying success by Platen. Schubert's song is too free with repetitions for a poem having a strict formal pattern. "Die Liebe hat gelogen" is a powerful song set to a pathetic poem of betrayal. The brief poem consists of only two four-line stanzas. Schubert's song is cyclic (ABA). He repeats the first stanza for the third section. In the B section he alters the words considerably, not for the better, but his twofold rendition of the short first stanza is brilliant:

Die Liebe hat gelogen,
Die Sorge lastet schwer,
Betrogen, ach, betrogen
Hat alles mich umher!

A daring musical treatment is given to the repeated "betrogen" in the third verse. Though the song is in the key of C minor, at this word Schubert makes an unexpected shift to C major:

Under the second "betrogen" is a forte-piano A major chord, which with its surprising C-sharp is out of the sequence. The climactic third verse of the poem is thus reinforced by a striking musical climax.

The restatement at the end of the song has another surprise. This time an augmented sixth in A minor[14] on the first "betrogen" progresses to a strong A minor chord for the repetition of the word and then on to C major, with a crescendo to fortissimo on "alles."

Schubert's two great song cycles, "Die schöne Müllerin" and "Die Winterreise," are composed to the weak poems of Wilhelm Müller (1794–1827), which do not begin to measure up to the glorious music. The settings ennoble the verses to which they are written to an extraordinary degree. With these songs even the literary-minded listener would do better simply to let the words serve as a general verbal background for some of the most enjoyable works in the entire literature of song.

Chapter *IV* Robert Schumann

"All my life I have ranked songs below instrumental music, and have never considered them great art."[1] Schumann (1810–1856) was twenty-nine when he wrote these words in 1839. Up to that time, except for some very early songs, he had composed only instrumental, chiefly piano music. As editor of the *Neue Zeitschrift für Musik* he had refused even to discuss vocal works, and he held to this position right up to the moment— less than a year later—when he suddenly broke into song.

Eighteen-forty is the miraculous Liederjahr, which produced an unprecedented and unexpected flood of songs, 138 of them, well over half of all his songs, including most of his famous ones. It was a real fulfillment, however long delayed, as shown by a letter to Clara in February 1840, "Oh Clara, what bliss it is to write songs; I had deprived myself of it for too long." His choice of poems and poets was guided by strong literary interests and a conviction that setting mediocre poems to music was a waste of time. "Why turn to mediocre poems?" he wrote in October 1940, "They will always avenge themselves on the music. To weave a musical garland around the brow of a true poet—there is nothing more beautiful. But to waste it on a commonplace writer, why make the effort?"[2] Though his judgment of the literary merit of the poems he chose was not infallible, their general level is certainly higher than that of Schubert or Brahms, and second only to Hugo Wolf. Heine and Eichendorff were his favorites, though it is paradoxical that he was less consistently successful in synthesis of poem and music with their poems than with a cycle by a truly second-rate poet, Adalbert von Chamisso, whose maudlin "Frauenliebe und -leben" poems have been elevated far beyond their uncertain intrinsic quality by Schumann's settings.

Heinrich Heine

Schumann felt a special relationship to the poems of Heine. He used forty-one of them in all, over thirty in the Liederjahr alone. An afternoon he had spent with Heine in Munich in 1828, when the poet was thirty-one and Schumann eighteen, had left a lasting impression on him. There is plenty of evidence that he knew Heine's works well, and that he recognized the kind of sophistication Schubert had missed in the poetry. As early as 1829 he wrote in his diary of "the bizarre quality [die Bizarrie] in Heine's verse: that burning sarcasm, that great despair; all the caricature of nobility and dignity."[3]

Sensing this quality in Heine's poetry was one thing; communicating it through his music was quite another. Schumann's romantic temperament directed him away from the caustic, ironic, cosmopolitan, sardonic, rational sphere of Heine into the more intimate, emotional, lyrical Biedermeier world. The result is often a sweetening and sentimentalizing of Heine's sharp, pointed verse. This is true in his most famous collection, "Dichterliebe," op. 48, sixteen songs to poems from *Buch der Lieder*. All the selections are taken from "Lyrisches Intermezzo."[4] The sixty-five poems in this section of Heine's anthology lead off with ten brief, artfully but not sweetly sentimental love poems. Gradually the more typical Heine irony begins to show. With no. 17 it develops that the poet's beloved has married someone else, and from this point on the poems become more and more bizarre, even macabre. By the end of "Lyrisches Intermezzo" Heine has progressed to outright self-parody.

Schumann's selection touches all of these phases, but he avoids the more extreme poems. In general his settings modify the more outspokenly ironic, parodic elements. "Im wunderschönen Monat Mai" is the first poem as well as the first song. The subtle intertwining of voice and piano in this irresistibly beautiful work shows Schumann's most important advance in song technique over Schubert. The mood in both poem and music is one of tender longing. Schumann once described his view of the proper relation of words to music in the lied by saying, "The poem should lie in the arms of the singer like a bride, freely, blissfully, totally."[5] This poem does:

Im wunderschönen Monat Mai,
Als alle Knospen sprangen,
Da ist in meinem Herzen
Die Liebe aufgegangen.

Im wunderschönen Monat Mai,
Als alle Vögel sangen,
Da hab' ich ihr gestanden
Mein Sehnen und Verlangen.

Behind the imagery of Heine's brief two-stanza poem there is a touch of Heine artifice, which the warmth of Schumann's strophic setting at least partially conceals: the double meaning of the last word in stanza one, "aufgegangen," refers not only to "Liebe" but on back to the buds as well. As his budding love is linked in the first stanza with the flowers, in the second stanza the poet's declaration of love is linked to the singing of the birds. But since this is the beginning point in both anthology and song cycle, only the critic could be aware of the first gentle appearance of an artifice that becomes explicit only in the next poem. It would be hypercritical to argue on this score that the word-tone relationship is less than ideal. In fact, this is another of those relatively rare occurrences: a perceptive musical interpretation by a great composer, of a fine poem by a great poet, which rises to heights of artistry that no song to a mediocre poem could achieve.

The first song ends on a tantalizing dominant seventh, and the listener finds himself in the second one before he can catch his breath. This is a masterstroke, because the two poems are closely linked. The second continues the imagery of no. 1, though the artifice in the verse is much more prominent. Flowers spring from the poet's tears and his sighs become a chorus of nightingales; he promises his beloved all the flowers and will have the nightingales sing at her window if she will return his love. A true word-tone synthesis would exhibit this sophistication, but Schumann's brief setting does not. It is through-composed in a mood of naïveté and sentimental innocence. There are more such discrepancies as the cycle continues. The third song, "Die Rose, die Lilie, die Taube," is a charming, exuberant trifle which, amusingly, is perhaps the only song that reverses the usual relationship of duration between poem and song. With its fast tempo and rapidity of delivery, the song takes less time to perform than a reading of the poem without the music. With the next two very beautiful songs, "Wenn ich in deine Augen seh' " and "Ich will meine Seele tauchen," there is no doubt that Schumann is moving away from the spirit of Heine. The verse is full of artifice; the songs are warmly expressive and emotional. The composer's love is considerably more innocent than the poet's. Heine's attitude, as always, was extremely deliberate. In a letter of December 15, 1825, to his friend Moses Moser he referred to his "lyrically malicious two-stanza manner."[6] There is actually nothing "malicious" in these two poems—that tone begins to appear a little later—but the remark and the poems themselves show that the poet maintains a distance which Schumann does not.

No. 6, "Im Rhein, im heiligen Strome," is probably Schumann's worst misreading of a Heine poem. The heavy, solemn setting completely misses the bold, perhaps blasphemous idea that the eyes, lips, and cheeks of the Madonna in a painting in the Cologne cathedral are exactly like his beloved's. From the beginning the tone of the poem is ironic:

> Im Rhein, im heiligen[7] Strome,
> Da spiegelt sich in den Well'n,
> Mit seinem grossen Dome,
> Das grosse heilige Köln.

When Heine writes of the Rhine as a "sacred river," the reader should put up his guard. The deliberate awkwardness, the silly naïvete of the language (repetition of "gross" and "heilig"), the ridiculous rhymes ("Well'n"–"Köln," later "Englein"–"Wänglein") ought to have warned Schumann away from his straight-faced, pompous, patriotic-religious treatment. The solemnity of the music to the first stanza is in fact so insistent that it could stand as the ironic beginning of a satirical setting, but the rest of the song proves Schumann's earnestness. In fact, he insists on it to the very end, with a seventeen-measure piano epilogue.

This curious song is followed by the famous "Ich grolle nicht." Now that the beloved has married for money, the poet becomes sardonic, bitter, and ironic:

Ich grolle nicht, und wenn das Herz auch bricht,
Ewig verlornes Lieb! ich grolle nicht,
Wie du auch strahlst in Diamantenpracht,
Es fällt kein Strahl in deines Herzens Nacht.

Das weiss ich längst. Ich sah dich ja im Traum,
Und sah die Nacht in deines Herzens Raum,
Und sah die Schlang', die dir am Herzen frisst,
Ich sah, mein Lieb, wie sehr du elend bist.

But the composer misses the tone. The song has a great deal of pathos and melodrama, building to an extremely demonstrative climax on the lines "Ich sah, mein Lieb, wie sehr du elend bist." The mood of the entire song is set by the first line, though in the poem this mood has changed by the third line to bitterness and scorn. The poem is cold and brutal; the possibility of the poet's breaking his heart cannot be taken seriously. Its last line is an unemotional judgment, an aphoristic summing-up, a moralistic rejection. The music, in contrast, builds to pathos. Not only is the song through-composed, but Schumann is so free with repetitions of the text that the stanzaic pattern of the poem is not at all in evidence. This adds to the feeling of emotional commitment that the music conveys.

By this point, two additional weaknesses of the cycle as settings of these poems have become clear. The poems are all brief, most having only two four-line stanzas, and the aesthetic relation between the stanzas usually hinges on some repeated or extended pattern or image. Most of Schumann's settings, brief though they are, are through-composed, which obscures this underlying pattern. And with Schumann's basically more emotional orientation, the through-composing adds to the intensity, or sentimentality, of the settings.

Also, Heine's poems are arranged with great skill and precision. For example, as shown, no. 2 grew directly out of no. 1. The sequence and juxtaposition is often an important part of the effect. "Ich grolle nicht" is followed in *Buch der Lieder* by another brief poem with the opening line, "Ja, du bist elend und ich grolle nicht," which uses the same imagery even more drastically. This poem in turn is followed by the sardonic "Das ist ein Flöten und Geigen," succeeded by one more poem that pours out venomous bitterness. Then come several delicate, fragile, self-pitying poems, beginning with "Und wüssten's die Blumen, die kleinen." Schumann not only breaks up pairs and sequences of poems that belong closely together, but he changes their order. After "Ich grolle nicht" he places the delicate "Und wüssten's die Blumen, die kleinen," and then the sardonic "Das ist ein Flöten und Geigen":

Das ist ein Flöten und Geigen,
Trompeten schmettern drein;
Da tanzt den Hochzeitsreigen
Die Herzallerliebste mein.

Das ist ein Klingen und Dröhnen
Von Pauken und Schalmei'n;
Dazwischen schluchzen und stöhnen
Die guten Engelein.

The setting for this poem, however, is one of Schumann's best transferences into musical terms of a Heine poem. The poet describes the wedding festivities of his beloved with self-pity: the instruments "schmettern" and "dröhnen"; the angels "schluchzen" and "stöhnen." Schumann has written an accompaniment with an insistent running line in the treble and a sardonic rhythmic chordal accompaniment:

If played with a slight overemphasis of the persistent pedal point A on the downbeat, the waltz rhythm of the right hand is ironically accentuated, while the rhythm of the bass chords that follow clashes with it. In this way, the piano part conveys precisely the overlay of bitterness with which the gaiety of the celebration is described. The vocal line strengthens this weird effect, which is subtle and understated but definite in both poem and music. This time, the setting, like the poem, is strophic, with slight variations.[8] It shows how much better the strophic form matches Heine's verse. A twenty-measure piano epilogue brings the song to a sardonic close.

This is the last fully successful word-tone fusion in the cycle. All the rest emotionalize, sentimentalize, or otherwise fail to capture the essence or intent of Heine's essentially rationalistic, witty poems. The text to no. 11, "Ein Jüngling liebt ein Mädchen," is the cold, almost brutal stereotype of a love triangle, with a typically Heinesque twist into the personal and mock-pathetic at the end. Schumann gets this one all wrong, setting most of the song to a jolly, lively, good-humored tune and shifting to the expressively pathetic at the end, with no trace of the latent self-mockery that is the point of the poem. This piece is followed by the effusively sentimental "Am leuchtenden Sommermorgen," which comes close to transforming Heine into Chamisso. In contrast, no. 13, "Ich habe im Traum geweinet," is dramatically conceived. Though a fine song, like most of the others, it is too overwrought to be a faithful extension of the highly calculated Heine poem.

The rapport between words and music in no. 15, "Aus alten Märchen," with its lilting, fairy-tale-like melody for the first six stanzas, is very close, but the abrupt transition in the last two strophes is much more pronounced in the musical setting than in the poem. The slow pace in this final section prolongs the lines so much that most of the electrifying impact of the concluding "zerfliesst's wie eitel Schaum" is lost.[9] "Die alten, bösen Lieder" is both the last song of the cycle and the closing poem of "Lyrisches Intermezzo." The poem is extremely sophisticated. It is several things at once: a parody of its own macabre content (the burying of his verses); a poem about poems; and a poem with a surprise ending—the coffin for his verse being giant size because his love and pain are also to be buried in it. There is a large share of self-mockery in this witty poem, none in Schumann's song. How vastly different are in fact the endings of the two cycles: "Lyrisches Intermezzo" closing with this showcase of Heine's wit, irony, and theatricality; "Dichterliebe" ending with a sweetly touching 15-measure piano epilogue that recalls the tender mood of the first song.

There are twenty-one other Schumann settings of Heine poems. "Die beiden Grenadiere,"[10] by far the best known, is a real masterpiece. The ballad has certain folk qualities deliberately affected by the poet, but it culminates in a highly theatrical, indeed sensational, vision of the dying French soldier who expects to rise from his grave and join Napoleon as he rides once more to victory. The pace of the poem is slow and labored in the beginning, as two dejected French soldiers returning from Russian captivity hear of the capture of Napoleon; it quickens with the bravura vision of the second soldier and builds to a thrilling climax in the final lines:

> Dann steig' ich gewaffnet hervor aus dem Grab,—
> Den Kaiser, den Kaiser zu schützen!

Schumann's adaptation of the music is brilliant. The song starts out deliberately, with a recitative-like melodic line. It begins to pulsate with suppressed excitement when the second soldier says "Gewähr mir Bruder eine Bitt', wenn ich jetzt sterben werde." From there it builds inexorably to "So will ich liegen und horchen still." At this point Schumann introduces the "Marseillaise," a theatrical touch that is the perfect match for Heine.[11] The melody of the French hymn persists, becoming more and more powerful right up to the final fortissimo:

It is amazing how well the rhythm of the "Marseillaise" with only slight alterations fits the words. The unexpectedly subdued four measures of accompaniment after the voice concludes undoubtedly suggest the collapse of the soldier, a bravura touch perfectly in the spirit of this highly theatrical ballad.

"Die feindlichen Brüder"[12] ("Oben auf des Berges Spitze") is another fine work, all too rarely performed. Both poem and setting are ingenious imitations of folk style. A combat between two brothers, in love with the same woman, ends in the death of both, and through the centuries, long after the castle has become a deserted ruin, the ghostly combat is repeated at midnight. Here again appears Heine's flair for the sensational, the mysterious, the macabre, blended with the naïveté and directness of the folk ballad. To convey this effect, Schumann has introduced a stereotyped flavor into the vocal line with a very simple accompaniment:

This melody, which sets the first two lines, is repeated exactly for lines three and four. In the second stanza, lines one and two are heard to an answering phrase, and then the third and fourth lines return to the original phrase again (AABA). The next section of the song is very similar, with a new melodic line repeated three times, as before, with a slightly altered cadence (CCDC$_1$). The third climactic section returns to the exact pattern of the beginning but highlights the climax by a repetition of the lines "Beide Kämpfer stürzen nieder,/einer in des andern Stahl" to a somewhat changed vocal line (AABAB$_1$). The final section, which begins "Viel Jahrhunderte verwehen," closes the song hauntingly with still another series of threefold repetitions of the same melody (AABA). Only the final line, as though to pictorialize the eternal recurrence of the combat, trails off with a cadence that repeats the first half of the line:

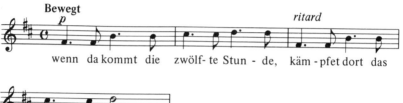

wenn da kommt die zwölf-te Stun - de, käm-pfet dort das

Brü - der - paar.

Except for this variation at the close, the initial musical phrase is repeated a total of nine times during the short song.

"Tragödie" is a love tragedy consisting of three poems that come from Heine's later collection, *Neue Gedichte* (1844), though these poems had been published separately in 1829. Schumann makes admirable syntheses of the first two, but as Heine's third poem shows a falling off, so does the setting. The first poem, "Entflieh mit mir und sei mein Weib," is the exuberant, impetuous, fiery demand of a confident lover. The Heine touch appears in the paradoxes: "In distant lands my heart will be your home and fatherland," and its reverse, "If you refuse, I'll perish, and you will be estranged even though you are in home and fatherland." The song, "rasch und mit Feuer," launches con brio into this bold proposal of the lover, its diatonic decisiveness expressing his confidence in the rightness of his plan. The warning that he will die if they do not flee is only slightly less confident in the melody. Schumann then repeats the first stanza, ending with an even more self-assured, optimistic flourish. The second song is in poignant contrast: the lovers have fled, wandered homeless and hopeless, and then died unknown. The restrained pathos in the poem is achieved by a foreshortened three-line stanza:

Es fiel ein Reif in der Frühlingsnacht,
Er fiel auf die zarten Blaublümelein,
Sie sind verwelket, verdorret.

The second stanza ends in the same way, with "Es wusst' weder Vater noch Mutter," and the final one with the pathetic assonance "gestorben, verdorben." The desolation of the poem is beautifully reflected by a touching melody and an accompaniment of great simplicity. The foreshortening in the third line is as prominent in the music as in the words:

The song is strophic, with three almost identical repetitions, except that the final word is simply but movingly highlighted by an unexpected rise in pitch:

The third poem describes their graves, near which sit another pair of lovers. It closes, "Sie weinen, und wissen selbst nicht warum." For some inexplicable reason, Schumann set this third poem as a duet for soprano and tenor.[13] For practical reasons, the first two songs are usually sung without the third, and they sound better this way.

"Belsazar" (Heine's spelling was "Belsatzar") is one of Heine's most brilliant early ballads. The tale of the blaspheming king of Babylon has the sensational quality Heine liked and knew well how to handle. He tells the story with utmost economy and a sure theatrical sense. It is a frenetically noisy scene of banqueting and carousing that he paints with such powerful words as "klirrten," "jauchzten," "leuchten," "keck," "blindlings," "lästert," "sündig," "brüstet sich," and "brüllt." The tumult reaches a climax with the king's blasphemous words:

> "Jehovah! dir künd' ich auf ewig Hohn,—
> Ich bin der König von Babylon!"

Up to this point Schumann matches Heine's narrative with an ingenious musical setting that owes much to the commotion and suspenseful excitement of its accompaniment. The rhymed couplets of Heine's poem come through the musical texture with prominence, and the whole picture builds to a powerful climax at the king's defiant:

The replacement of the fast-moving accompaniment at these words by percussive eighth-note chords on the first and third beats adds to their shock effect. The poem goes on from here to create one of the most effective atmospheric climaxes in German lyric poetry, as the ghostly hand writes the fiery letters on the wall:

Und schrieb, und schrieb an weisser Wand
Buchstaben von Feuer, und schrieb und schwand,

After this high point, the poem rushes to its closing couplet:

Belsatzar ward aber in selbiger Nacht
Von seinen Knechten umgebracht.

But the magic disappears from Schumann's setting. The music, unable to convey the unearthly atmosphere of the ghost-writing, becomes almost routine. After the disappointing hushed climax of the handwriting on the wall, the pace of the song slows. It takes Schumann much too long to reach the final murder of the king by his vassals. This poem, incidentally, was the first Heine poem Schumann set, and one of the first songs of his miraculous Liederjahr.

Op. 24, a cycle of nine Heine poems, was also among the first compositions of 1840. These early poems are grouped together as "Lieder" in the section "Junge Leiden" of *Buch der Lieder*. They are certainly less skillful than the others, though they contain ingredients by now familiar in Heine. None of Schumann's settings achieves a real rapport with the texts. Beautiful songs they are, particularly "Schöne Wiege meiner Leiden," no. 5, and the last one, "Mit Myrten und Rosen," but they treat the poems too naïvely, lyrically, and sentimentally, and miss the wit, the calculated imagery, the paradox, and the epigrammatic character. The same is true of two of the three Heine songs in "Myrten," op. 25, Schumann's second song cycle, comprising twenty-six songs by various writers. The popular setting of "Die Lotosblume," no. 7, misses the real character of the poem. The cool, exotic narrative of the lotus flower, which avoids the sun and yields itself to the moon, is set to a warm flowing melody, typical of Schumann, which toward the end becomes impassioned just where Heine's poem becomes enigmatic. The poem belongs with the one that precedes it in Heine's *Buch der Lieder* ("Auf Flügeln des Gesanges," which Mendelssohn domesticated in a mediocre setting), and together they form a highly exotic interlude, with palm trees, the Ganges River, and gazelles. Both poems feel very uncomfortable in the Biedermeier surroundings provided by Schumann and Mendelssohn. No. 21, "Was will die einsame Träne mir," misses the wit and irony of its poem. But in the famous "Du bist wie eine Blume" Heine meets Schumann halfway. The composer's sentiment and lyricism are appropriate here, for though the song is somewhat sentimental, so is the poem. It is, in fact, not typical of Heine. The scholar must stretch his analysis to find Heine's artful gesture and stylization, and he might never be able to do so if he did not know who had written the poem.

The remaining Heine songs are disappointing as musical adaptations of their poems. In most, the composer is saying something different from the poet, particularly in "Abends am Strande" ("Wir sassen am Fischerhause"), an advanced, almost experimental poem, in which Heine joins together a succession of entirely unrelated elements in a parodistic, almost nihilistic vein. The songs originally intended for the "Dichterliebe" also fall wide of the mark. "Lehn deine Wang" is by many degrees too passionate; "Es leuchtet meine Liebe" is a sophisticated parody that Schumann treats in a fairy tale manner; "Mein Wagen rollet langsam" is a cold, bitter poem, which the musical setting tries to make cute and charming. It is ironical that Schumann's direction to the accompanist should be to play "nach dem Sinn des Gedichts."

Joseph von Eichendorff

The poet Eichendorff (1788–1857) was much more congenial to Schumann's temperament, though apparently less fascinating to him. He composed only sixteen of Eichendorff's poems (as against forty-one of Heine's). Twelve of these comprise his well-known "Liederkreis," op. 39. Unlike the earlier Heine "Liederkreis," op. 24, or the later "Dichterliebe," the Eichendorff cycle is made up of poems that did not originally belong together. The unity of the songs is thus not as firm, though there is some evidence in the key relationships that Schumann attempted a kind of musical unity.[14]   However, there is a pleasing variety in the succession of songs, and in his choice Schumann shows he knew good poems, for included are some of Eichendorff's very best.

The cycle opens with the hauntingly melancholy "In der Fremde" ("Aus der Heimat hinter den Blitzen rot"). This piece shows at once the real affinity between poet and composer. The subdued, richly beautiful vocal line, over a low arpeggioed accompaniment in F-sharp minor, exudes the same kind of fragile sadness as does the poem. But in spite of the pervasive mood of melancholy, poem and music both convey a basic affirmation of man in nature, an acceptance that blunts the edge of the sadness and fills the song with a sweet contentment. This is the very essence of Eichendorff's art and of Schumann's as well. The grace note embellishment on "Wolken," "keiner," and "kennt" adds an ingenious touch of poignancy to the smoothly flowing lines:

No. 2, "Intermezzo," accomplishes less. The poem is a slight, simple, gentle mood picture:

Dein Bildnis wunderselig
Hab' ich im Herzensgrund,
Das sieht so frisch und fröhlich
Mich an zu jeder Stund'.

Mein Herz still in sich singet
Ein altes, schönes Lied,
Das in die Luft sich schwinget
Und zu dir eilig zieht.

The song to this tender love poem seems overwrought. It forces a magnitude on the verses that robs them of their fragility and seems to engulf them in a more expansive musical lyricism. A sign of this distortion is that Schumann builds the second brief stanza into an insistent climax, though there is none in the poem. Then he repeats the first stanza in its entirety, adding a rich, though brief piano epilogue.

No. 3, "Waldesgespräch,"[15] is dazzling. This is Eichendorff's famous Lorelei ballad. There is a stereotyped folklike ring to poem and music, both of which build up to a highly dramatic climax. Before the voice enters, the piano accompaniment sets the tone with a simple lyrical passage that has a kind of "Once upon a time" quality:

The voice begins with the gallant words of the rider in the woods at night, who offers to conduct safely home the beautiful girl he unexpectedly encounters. The mood is robust and self-confident, with just a touch of ominousness as an undertone. The accompaniment changes to subdued smooth arpeggios for the girl's reply. She hints mysteriously at unfaithfulness and sadness, ending with an unexplained but meaningful warning to the rider to flee from her. The return to the opening musical phrase with the reply of the rider fits the dialogue of the poem ideally. The vocal line expresses a growing tension in the rider's wonderment at the richness of her beauty and accoutrements. Then it breaks out with an urgent, recitative-like line, accompanied by strong staccato chords, on his recognition that she is the witch Loreley:

Note the remarkable psychological precision of this phrase. The strongest emphasis is on "bist," both because it is on the downbeat of the measure and because of the downward leap after it. The stress conveys the rider's certainty of the girl's identity. "Die Hexe Loreley" is sung in hushed, almost muffled tones. Compare the subtle impact of this phrase with a more conventional melodic and rhythmic solution that would build to a climax on the word "Loreley."

With the final reply of the girl, the subdued arpeggios return in the accompaniment. The pitch is transposed a third higher, which makes the line somewhat more assertive. Music and poem both become threatening. There is a conventional repetition of the first line, "Es ist schon spät, es ist schon kalt," now with a more fearful implication and on a climactic, soaring vocal line.[16] The denouement comes with the devastating "Kommst nimmermehr aus diesem Wald," highlighted by a series of abrupt chords that replace the previous flowing movement, and by a repetition of the key word "Nimmermehr" three times, followed by a decisive cadence that seems to seal the fate of the rider. Schumann ends with a repetition of the theme that began the song, which provides a fairy tale frame entirely appropriate to the poem. This quality, incidentally, is often missed by the singer, who is tempted to make the narrative more intensely dramatic and realistically vivid than poet and composer intended (as though it were another Schubert's "Erlkönig"), and to disregard the everpresent leveling quality of the folktale atmosphere. If the singer makes the climax too intense, its occurrence on the line "Es ist schon spät, es ist schon kalt" is not appropriate, and the piano epilogue seems incongruous. But the performing artist, not Schumann, is to blame for this. All elements of the song itself are in perfect balance.

No. 4, "Die Stille" ("Es weiss und rät es doch keiner"), and No. 6, "Schöne Fremde" ("Es rauschen die Wipfel und schauern"), suffer from overnourishment, so to speak. These slight but beautiful verses of Eichendorff are overwhelmed by enthusiastic musical settings that turn them into something they are not intrinsically; the poems are out of focus. Beautiful songs they are, but not satisfying as a word-tone union.

No. 5, "Mondnacht," perhaps the best known of all Schumann's songs, is another magnificent synthesis. This is one of the great lyric poems of German literature:

Es war, als hätt' der Himmel
Die Erde still geküsst,
Dass sie im Blütenschimmer
Von ihm nun träumen müsst!

Die Luft ging durch die Felder,
Die Ähren wogten sacht,
Es rauschten leis die Wälder,
So sternklar war die Nacht.

Und meine Seele spannte
Weit ihre Flügel aus,
Flog durch die stillen Lande,
Als flöge sie nach Haus.

This is art that conceals art, for in form and content it is simplicity itself, and it achieves a sense of quiet but joyful union with nature, a kind of ingenuous pantheism. The song begins with a fragile piano introduction, which at once sets the tone of moonlit serenity. The vocal line grows directly out of this and expands on the same mood with utmost clarity. The musical portrait of the first stanza complements the serenity of the word portrait. There is a repetition of this music for the second strophe, with a gentle touch of reinforcement in the accompaniment. The third strophe contains a miracle of word-tone fusion. Poem and music seem to expand as the wings of the poet's soul spread out, and a richly satisfying climax is reached on the words "flog durch die stillen

Lande." The climactic vocal line is not much changed; the expansion occurs chiefly in the accompaniment. The climax reached, the final cadence brings the poem and song to an end with the richly satisfying fulfillment of "als flöge sie nach Haus." There is a serene epilogue for piano.

No. 7, "Auf einer Burg" ("Eingeschlafen auf der Lauer"), is a subdued poem in two parts. The first part portrays the legend of the old emperor Frederick Barbarossa as he waits through the centuries to be reawakened. This is followed by a peaceful landscape scene with a wedding celebration in the far distance. Schumann attempts a hushed, highly atmospheric musical evocation of the Barbarossa legend, but without much success. The adagio pace is too slow to sustain the scanty vocal line and harmony; the picture falls apart. Even worse, Schumann attempts to portray the placid landscape with a strophic repetition of the music to the Barbarossa portrait. This strange mismatch is distorted even further by a pathetic highlighting of the last word, "weinet." Though the bride does weep in the poem, she is probably crying from happiness or simply from tension. The composer treats her crying as a kind of Heinesque surprise ending.

The next two pieces, no. 8, "In der Fremde" ("Ich hör' die Bächlein rauschen"), and no. 9, "Wehmut" ("Ich kann wohl manchmal singen"), are typical Eichendorff poems with a sweetly sad atmosphere mixed with a vague longing. Schumann's music to "In der Fremde" is several shades too joyous and springlike, missing the sweet sadness almost entirely. Again, as in no. 7, the last line of the song becomes a reversal of what precedes, whereas the poem is all one mood. The closing words, "Und ist doch lange tot," add only a final intensification of the sadness. The very slow "Wehmut" has the opposite fault, for its measured pace misses the overlay of happiness and contentment.

No. 10, "Zwielicht" ("Dämmrung will die Flügel spreiten"), is one of Eichendorff's great poems, and Schumann makes a fine song out of it, although he has to solve a very difficult problem to do so. This poem evokes the threatening aspect of nature, expanding it into a powerful portrait of the dangers that lurk everywhere in life. The first stanza is a menacing picture of nature at twilight:

Dämmrung will die Flügel spreiten,
Schaurig rühren sich die Bäume,
Wolken ziehn wie schwere Träume—
Was will dieses Graun bedeuten?

Each line is ominously suggestive: dusk spreading its wings (the ugliness of "spreiten" is a fine touch); the trees moving weirdly; the clouds passing like oppressive dreams; and the final, "What does all this horror mean?" Schumann sustains this mood by a dark and sinuous linear accompaniment. The unusual intervals of the vocal line evoke the same sense of dread and apprehension:[17]

The heavy emphasis on "schwere Träume" achieves precisely the same effect as in the poem, and the apprehensive question that follows sums up the atmosphere of dread.

The second stanza of the poem warns in vague terms of the menace of the hunters to the helpless deer. The song is strophic, so this stanza is an exact repetition except for the subtle addition

of a few low bass tones in the accompaniment. The third stanza
contains the frightening admonition to trust no friend on earth,
for he may be planning treachery. This is a bold transference of
the foreboding twilight atmosphere into terms of human relationships:

Freundlich wohl mit Aug' und Munde,
Sinnt er Krieg im tück'schen Frieden.

Schumann begins the third strophe like the others, but intensifies
it as it progresses. The parallelism of the third and fourth verses is
exactly mirrored in the vocal line:

freund - lich wohl   mit   Aug' und Mun - de,   sinnt   er   Krieg   im

tück' - schen Frie - den.

The vagueness and impressionistic quality of the earlier strophes
has been replaced by a frightening precision; it is as though a veil
of mist was suddenly rent, to reveal treachery. In the final gen-
eralizing strophe, the vague threatening atmosphere returns, and
the poem ends with a warning: Be on guard! ("Hüte dich, sei wach
und munter"), which is brilliantly evoked by the music:

hü - te dich,   sei   wach und   munter!

The triumph of the musical setting of this difficult poem is the way that the song matches the atmosphere of the poem. The musical restraint Schumann exercises makes it the highlight of the cycle in terms of word-tone values.

No. 11, "Im Walde" ("Es zog eine Hochzeit den Berg entlang"), suffers the familiar fate of overexploitation and overemphasis. The final joyful song, no. 12, "Frühlingsnacht" ("Überm Garten durch die Lüfte"), is an exuberantly brilliant setting of an irresistibly happy poem, culminating in the outburst, "Sie ist deine, sie ist dein," a satisfying bravura close to this cycle of twelve Eichendorff songs.

The moving "Frühlingsfahrt," op. 45, No. 2,[18] begins in a cheerful folk style:

The carefree atmosphere of the text is buoyantly realized in the music:

The happy fate of the first journeyman, who becomes a contented family man, is set to the same optimistic tune, though with a slightly more placid accompaniment. The sad life of the second is then contrasted in tone, though the contour of the original tune is discernible:

ver - lok - kend Si - re - nen, und zo - gen ihn

in die buh - len - den Wo - gen,

The final pious stanza returns to the original melody with a measured, subdued accompaniment. The closing prayer of the last line is straightforward and simple.

"Der frohe Wandersmann" is quite similar, except that there are no shadows at all to this hearty song on the lips of the young boy as he makes his way confidently out into the world:

den schickt er— in —— die wei - te Welt,

"Frauenliebe und -leben"

The cycle "Frauenliebe und -leben," op. 42, though composed to mediocre poems by Adalbert von Chamisso (1781–1838), is probably Schumann's greatest achievement in song. The cycle of nine poems, of which Schumann composed only eight, first appeared in 1831. Each poem deals with a central moment in the love life of a woman, from the first awakening of love to old age. Although they are not first-class lyrics, they show an amazing empathy, each of them being a believable expression of the moment it portrays. The poems thus lend themselves readily to musical embellishment, and there is no question that Schumann's task here was far easier than in Eichendorff's "Zwielicht," for instance, or in the Heine poems. There is also a strong affinity between the spirit of these poems and Schumann's temperament. He responded fully to the unembarrassed emotionalism, the sentimentality bordering on bathos, the Biedermeier glorification of the homely and domestic. The happy prospect of his impending marriage to Clara must have served as a further inspiration.

The songs portray unabashedly the successive moments in the woman's life, her virginal worship of the beloved from afar; the more urgent, joyful awakening of her love; bewilderment at his declaration of love; their betrothal; her excitement and timid anticipation on the wedding day; her confiding to her husband that they are going to have a baby; her joy in motherhood; and her desolation at the early death of her husband. In all of these songs one has the happy sense that the musical settings are the ultimate fulfillment of their moods, that with the music the words find their fullest, richest expression.

If the poems were better, one could criticize Schumann for having omitted the final one and thus impairing the theme of the lyric cycle.[19]   In the ninth and last poem, the now aged woman, talking to her granddaughter on the day of her own betrothal, recalls in serenity the joys and sorrows of her life and concludes: "Glück ist nur die Liebe. Liebe nur ist Glück." Since Schumann composed a longish piano epilogue, identical with the accompaniment of the first song, this is sometimes pointed to as a substitute for the final poem, which indeed it is in a mechanical sense, but certainly not in the more comprehensive sense of the lyric cycle. Schumann's cycle leaves the woman at her moment of desolation. The reminiscence of her virginal love provided by the piano epilogue mitigates this grief to some extent, but it is certainly not the equivalent of Chamisso's closing stanzas, which portray the woman, after a long widowhood lasting through two generations, as attaining the serenity of distance and old age.[20]

Goethe

The imposing figure of Goethe was no longer on the scene by the time of the Liederjahr, the poet having died at the age of eighty-two when Schumann was twelve. A new generation, all more or less his contemporaries, including Eichendorff, Heine, Ludwig Uhland, Friedrich Rückert, Nikolaus Lenau, and others, commanded the attention of the composer. He spoke of the "progressive poetry" of these younger poets and claimed that "there arose a more artistic and profound type of song, of which earlier generations could not have known, for it was only the new poetic spirit which was reflected in the music."[21] This comment shows how committed Schumann was to romantic poetry. Nevertheless, the influence of Goethe was still potent enough to elicit eighteen songs from him.

Four of his Goethe songs are in "Myrten," op. 25, the second series of songs he composed in the Liederjahr. The poems are from the *West-östliche Divan*, the late collection inspired by the Persian poet Hafiz.[22] The pronounced eastern flavor in the collection is not in Schumann's settings, and the songs are as far from the spirit of the poems as Biedermeier is from Baghdad. The first one, "Freisinn" ("Lasst mich nur auf meinem Sattel gelten!") has a kind of verve, albeit a German romantic one; the second, "Sitz ich allein," conjures up a German Biergarten rather than a Persian tavern. The third and best known is "Talismane" ("Gottes ist der Orient"). Here the eastern flavor is so prominent in the words, with the first two lines coming directly from the Koran, that its absence in the thoroughly western music is a serious defect. Schumann took three separate four-line religious incantations from the early pages of the anthology as the basis for the song. The first two fit together, but the third is strangely different and unrelated.

The lovely Suleika poem "Wie mit innigstem Behagen" was the inspiration for the fourth song. This, too, is a strange choice, for the poem is a reply to the one preceding it, as the first two lines immediately show:

Wie mit innigstem Behagen,
Lied, empfind ich deinen Sinn.

Schumann manages to make a fervent love song of it, which borders on the sentimental, particularly in the ardent repetitions (not in the poem) of "ihm zur Seite" and "Kuss auf Kuss." This effusive mood, not right for the sense of the poem but compelling enough to carry the listener along, runs into a last stanza that embarrassingly reveals how inappropriate the setting is for the poem:

Süsses Dichten, lautre Wahrheit
Fesselt mich in Sympathie!
Rein verkörpert Liebesklarheit
Im Gewand der Poesie.

In op. 96, a late group, there is a setting of "Über allen Gipfeln," but it simply does not bear comparison with Schubert's.

Schumann composed all the *Wilhelm Meister* songs except the minor "Ich armer Teufel, Herr Baron" in 1849, long after the Liederjahr. They were published as op. 98a.[23] By this time his style had undergone noticeable change. The songs are richer in texture, the harmony is more complex, the musical declamation more subordinate to the poetic line, and the songs in general more dramatically conceived. All are through-composed except "Kennst du das Land," which is strophic.

There is no relation whatsoever between Schumann's songs and Goethe's novel. The atmosphere in the music is closer to Schumann's own romantic temperament than to that of the harpist or Mignon, though Philine's song is a delightful exception. The composer's often overrated literary sophistication notwithstanding, some of the *Wilhelm Meister* poems defeated him. He did not know how to interpret certain passages. In "Wer nie sein Brot mit Tränen ass" he introduces awe-inspiring arpeggios in the accompaniment to the lines "Ihr führt ins Leben uns hinein, / Ihr lasst den Armen schuldig werden," while the vocal line is highlighted by two minor seventh leaps to a high C on the words "Leben" and "Armen." It is difficult to see what the composer had in mind. If he was depicting the mystery of the relationship between God and man, this is foreign to the poem. In "Wer sich der Einsamkeit ergibt" Schumann was led by the words "Es schleicht ein Liebender lauschend sacht, / Ob seine Freundin allein" to a more animated, cheerful musical line, which is much removed from the atmosphere of the full poem. This prevents him from portraying the relevance of the next line, "So überschleicht bei Tag und Nacht / Mich Einsamen die Pein." Nor does the music give any indication that Schumann understood the significance of the closing lines, "Ach, werd' ich erst einmal / Einsam im Grabe sein, / Da lässt sie mich allein!" "An die Türen will ich schleichen" is very difficult to interpret without reference to the novel, which casts it in a special light.[24]   Schumann sets the words rather simply, though the harmonies of his accompaniment are complex. Not much happens in the song, and the last lines, "Eine Träne wird er weinen / Und ich weiss nicht, was er weint," have no point. The through-composed ballad "Was hör' ich draussen vor dem Tor" is the most rambling of all the harpist's songs and as pointless as Schubert's.

The songs for Mignon are more impressive. "Heiss mich nicht reden" is a passionate outburst of great power. The music conveys a tense urgency in its opening chords and throughout the entire first stanza:

This atmosphere gets Schumann into serious difficulty in the second strophe of the poem, for though the first allows a passionate interpretation, the epigrammatic second does not, and the musical composition thus becomes pointless:

The third stanza lends itself to Schumann's music better. From "Ein jeder sucht im Arm des Freundes Ruh" the song communicates the pathos felt by the lonely girl, leading up to a poignant climax on "Allein ein Schwur drückt mir die Lippen zu."

When the poem is over, Schumann is not ready to stop but pulls out the phrase "nur ein Gott" for a separate, impressive repetition:

He then combines other lines from the poem to make a dark adagio coda. The whole composition is a tour de force (like Schubert's "Erlkönig"), exploiting emotional potentialities in the poem in a way that Goethe would never have dreamed possible. The song is so compelling, except for the second stanza, that one cannot help wishing he had simply left that stanza out. Schumann took even greater liberties elsewhere.

The finest of Schumann's *Wilhelm Meister* songs is surely the little-known "Nur wer die Sehnsucht kennt." For this poem, the most congenial to his temperament, he captures the true pathos of the words better than either Schubert or Wolf, or Tchaikovsky for that matter. Rich dark harmonies and a stunning vocal line set the mood at the outset, and it is sustained throughout the song. The texture is uniform. Schumann avoids the potentially disruptive effect (as Schubert did not) of the two strong lines, "Es schwindelt mir, es brennt / Mein Eingeweide," by underplaying them, though he does not slight them; the high A-flat on "brennt" is a minor peak. He saves the main climax for the recurrence of the lines "Nur wer die Sehnsucht kennt / Weiss was ich leide." Schumann repeats almost the entire short poem to make the second half of his song, significantly omitting the two lines with "schwindelt" and "Eingeweide."

Of the remaining Mignon songs, Schumann clearly did not know what to do with "So lasst mich scheinen, bis ich werde." Nor is his "Kennst du das Land" in any way a refutation of his own remark that Beethoven's is the only satisfactory musical rendition of this poem.

Schumann was the first since Reichardt to compose Philine's saucy "Singet nicht in Trauertönen," and he easily wins against his only major competitor, Hugo Wolf, who somehow fails to catch the insouciant charm of the poem. In Schumann's collection the song follows "Wer sich der Einsamkeit ergibt" and is followed by "An die Türen will ich schleichen," and the contrasting mood and atmosphere are like a breath of fresh night air. The accompaniment and vocal line are both gay and pert, with just the touch of boldness that permeates the words and their playfully amorous implication:

Although the setting is not strophic, the simple stanzaic pattern which gives charm to the poem comes through the texture of the song. For some reason Schumann omits the second of the eight four-line stanzas. The song ends with a delightful touch of bravura at the repeated final line:

Other Poets

Schumann's op. 90 comprises six songs to the poems of the melancholy Nikolaus Lenau (1802–1850), composed in the same year that the poet died in an insane asylum in Vienna. Like almost all the other late songs of Schumann, these fragilely beautiful pieces are not as well known as they deserve to be. Four of them, especially the lovely "Meine Rose," are splendid examples of the interplay of melody between accompaniment and voice line, as in the popular "Der Nussbaum" (unfortunately a gorgeous song to a bad poem by Julius Mosen). Although the interwoven melodies catch the generally melancholy atmosphere of the poems,[25] the songs are disappointing from the point of view of word-tone synthesis, for the poems are far from Lenau's best. And Schumann takes liberties with them, changing some words, adding others, leaving several out.

A year later Schumann set the four "Husarenlieder" of Lenau for low male voice, op. 117, and here again fine songs are not matched in quality by their verse. The poems are lusty, not to say bloodthirsty warrior's tirades, the last one containing the grim bravura gesture: "Er wischt an die Mähne sein nasses Schwert,/ Und weiter springt sein lustiges Pferd / mit rotem Huf." The first three nevertheless have a boisterous gaiety, which Schumann thoroughly captures.

Schumann composed five songs of Eduard Mörike (1804–1875). They are eclipsed by Wolf's masterpieces, but they show poetic sensitivity. The three of them that must compete directly with the popular Wolf settings—"Das verlassene Mägdlein," "Der Gärtner," and "Er ists"—are little gems. Unfortunately the stunning setting of the brief poem "Er ists" is marred by too much repetition of the final words, "Frühling, ja du bists! / Dich hab' ich vernommen!" which in the song are expanded to: "Frühling, ja, du bists! Ja, du bists, du bists! Dich hab' ich vernommen, ja, du bists! Dich hab' ich vernommen. Frühling, ja, du bists, ja, du bists! Ja, du bists, du bists, du bists! Dich hab' ich vernommen, ja, du bists!"

"Jung Volkers Lied" and "Die Soldatenbraut," the other two Mörike poems set by Schumann, are both fine works, which Wolf did not set to music. Since Wolf on principle did not compose poems used by his predecessors in songs he felt could not be surpassed, he may have omitted these two for that reason, though on this point there is no direct evidence. "Die Soldatenbraut" especially is interpreted by Schumann with unusual subtlety. The girl's happy anticipation of her beloved's release from the army (suggested by a gay march rhythm), her certainty of his bravery and his steadfast love for her, and a gentle touch of pertness are all portrayed in the music of the first two stanzas:

Her vision of their marriage is conveyed in a warmer, mellower tone, which turns to the slyly humorous with the mention of "Hauskreuz," which implies that she will handle him firmly when they are man and wife.[26] A short piano interlude offers a brief glimpse of the wife-dominated but loving household. After a return to the first stanza, a final gay piano interlude and an unexpected closing repetition of "Für mich aber ebenso gut" end the song on a note of supreme confidence in the steadfastness of her beloved.

The poetry of Friedrich Rückert inspired Schumann to no fewer than twenty-two songs (three of the twelve in op. 37 are by Clara). Of this entire group, only two—"Widmung" ("Du meine Seele, du mein Herz") and "Volksliedchen" ("Wenn ich früh in den Garten gehe")—are heard very often, which is a pity, for it includes some beautiful songs. Unfortunately, Rückert was a prolific poet who rarely produced first-rate verse. Though Schumann's choices avoided the poet's weakest products, only one of the poems, "Du meine Seele," rises above mediocrity, and not much at that. This piece, the composer's first Rückert song and one of the earliest of the Liederjahr, is one of Schumann's most inspired compositions.

Chapter V Johannes Brahms

In the songs of Johannes Brahms the incidence of word-tone fusion is far less than with any other composer discussed in this book. Brahms is more of an absolute musician than the others. This statement, however, must not be understood to imply that he ran roughshod over the texts of his songs. There is evidence that he had a very high regard for the poem he was setting. He believed that the musician had a serious responsibility to the text. One of his pupils, Gustav Jenner, remarked on Brahms's insistence that the composer know his text thoroughly and carefully analyze its structure and metrical system. He urged his pupils to carry around in their heads for a long time any poem that they wanted to compose "to recite it aloud often, and to pay close attention to everything, most especially the declamation . . . When he discussed a song with me, he would first investigate whether the musical form was absolutely in keeping with the text. He sharply censured mistakes of this nature as a lack of artistic sense or the result of insufficient comprehension of the text."[1]

This attitude Brahms shares with other song composers in both centuries. That his own songs nevertheless contain few examples of a genuine synthesis of poem and music is the result not so much of his intention or of a conscious decision, as of an innate subconscious orientation. Once the song is set in motion, the musical values become automatically more assertive and determinant than the text; though there remains a very definite connection, this relationship matters less. In most songs of Brahms the attention of even a listener who is word-tone conscious is drawn irresistibly to the musical development. Time and again, such a listener discovers that as the song progresses, his attention strays from what the poem says; a certain formal quality of the music insistently demands his attention.

Brahms's respect and admiration for the classical musical forms in all phases of composing, including his four symphonies, is well known. This tendency toward self-contained musical symmetry and structure is evident in most of his songs, too, from the simplest to the most complex.[2] Formal musical patterns are a serious threat to word-tone union, for they can easily become so self-assertive that they interfere with the blending of word and tone into a single expressive unit. Recognition of this risk led Wagner to his "endless melody" and was a basis for much of his extensive theorizing about word-tone synthesis.[3] That set musical forms do not of necessity prevent a word-tone synthesis can be shown in many songs by many composers; it is only a matter of degree. The formal structures of Brahms's songs are in the main more independent and often more subtle and elaborate than those of any other eighteenth or nineteenth century composer. According to Paul Mies, "unity and a self-contained quality are a chief stylistic characteristic of the Brahms songs."[4] Whatever the hypothetical ideal balance between musical form and the demands of the poetic text, it can be safely said that Brahms approached it less closely than Schubert, Schumann, or Wolf.

Added to Brahms's insistent formal musical impulse is his strong expressive tendency. This results in an opulence of harmony and melodic line, and a highly emotional quality in his music. Whereas in Schubert, Schumann, and in Wolf, a high degree of emotionality is usually related closely to the poetic text, with Brahms it tends to be associated with the formal development of the music, and more often than not it draws the attention still further away from the words.

The matter of poetic-musical rhythm is a much-debated point in Brahms's songs. On the one hand, it is often asserted that he was careless about the rhythm of his texts; that he permitted the dynamics of the vocal line to be the determining factor. On the other hand, claims are made that Brahms was scrupulously attentive to rhythmic demands of the text, and that his melodic lines, while seeming to ignore them if cursorily examined, prove on sympathetic investigation to conform faithfully to the poetic rhythm.[5] Many examples can be cited in which the bar-line and the normal stress patterns of the musical measures are not a determining factor in the melodic or rhythmic pattern that comes across during performance. This means that a perceptive singer can mold the melodic line more closely to the poetic rhythm than would seem likely to one who is studying the song from the score.

Another factor of importance is Brahms's inclination to pay

more attention to the underlying metrical patterns of a lyric line than to the individual irregularities of rhythm superimposed on it.[6] When the more assertive musical rhythm underscores the underlying metrical pattern of the poem, attention is inevitably drawn away from the individuality and meaning of the words. Such reinforcement occurs to some extent in all songs, but in most of those by Schubert or Schumann it is not so clearly favored over the individuality of the specific line as it is in Brahms.

There are fewer songs by Brahms, about 200, as compared with over 600 by Schubert, more than 250 by Schumann, and over 300 by Wolf. Moreover, he was either unconcerned with or insensitive to the literary quality of poems he chose as texts. He composed many songs to poems so inferior that they are automatically excluded by the quality of the verse alone from consideration in the present context. Well over half of his songs use mediocre-to-bad poems by such writers as Klaus Groth, Max Kalbeck, Carl Lemcke, Friedrich Halm, Hans Schmidt, Josef Wenzig, Carl Candidus, and—a favorite of Brahms—G. F. Daumer. Only about sixty songs are set to worthy verse: fifteen to poems of Ludwig Tieck; six each to Heine, Eichendorff, and Hölty; five each to Goethe and Platen; three to Gottfried Keller; two each to Mörike, Paul Fleming, and Detlev von Liliencron; one each to Clemens Brentano and Theodor Storm.

For all these reasons, any discussion of the word-tone relationship in Brahms deals with a phenomenon that is not so central with him as it is with any of the other composers. Konrad Giebeler, in a book on the relation of text to music in Brahms's songs, states, "We will investigate the relation between music and text without presupposing the idea of a fusion of the two to be valid for Brahms."[7] Though this is not precisely my own procedure, I approach it more closely with Brahms than with any other composer.

August von Platen

There is no single poet who comes to mind so readily in the case of Brahms as does Goethe for Schubert or Heine for Schumann. Ludwig Tieck comes closest because of the fifteen songs in the "Magelone" cycle, which reveal a real affinity between the two artists. But just as Schumann, in my view, produced finer word-tone compositions with poems of Eichendorff than with those of Heine, so Brahms shows a closer affinity to the poems of August von Platen (1796—1835) than to those of Tieck. Different as their personalities and temperaments were, Brahms and Platen share important artistic characteristics. Platen's concern for formal symmetry is, if anything, even greater than Brahms's. This quality is combined in both artists, not with a tendency toward personal reserve and objectivity, but with a high degree of emotionality and expressivity. As Brahms was attracted to poems of pessimism and melancholy, so despair and gloom—weltschmerz—are the overriding tones of Platen's lyric. And both artists had strong ties to the folksong.

All five Platen songs are contained in op. 32, published in 1864. The most brilliant of these is no. 1, "Wie rafft' ich mich auf." The poem, one of Platen's best, is in four identical stanzas of considerable complexity:

> Wie rafft' ich mich auf in der Nacht, in der Nacht,
> Und fühlte mich fürder gezogen,
> Die Gassen verliess ich, vom Wächter bewacht,
> Durchwandelte sacht
> In der Nacht, in der Nacht,
> Das Tor mit dem gotischen Bogen.

The most striking feature is the insistent repetition of "in der Nacht." The fifth line of each stanza is identical, and stanza four, like stanza one, has the repetition also in its first line. Thus, the phrase "in der Nacht" occurs twelve times in twenty-four lines. There is also the pervasive "acht" rhyme, which ends every line but the second and sixth in all four stanzas, making sixteen "acht" rhymes in twenty-four lines. Internal assonance to the same dark vowel is produced by a subtle emphasis on "a" sounds in the other words (in the first stanza, "rafft'," "Gassen," "durchwandelte"). The three-beat rhythm of the poem, a unique one dominated by the anapests of the repeated phrase, contributes to the feeling of movement, anxiety, and restlessness, which is the theme of the poem. This is expressed in successive images: the poet's nocturnal wandering in stanza one; the brook in the second stanza, whose waves flow ceaselessly onward, "doch wallte nicht eine zurücke"; and the poignant outcry at the transitoriness of life in the climactic last stanza, "O wehe, wie hast du die Tage verbracht!"

In its overall effect, Brahms's setting provides a superb counterpart to the main thrust of the poem, and matches many of the more specific points as well. The repetition of "in der Nacht" in the first line is striking:

All twelve repetitions of this key phrase are brought into relief without interrupting the flow of the thought or the melodic line.

Brahms, more than any other composer, indulges in the device of repeating words and phrases of the text when he needs them to work out his melodic pattern. When the poem already uses repetitions as a conscious poetic device, however, the composer introduces a confusing element when he asks for additional repetitions. A characteristic example occurs with the second line of this poem. Brahms composes "und fühlte mich fürder, *mich fürder gezogen, und fühlte mich fürder gezogen*" (italics indicate repetitions not in the original). There are fortunately no other such repetitions in the first strophe, and none at all in the second and third (except for a less obtrusive repetition of the final line in each case). The fourth stanza is treated like the first, except for a repetition of the climactic line, "O wehe, wie hast du die Tage verbracht," which is so powerful and so deeply expressive of the melancholy despair in the poetic line that it becomes an example of enhancement by repetition in the musical setting, such as seen, for instance, in Schubert's "Meine Ruh ist hin" or his "Gruppe aus dem Tartarus":

we - he, wie hast   du die   Ta - ge ver-bracht,

The melodic line brings out, instead of submerging as it so often does, the sense and import of the poetic lines, and the music of the individual sections matches the poem closely. The total result is a work of art that powerfully enhances the intrinsic effect of the poem.

"Der Strom, der neben mir verrauschte" (op. 32, no. 4) is a ghasel, a form adapted from oriental verse and rarely attempted in German. One can understand its attraction for Platen, the extremely form conscious post-romantic, and indeed in a few instances, such as this, it becomes a forceful medium for his always melancholy poetic expression:

> Der Strom, der neben mir verrauschte, wo ist er nun?
> Der Vogel, dessen Lied ich lauschte, wo ist er nun?
> Wo ist die Rose, die die Freundin am Herzen trug,
> Und jener Kuss, der mich berauschte, wo ist er nun?
> Und jener Mensch, der ich gewesen und den ich längst
> Mit einem andern Ich vertauschte, wo ist er nun?

The poetic principle in the ghasel is a rhyme in lines one and two, and from then on in each second line. The rhyming words (in this case "verrauschte," "lauschte," "berauschte," and "vertauschte") can occur anywhere in the line, but must be followed in every instance by identical words (here: "wo ist er nun?"). In this ghasel Platen imbues the repetitions, which need not have any particular function besides the decorative, with intense meaning. They take on additional urgency with each recurrence.

Brahms makes this the central feature of his song, setting each "wo ist er nun?" to an upward-sweeping melodic line:

Each repetition begins a half or whole step higher, with the final one ending on a brilliant high G. The piano accompaniment prolongs the intensity with an imitation of the vocal line in the ensuing pauses. The declamation is much closer to the poem than is usual with Brahms, and at the enjambment of the climactic lines five and six the vocal line sweeps through to an urgent end. The gloomy but rich, fast-moving accompaniment strengthens the mood. It is a pity to have to point out that Brahms's familiar habit of repetition intrudes awkwardly at two crucial points ("wo ist, *wo ist, wo ist* er nun" at the end of lines four and six), to vitiate somewhat the close rapport between verse and setting.

"Ich schleich umher betrübt," no. 3, and "Wehe, so willst du mich wieder," no. 5, are lesser poems, the first set simply and the second with great brilliance, but in neither case is there the sense of a union between setting and poem as in the two just described. "Wehe, so willst du mich wieder" is of special interest because of the extreme virtuosity with which Brahms matches his 9/8 rhythm to the requirements of the dactyls and to the individuality of the separate lines. The final poem, "Du sprichst, dass ich mich täuschte," no. 6, is an epigrammatic lyric with a Heinesque surprise twist at the end. Stanzas one and two close with the line "allein du liebst nicht mehr," which in the third line shifts to the imperative "und liebe mich nicht mehr." Brahms makes little of this important point.

Heinrich Heine

"Der Tod, das ist die kühle Nacht" (op. 96, no. 1) is possibly Brahms's finest word-tone synthesis. This beautiful impressionistic poem is from Heine's *Buch der Lieder:*

Der Tod, das ist die kühle Nacht,
Das Leben ist der schwüle Tag.
Es dunkelt schon, mich schläfert,
Der Tag hat mich müd' gemacht.

   Über mein Bett erhebt sich ein Baum,
Drin singt die junge Nachtigall;
Sie singt von lauter Liebe,
Ich hör' es sogar im Traum.

It is set with baffling simplicity and extreme precision. The tempo is marked "very slow" so that the duration of the song is much longer than of the poem alone. Yet this lyric, unlike most poems of Heine (but like "Über allen Gipfeln ist Ruh" of Goethe), has great tolerance for extension in time, and there is absolutely no sense that poetic values have been neglected because of the deliberate pace.

The melody of the first line, over a subdued accompaniment of tonic and diminished seventh chords, voices a peaceful affirmation of death as the cool night:

The answering second line descends to describe the oppressive day, with just a slight emphasis on the color word "schwül." The two parts of the next verse, "Es dunkelt schon" and "mich schläfert," are separated by a long pause in the vocal line but joined into a unit by the accompaniment. A stressed "Der Tag" on the highest and longest note yet reached has the appropriate plaintive quality, and the falling figure on "müd' " adds a further touch of weariness.

With the second stanza, the accompaniment changes to simple arpeggio figures in the left hand and broken chords in the right, with a suggestion of the nightingale's song in the repeated top note of the chords. The vocal line is brighter, smoother, richer, and more melodious, building to a simple climax on "Sie singt von lauter Liebe":

sie   singt   von lau - ter   Lie - be,

After a quieting repetition of "von lauter Liebe," the voice descends to the pensive, somewhat enigmatic final line, each half of which is repeated. With a subdued four-measure epilogue in the accompaniment, the song is over. In both poem and song there is the same understatement, simplicity, and finesse, with the listener left to make his own bridge between the two loosely connected ideas.

There are five more Heine songs. "Es liebt sich so lieblich im Lenze" (op. 71, no. 1—Heine's title was "Frühling") is a charming song, showing the same combination of folk song mood and sophistication that Heine put into the poem. But it does not reflect the poet's equally typical and here central quality of irony, introduced in the jingly first line, which recurs as a refrain throughout the poem. The irony is strongest in the implied eroticism of the shepherdess' naïve question, "Wem geb ich meine Kränze?" Brahms also made some "improvements" to Heine's text.[8]

"Sommerabend" and "Mondenschein" (op. 85, nos. 1 and 2) are linked together melodically. The poems, however, are unrelated, though they do come together near the end of "Heimkehr" in *Buch der Lieder.* Brahms's comment in a letter to Otto Dessoff on the reason he combined the poems shows clearly that he did not have a serious word-tone intent when he composed them: "The two poems happen to stand together in Heine, the moon is shining in both of them, and it is annoying to the musician to have to say four pretty lines only once when they can be repeated so respectably and nicely!"[9]

In "Meerfahrt" (op. 96, no. 4) Brahms has written an impressive song, daring in its harmonic and melodic effects. But as a setting of the Heine poem, the music is overwrought. The lover and his beloved are in a small boat on the sea at night, passing a mysterious island. But the island is not forbidding, as Brahms makes it in his music; rather, it is "die Geisterinsel, die schöne." The couple hear ghostly music—but "liebe Töne," not frightening ones—and see the mists dancing. The final lines laconically but powerfully state the lovers' isolation from all joy:

Wir aber schwammen vorüber,
Trostlos auf weitem Meer.

Brahms apparently misunderstood the poem, for he portrays the ghostly island in macabre tones. His song builds an uncanny crescendo to a frightening climax on words that are not frightening at all:

Dort klangen liebe Töne
Und wogte der Nebeltanz.

Ludwig Tieck

Brahms composed only one song cycle, the fifteen songs, op. 33, to poems from *Die schöne Magelone* by Ludwig Tieck (1773–1853). Tieck's work is a retelling of a folk legend in romantic prose, with poems liberally interspersed throughout the narrative. Each poem is the lyric expression of a mood, a scene, or a situation, so that there is a continuity to the song cycle, though it is necessary to know Tieck's work quite well to be aware of this. Otherwise Brahms's cycle just sounds like a collection of beautiful songs. In Schubert's "Die schöne Müllerin" or "Die Winterreise," the progression of the narrative is embodied in the poems themselves. Schumann's "Frauenliebe und -leben" is similarly self-contained. His "Dichterliebe," though somewhat less compact, is not dependent on any outside material. Brahms's "Magelone" is the only major cycle that requires close acquaintance with its source to be reasonably well understood as a unit.

All of the songs in each of the Schubert and Schumann cycles are expressions of a single personality. In Brahms's "Die schöne Magelone," four people share the songs. A minstrel sings the first one, "Keinen hat es noch gereut"; Graf Peter sings most of the others. Magelone sings "Wie schnell verschwindet / So Licht als Glanz"; and the Sultan's daughter delivers "Geliebter, wo zaudert / Dein irrender Fuss." The final song, set to verses that end Tieck's tale, is sung as a duet by the reunited Peter and Magelone, now happily married, who repeat it in a little anniversary ceremony each spring.

Tieck was a virtuoso with a dazzling command of meter, rhythm, and sound effect. Most of these lyrics are technically complex in a way that none of the poems used by earlier composers were. They present problems in word-tone relationship to a degree not previously encountered. It cannot be said that Brahms rose successfully to these challenges, though as sheer music the cycle contains some of the most opulent sounds in all of his songs.

Tieck was an erratic writer, and the quality of the poems is uneven, the best of them being splendid lyrics, the poorest weak indeed. In the songs there are individual moments, sometimes entire stanzas, where word and tone are in splendid balance, but this is not sustained in any except no. 9, "Ruhe, Süssliebchen." In all the others, familiar Brahms characteristics—a closely knit musical structure which attains an independence that either fits the word awkwardly or causes the sense of the words to go unnoticed, as well as a fatal tendency to repeat words or phrases for the sake of the musical structure—usually prevent a close rapport. In view of the intricacy of the metrical patterns, these repetitions often make a shambles out of an ingeniously devised poetic structure. The last lines of the final poem, for instance, are:

Sie scheide
Von Leide
Auf immer
Und nimmer
Entschwinde die liebliche, selige, himmlische Lust!

Out of this Brahms makes: "Sie scheide von Leide auf immer, und nimmer, und nimmer, und nimmer entschwinde, und nimmer entschwinde die liebliche, selige, himmlische Lust, die himmlische Lust. Sie scheide von Leide auf immer, und nimmer entschwinde die selige, himmlische Lust! Sie scheide von Leide, und nimmer entschwinde die liebliche, selige, himmlische Lust!"

Most of the numbers of this cycle are considerably longer than Brahms's songs usually are. This is in part because the poems tend to be rather long, but mainly because the musical structures are more complex—as the often excessive repetitions would indicate. The unusually elaborate piano accompaniments, which sometimes achieve quasi-orchestral effects, also add to the length. The songs often fall into contrasting subsections, even when there is little or no occasion for this in the poem itself, as in "Liebe kam aus fernen Landen." In this poem Tieck held his virtuosity in check and produced seven regular four-line stanzas of trochaic tetrameter. It is a love poem, supposedly written by the hero Peter and sent by messenger to his new-found beloved, Magelone. The elaborate musical structure is wholly inappropriate to the poem. In no. 6, "Wie soll ich die Freude, die Wonne denn tragen?" the six stanzas of the poem are extremely varied, with constantly changing rhythmic and rhyming patterns, and greatly differing line lengths. The twelve-page song, the longest in the cycle, does not solve the problems posed by these intricacies.

No. 9, "Ruhe, Süssliebchen," is the only word-tone gem of the cycle. The poem is a sweet lullaby and love song sung by Peter as he watches over the slumbering Magelone just before their cruel separation. The meter is irregular, chiefly dactyls and trochees. There are prominent sound effects in the verse:

Es säuselt das Gras auf den Matten,
Es fächelt und kühlt dich der Schatten.

The melody begins expansively, taking in the first two lines of the poem and accommodating the rhythm with precision:

The accompaniment is gentle and swaying, *sempre pianissimo e dolce.* The song continues in the same gentle, warm vein until a kind of refrain is reached, beginning:

In the second stanza, the knight turns to the birds of the forest, bidding them not to disturb the slumber of his beloved. The accompaniment is a melodious evocation of softly rustling leaves:

The more animated final stanza bids the brook weave beautiful phantasies of love into her dreams. Again the accompaniment changes to an expansively flowing rhythm, as the voice sings:

The motif of the refrain—somewhat altered, fuller, and more rapid —closes the beautiful song on the words:

Durch den flüsternden Hain
Schwärmen goldene Bienelein,
Und summen zum Schlummer dich ein.

Ludwig Hölty

That Brahms composed six Hölty songs is ample proof that he was attracted to poems with elaborate structures. He greatly admired the poet. In 1869 he wrote to a friend about "my dear Hölty, for whose beautiful moving words my music is not fine enough, otherwise you would see his verses oftener in my works."[10] Two of his settings are to asclepiadic odes ("Die Mainacht" and "Der Kuss"); a third ("Die Schale der Vergessenheit") has alternating asclepiadic ($-\cup-\cup\cup--\cup\cup-\cup-$) and glyconaic ($-\cup-\cup\cup-\cup-$) verses; a fourth ("An ein Veilchen") is constructed on the verse pattern $-\cup-\cup\cup-\cup-\cup-\cup$; while the other two ("An die Nachtigall" and "Minnelied") are in simpler verse forms.

Brahms's best-known Hölty song is "Die Mainacht" (op. 43, no. 2), one of his most enchanting works. The claim has been prominently made that the song carefully follows the complex rhythm of Hölty's asclepiadic ode. In a discussion of "Die Mainacht," Karl Geiringer writes, "It is instructive to observe the sovereign mastery with which Brahms at the height of his powers treats this complicated form."[11] This is just not so, and a correction is in order.

The metrical structure of an asclepiadic ode is as follows:

(1) $-\cup-\cup\cup--\cup\cup-\cup-$
(2) $-\cup-\cup\cup--\cup\cup-\cup-$
(3) $-\cup-\cup\cup-\cup$
(4) $-\cup-\cup\cup-\cup-$

There are three strophes in the song (the original had four, but Brahms omitted the second). The first is set with great beauty and remarkable fidelity to the nuances of the metrical structure of the ode, so that for the first strophe poem and music are indeed in perfect accord:

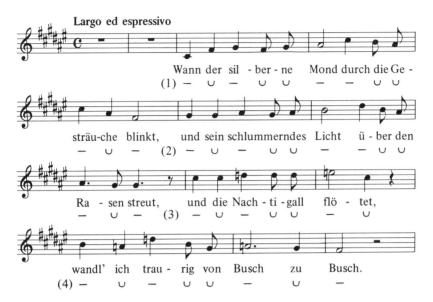

But, beginning with the next strophe, the musical development takes Brahms further and further from the ode form. The second line is broken in two:

The fourth line is set to a gorgeously expansive melodic line with rich accompanying harmony. By this time the music has taken over, and the poetic form is engulfed in musical sound and structure. The final stanza strains the ode yet further out of shape. The word "heisser" is repeated, but the lines have only the faintest resemblance to an asclepiadic in any case:

Often in songs of Brahms, the composer faithfully parallels the form of the poem at the beginning of the song, but as the music develops, it pulls away from the poetic structure and creates its own pattern. "Die Mainacht" is a classic case. Yet this tendency is not entirely inevitable, as proved by Brahms's equally well-known "Sapphische Ode," set, unfortunately, to an undistinguished rhymed sapphic ode by Hans Schmidt. In this beautiful song the meter of the ode is faithfully adhered to from beginning to end, and the music, if anything, actually strengthens the metrical pattern of the poem.

The other asclepiadic ode of Hölty, "Der Kuss," is an early song, Brahms's first to verses by this poet. The ode form is virtually unrecognizable as such in the 3/8 rhythm of the song.[12] "Die Schale der Vergessenheit" is a large-scale impassioned song in which the music takes its own course and even the sense of the words, surely the meter, is pretty much overwhelmed by the rich flood of musical sound. None of the Hölty songs comes close to the kind of affinity between words and music that is represented by "Der Tod, das ist die kühle Nacht," for instance. Brahms's admiration of Hölty's poetry notwithstanding, the delicate, sensitive verse of that gentle, shy youth cannot compete with the rich sentiment and expressivity of Brahms's song style.

Goethe

There are only five Goethe songs. Brahms alone among
major song composers was not tempted by the *Wilhelm Meister*
poems. But these five represent in capsule the predilections, the
strengths, and the weaknesses of Brahms as a composer of lyric
verse. In "Die Liebende schreibt" the formalist chooses, of all
things, a sonnet, with almost predictable results. It seems intrinsically impossible to accommodate such an elaborate, tightly knit
poetic form to musical delivery in the nineteenth century idiom,
and certain it is that this song, whatever its merits, destroys the
form of the sonnet. In contrast, "Trost in Tränen" was adapted
by Goethe from a folk song. The poem of eight stanzas (Volks-
liedstrophen) is a dialogue, with the speakers alternating at each
strophe. The first speaker tries to talk his friend out of his sadness
("Wie kommt's, dass du so traurig bist?"), but the friend prefers
his tears ("Verweinen lasst die Nächte mich / So lang ich weinen
mag"). The song matches the poem stanza for stanza, with the
music for the first speaker being more assertive and in the major,
and the music for the second, though parallel in movement, being
in the minor and having just a touch of intensification toward the
end of each strophe.

In an utterly different vein is the rollicking "Unüberwindlich"
("Hab' ich tausendmal geschworen"),[13] a drinking song in two
stanzas about the irresistibility of wine and women. From the first
to the second stanza there is a marvelous switch from "Flasche"
to "Falsche," which leaves one in doubt as to whether the first
stanza is only about wine after all. The second stanza is clearly not,
ending with a swift reference to the plight of Samson:

Deine Scher' in meinen Haaren,
Allerliebste Delila!

Why this song is not better known is a mystery, for the music is as
intoxicating as the poem. Both are tongue-in-cheek. The music
begins with a quotation from Domenico Scarlatti:

D. Scarlatti

This theme is used for a delightful buffo aria. The first stanza culminates in a hilarious pictorialization of a woozy head, using the Scarlatti theme:

wird der Pfropf her - aus - ge - ho - ben, sie ist leer, und ich nicht mein,

The Samson and Delilah lines are fitted to the same melodic line, proving that it is not only wine that causes dizziness. One is almost persuaded to think that the poem was written for this setting.

"Dämmrung senkte sich von oben" is, from the point of view of word-tone synthesis, Brahms's most impressive achievement, though, strangely enough, it too is little known.[14] The poem is a very late one from Goethe's "Chinesisch-deutsche Jahres- und Tageszeiten," a brief collection of poems written in 1827 when the poet was 78:

Dämmrung senkte sich von oben,
Schon ist alle Nähe fern;
Doch zuerst emporgehoben
Holden Lichts der Abendstern!
Alles schwankt ins Ungewisse,
Nebel schleichen in die Höh;
Schwarzvertiefte Finsternisse
Widerspiegelnd ruht der See.

Nun im östlichen Bereiche
Ahn ich Mondenglanz und -Glut,
Schlanker Weiden Haargezweige
Scherzen auf der nächsten Flut.
Durch bewegter Schatten Spiele
Zittert Lunas Zauberschein,
Und durchs Auge schleicht die Kühle
Sänftigend ins Herz hinein.

The serenity of the aging poet speaks from the measured rhythms of these beautiful lines. In the first strophe one senses a readiness for death, a detachment from life ("Schon ist alle Nähe fern"). This mood reaches a climax in the "schwarzvertiefte Finsternisse" (so great is the equilibrium of the poem that the reader could easily miss the creative use of language in the striking "schwarzvertiefte"). The moon in the second strophe, potentially a harbinger of death like the evening star in stanza one, is the pivot around which the atmosphere shifts from death to life. The moon brings light and movement to the darkness. The four lines that follow are brighter, more animated. The words, in their rococo association, reach back well over fifty years to the poet's earliest period:

Schlanker Weiden Haargezweige
Scherzen auf der nächsten Flut.
Durch bewegter Schatten Spiele
Zittert Lunas Zauberschein.

The final two lines strike a balance conveying the equanimity of the poet: readiness for death, willingness for life, serene composure.

Brahms was only forty when his song to this masterful lyric was published. Yet the music conveys fully the sense and atmosphere of the inspired verses. The low, quiet opening notes of the accompaniment, quite uncharacteristic of Brahms, set the tone of mature reflection, and the first notes of the voice line reflect the placidity of the verse:

The music of the first phrase is in B-flat minor; the following modulation to the key of F could be to F major, though miraculously Brahms omits the third of the chord on "fern," leaving the resolution indecisive. The evening star and its lovely light are brought in with slightly more brightness and color, now definitely in the major. Afterwards comes a sixteenth-note line in the right hand of the accompaniment, in counterpoint to left-hand octaves that repeat the beginning of the vocal line:

This passage makes a transition to the important lines "alles schwankt ins Ungewisse," which is vocally a repetition of the opening line, restating the theme that has just been heard in the bass, but supported this time by a more somber sixteenth-note counterpoint in both hands of the accompaniment. The vocal line to the next words, "schwarzvertiefte Finsternisse," repeats the melodic phrase heard earlier to the evening star, but significantly lowered a minor third, making it darker, more mysterious.

The opening lines of the second stanza, which form the pivot of the poem, are exactly that in the music as well:[15]

Nun   am   öst - li -chen Be - rei - che   ahn— ich

Mon-den-glanz ___   und   Glut,

The steadily ascending vocal line suggests both the serene herald of death and the rising light. To the rococo lines is set gently florid rococo music, precisely echoing the cadence of the words:

schlan - ker_   Wei - den_   Haar - ge - zwei - ge_

Finally, there is a shift to the major on "Durch bewegter Schatten Spiele / zittert Lunas Zauberschein," lines that combine the animation of willow trees with the magic glow of the moon, bringing to a climax the growing affirmation of life expressed in the second stanza. For this section Brahms repeats in the major and a major fifth higher the musical line that he had used twice before, first for the evening star, then lowered a third and still in the minor for the dark shadows ("schwarzvertiefte Finsternisse"). The poem and the music thus reach their climax on the same lines, and each unites in its climax the leading motifs of the first stanza.

The final lines, which Brahms repeats, descend calmly from this high point to the placidity of a serene acceptance. The song closes with alternate vocal lines, either one a suitable ending:

sänf - ti - gend ins   Herz_____   hin - ein. ___

Other Poets

Brahms composed only two poems of Mörike, selecting one from each end of the lyric spectrum. "Agnes" is a lament in the manner of a folk song:

Rosenzeit! Wie schnell vorbei,
  Schnell vorbei
Bist du doch gegangen!
Wär mein Lieb nur blieben treu,
  Blieben treu,
Sollte mir nicht bangen.

But there is sophisticated art concealed in these lines, particularly in the contrast between the lively rhythm and bright musicality and the plaintive theme. This contrast extends to the song, whose line is at once simple and artful:

Notice especially the ingenious alternation of 3/4 and 2/4. The vocal line is almost strophic, repeated with very slight variations four times for the four stanzas of the poem. The accompaniment, however, differs markedly for each stanza, paralleling the changing tone of the words.[16] Brahms also composed a gorgeous song to Mörike's complex "An eine Äolsharfe," which is discussed together with Wolf's setting in the next chapter.

Brahms composed settings for two poems by the seventeenth century poet Paul Fleming (1609—1640), one of which, "O liebliche Wangen," is a recital favorite.[17] One perceives at once the artfulness in the words that must have caught Brahms's eye:

O liebliche Wangen,
Ihr macht mir Verlangen!
Dies Rote, dies Weisse
Zu schauen mit Fleisse,
Und dies nur alleine
Ist's nicht, das ich meine:
Zu schauen, zu grüssen,
Zu rühren, zu küssen!
Ihr macht mir Verlangen,
O liebliche Wangen!

But the poem becomes engulfed in the surge of impetuous music. There is artistic and even ironic detachment in the words, but certainly none in the music, and one does best to try to forget that these verses are not really the romantic outpouring that Brahms's song makes them out to be. The poem, a highly stylized construction, was written, incidentally, to fit an Italian air, which was quite different, one may be sure, from the Brahms song.

Though it is undeniable that Brahms was attracted to elaborate metrical forms in the texts to his songs, many were the ties that linked him with the folk song as well, so it is not surprising that in the art songs he sometimes moved far from Hölty, Platen, and Tieck to choose from among the myriad folklike songs and poems produced in the nineteenth century. Five of his earliest songs are to Eichendorff texts, two of which had already been set by Schumann ("In der Fremde" and "Mondnacht").[18] But there is no contest here; Schumann is far and away the superior interpreter of Eichendorff.

Much more effective are the four songs of Johann Ludwig Uhland (1787—1862). Three of these appeared together in op. 19, published in 1862. The most irresistible is no. 4, "Der Schmied." The happy girl is immensely proud of her beloved smith, hard at work in his smithy. When she walks past, the bellows roar, the flames shoot up. Brahms's voice line and accompaniment conjure up this picture unfailingly with the first measures:

It is all there: the busy smith, the pride and love of the girl, and the charming folk näiveté. Nos. 2 and 3 are taken from Uhland's *Wanderlieder*. Their titles alone—"Scheiden und Meiden" and "In der Ferne"—tell the story. Brahms linked the two songs by using the same motif in both. It is amazing to note here that the composer who could produce a flood of the most opulent sounds is also capable of the greatest restraint when he wants to reflect the straightforward simplicity of the folk motifs and rhythms of the verse:

The graceful "Maienkätzchen" to a brief poem by Detlev von Liliencron (1844–1909) is a very late song, which shows the

same control. Brahms did not always exercise such restraint, however, and there are other simple folk-motif poems that he sets
more elaborately. Clemens Brentano's "O kühler Wald" and
Theodor Storm's "Über die Heide," as well as the early Uhland
song "Heimkehr," are examples.

Finally, there are three songs to poems of Gottfried Keller
(1819–1890). One wishes there were more, not because of
"Abendregen," a poor choice of text and a rather dull song, but
because of the other two, "Therese" and "Salome."[19] These are
among sixteen early poems Keller published in a cycle called "Von
Weibern," each poem headed by a different girl's name. Feminine
wiles, wisdom, and superiority in the battle of the sexes are
celebrated in the first eight poems. Therese is a mature woman
who gives charming advice to a young boy beginning to feel interest in the opposite sex:

Du milchjunger Knabe,
Wie schaust du mich an?
Was haben deine Augen
Für eine Frage getan!

Salome is a cocky young girl in love, who asks the other girls to
keep their hands off her lover; she will tame him herself:

O ihr teuren Gespielen!
Überlasst mir den stolzen Mann!
Er soll sehn, wie die Liebe
Ein feurig Schwert werden kann!

There is humor in these unusual poems, a similarity to the folk
song in form, language, and theme, but also a subtle sophistication
and tongue-in-cheek irony. Keller himself had trouble describing
them in a letter to his close friend, the musician Wilhelm
Baumgartner, in July 1852: "They are not supposed to be
portraits of passion, but just feminine whims and destinies, and
not even these expressly, but just light whimsical tones that come
from I don't know where myself."[20] Brahms clearly sensed their
intent, perhaps because of certain affinities between poet and
composer: both were bachelors, both were more interested in the
opposite sex than they were willing to admit, and both had a

"folksy" sense of humor. Many years later Keller confessed to a drinking companion that he could never listen to Brahms's "Therese," because it always made him weep, reminding him that he too stood as helpless before life as the young boy in the poem before the beautiful woman.[21] The two songs are splendid extensions into music of the essence of the poems.

Chapter *VI* Hugo Wolf

If Schumann's muse was inspirational, Brahms's steady and reliable, then Wolf's (1860–1903) was explosive. The fifty-three songs of his Mörike volume were produced in a frenzy of creativity between February and November 1888. This pattern was typical, applying to both his Goethe songs and virtually all the others. In 1895, after years of frustration, he completed his only opera, *Der Corregidor*, in full orchestra score within nine months of demonic creativity. By less than two years later (the same year in which Brahms died at the age of sixty-four) he had written his last compositions, the three Michelangelo songs. Wolf, who was then thirty-seven, lived on in insanity for six more years.

Eduard Mörike

Wolf's affinity for Mörike indicates that he was more sensitive to lyrical subtleties than any other song composer, for Mörike is a complicated poet. Only within the last twenty years has literary criticism begun to recognize the stature of his best poems. The shifting evaluations of Mörike from his own day to the present are examined in a recent book by S.S. Prawer, who points out for the first time that Hugo Wolf showed in his songs an appreciation of Mörike far ahead of his time.[1] By the same token, Wolf set himself a perilous task in attempting to set to music so difficult a poet. Early as he is, Mörike represents, even if only intuitively, a major step on the road toward late nineteenth and twentieth century symbolist poetry. His subtle interweaving of thought, mood, emotion, impression, and suggestion; the enchanting mellifluousness of his words, phrases, and rhythms, are unrivaled in any lyric poetry that had gone before, as witness these examples:

O flaumenleichte Zeit der dunklen Frühe. . . . .

Es dringt der Sonne goldener Kuss
Mir tief bis ins Geblüt hinein. . . . .

Und Frühlingsblüten unterweges streifend,
Übersättigt mit Wohlgerüchen.. . . .

Hört man der Erdenkräfte flüsterndes Gedränge,
Das aufwärts in die zärtlichen Gesänge
Der reingestimmten Lüfte summt.. . . .

The implications of Mörike's style for word-tone synthesis are
serious. Many of his lyrics are in effect miniature but complex
syntheses. To incorporate them into a late nineteenth-century
musical setting is to run the risk of damaging certain indispensable
features. Nevertheless, in a number of his Mörike songs, Wolf
succeeds in integrating the musical dimension into the already
complex structure. In others, he fails. An examination in detail of
some of the poems and songs will show his amazing if erratic
sensitivity to the intricacies of Mörike's poetic muse. Two of
Mörike's most complex poems offer a good starting point, for
one of them, "An eine Äolsharfe," eluded Wolf, whereas with the
other, "Um Mitternacht," an equally difficult poem, Wolf created
a genuine synthesis where word and tone are inseparably fused into
a larger whole without sacrificing the values of the poem.

The most important feature of any lyric poem is likely to be
not its literal meaning but rather its connotations, ambiguities, or
"paradoxes," to use Cleanth Brooks's excellent term.[2] These are
more often revealed by rhythm, rhyme, sound values, and images
than by what the poem literally says. It was the French symbolists
—Verlaine, Rimbaud, and Mallarmé—following the direction set by
Baudelaire, who were bold enough to carry this tendency to its
logical extreme, ignoring literal meaning to an unprecedented
degree and raising to absolute prominence the poem's connotations, free associations, and ambiguities—in short, its purely lyric
aspects. This kind of verse, often called *poésie pure* or absolute
poetry, set the patterns that dominate much of the poetry of the
twentieth century. Although the major part of Mörike's lyric production came long before *Les fleurs du mal* (1857), not to speak
of the later symbolists, and thus could not conceivably have been
influenced by them, yet in "An eine Äolsharfe" (1837) and "Um
Mitternacht" (1827), as well as in many other poems, Mörike
anticipates these techniques to an amazing extent. This quality
has   only   recently   come   to   be   understood   by   literary

scholars, with the help of such perceptive critics as Walter Höllerer.[3] In these important poems, the center of gravity shifts, so to speak, away from the literal meaning toward the more subtle lyric aspects, to a degree that is true of no other German poet until Hugo von Hofmannsthal and Stefan George at the turn of the century, whose works clearly came under the influence of the French symbolists.

Only by being aware of this shift can one really understand "An eine Äolsharfe":

Angelehnt an die Efeuwand
Dieser alten Terrasse,
Du, einer luftgebornen Muse
Geheimnisvolles Saitenspiel,
Fang an,
Fange wieder an
Deine melodische Klage!

Ihr kommet, Winde, fern herüber
Ach! von des Knaben
Der mir so lieb war,
Frisch grünendem Hügel.
Und Frühlingsblüten unterweges streifend,
Übersättigt mit Wohlgerüchen,
Wie süss bedrängt ihr dies Herz!
Und säuselt her in die Saiten,
Angezogen von wohllautender Wehmut,
Wachsend im Zug meiner Sehnsucht,
Und hinsterbend wieder.

Aber auf einmal,
Wie der Wind heftiger herstösst,
Ein holder Schrei der Harfe
Wiederholt, mir zu süssem Erschrecken,
Meiner Seele plötzliche Regung;
Und hier—die volle Rose streut, geschüttelt,
All ihre Blätter vor meine Füsse!

The poem tells about an aeolian harp, or wind harp, which the dictionary defines as a "box-shaped musical instrument having stretched strings usually tuned in unison on which the wind produces varying harmonics over the same fundamental tone." Yet one can easily miss the essence of the poem by concentrating exclusively on the harp. This is undoubtedly what misled Hugo Wolf. On a more significant level, the harp is secondary to the essential communication of the poem, the blending of several strands of connotation: spring and death, sound and feeling, poet and harp, which hover about the lines in an elusive manner.

In the second strophe the poet speaks of the winds as though they were wafting from the distant grave of the boy he loved (Mörike's younger brother, though the fact is of no significance in the poem). Whereas the suggestion is a literal absurdity, it is of the utmost lyric importance, for the motif of death is about to undergo an infinitely subtle interweaving with the motif of spring and burgeoning life. Earlier the theme of rebirth was delicately touched on in the description of the grave as becoming freshly green ("frisch grünendem Hügel"), just as the motif of death was gently anticipated by the "ach" and the past tense "war." The next two extraordinary lines, which tell of the wind wafting through the spring blossoms and becoming saturated with fragrance, are a miracle of richly fluted melodiousness:

Und Frühlingsblüten unterweges streifend,
Übersättigt mit Wohlgerüchen

They must be read at a slow pace, so that the full vowels and consonant combinations of "Frühlingsblüten," "übersättigt," and "Wohlgerüchen" have their intended effect.

Once the motifs of death and life have been intertwined, the magical identification of the poet's feelings with the tones of the harp are subtly accomplished by the juxtaposition of the next two lines:

Wie süss bedrängt ihr dies Herz!
Und säuselt her in die Saiten

This identity makes possible the delicate tracery of the last three lines of the strophe, in which the motifs of harp, poet, and wind are merged. The line "Angezogen von wohllautender Wehmut," another literal absurdity, blends the three themes. It is followed by two lines that evoke a brilliant crescendo and diminuendo of emotion:

Wachsend im Zug meiner Sehnsucht,
Und hinsterbend wieder.

These interwoven motifs reach a peak of synthesis in the shorter
third strophe, where a sudden gust of wind, evoked by the strong
aspirates and full stresses of "heftiger herstösst," is matched by the
simultaneous sforzando of the wind harp ("ein holder Schrei")
and an identical agitation in the soul of the poet ("meiner Seele
plötzliche Regung"). Note how the "holder Schrei" of the harp is
echoed by the "süssem Erschrecken" in the poet's heart, and the
"plötzliche Regung" of his soul echoes the "heftiger herstösst"
of the wind. This leads to the rich but understated image of the
mature rose whose petals, shaken by that same gust of wind, fall
at the feet of the poet. In this image the motifs culminate in a
final union, for here the sudden gust of wind, the surge of emotion
in the poet, the quickening sound of the wind harp, and the fallen
petals of the rose all express in symbol and image the elusive
themes of the poem.

Wolf's song is a disappointment to the listener who understands
the poem, though as chamber music it is hauntingly beautiful. The
subtle interweavings of the poem are not realized in the setting and
thus cannot be part of the communication of the song. It is clear
that Wolf used the wind harp as the theme of his song, as did
Brahms before him, and subordinated everything else to it. The
central motif is a haunting evocation of the beautiful sounds of
the harp's strings set in motion by the wind:

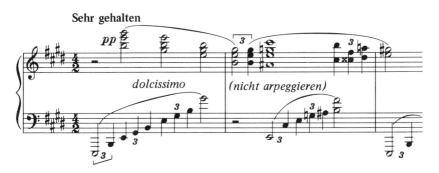

Brahms's harp motif is less striking, but also very effective. It is
capable, like Wolf's, of subtle harmonic changes:

Poco lento

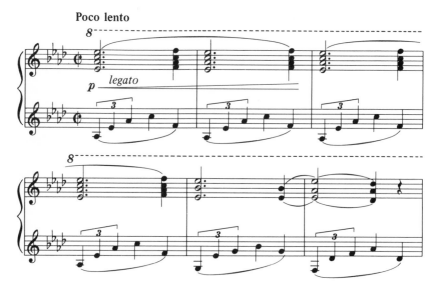

Neither vocal line binds together the wonderfully evocative associations of the poem. The three most expressive passages in both songs, in fact, are those that might be selected from a cursory reading of the poem. The first occurs at the words "wie süss," which Brahms repeats once. Wolf uses the phrase no less than three times, one of the rare instances in which he permitted himself repetitions that were not in the original. A still further repetition of the entire phrase "Wie süss bedrängt ihr dies Herz" makes this passage exceptional in Wolf's songs. The expressive lines "wachsend im Zug meiner Sehnsucht / Und hinsterbend wieder" are appropriately set by both composers, but without the exquisite preparation offered by the poet. It is the literal meaning of "wachsend" and "hinsterbend" that Brahms and Wolf compose, though Wolf is more explicit in the swelling and subsiding of the musical phrase. Finally, as one might expect, there is an intensification at "wie der Wind heftiger herstösst," but it lacks any subtler significance. To emphasize these words, Brahms moves momentarily into a recitative. Hugo Wolf's entire song is bathed in the fragile beauty of the wind harp motif, which persists in the accompaniment throughout in manifold transformation. It ends with a long piano epilogue in which the wind harp theme achieves its fullest harmonic development.

Frank Walker's biography of Wolf tells of a visit by the composer to the castle of Hoch-Osterwitz in southeastern Austria,
which substantiates my interpretation, indirectly at least: "As
they walked through the deserted halls Wolf suddenly stopped
short and listened intently. Strange sounds came to his ear, as if
somebody were playing a piano in the distance. He walked towards
the sound and discovered its source in an Aeolian harp, set in the
window of the last chamber of the castle. For a time he listened
enchanted, then said, 'That is really wonderful. Look, I have
never heard an Aeolian harp in my life until this moment, and yet
I divined it just so, exactly as the Aeolian harp there sounds, so it
is in my song.'"[4]

If Wolf's "An eine Äolsharfe" is not a true extension of the
essence of the poem into musical terms, his greatest success with
this extremely difficult kind of composition is his setting of
Mörike's "Um Mitternacht":

Gelassen stieg die Nacht ans Land,
Lehnt träumend an der Berge Wand,
Ihr Auge sieht die goldne Waage nun
Der Zeit in gleichen Schalen stille ruhn;
　Und kecker rauschen die Quellen hervor,
　Sie singen der Mutter, der Nacht, ins Ohr
　Vom Tage,
　Vom heute gewesenen Tage.

Das uralt alte Schlummerlied,
Sie achtet's nicht, sie ist es müd;
Ihr klingt des Himmels Bläue süsser noch,
Der flüchtgen Stunden gleichgeschwungnes Joch.
　Doch immer behalten die Quellen das Wort,
　Es singen die Wasser im Schlafe noch fort
　Vom Tage,
　Vom heute gewesenen Tage.

Here again is a poem whose subtle evocative quality almost
defies prosaic paraphrase. The delicate atmosphere is achieved
by the personification and juxtaposition of blissful night and
the restless springs. At midnight the contented dreamy eye
of night sees the golden scale of time in exact balance, while

the animated springs sing of the day that is past. The juxtaposition of the senses of sight and sound ("ihr Auge sieht"; "und kecker rauschen") is central to the imagery. The night does not hear this ancient slumber song, having grown accustomed to it ("sie achtet's nicht, sie ist es müd"). Its attention is centered elsewhere, as the next two lines reveal with magical synaesthetic effect:

> Ihr klingt des Himmels Bläue süsser noch,
> Der flüchtgen Stunden gleichgeschwungnes Joch.

"Klingt," "Bläue," and "süsser" achieve a blending of three senses. The beautiful refrain, "Vom Tage, / Vom heute gewesenen Tage," is the most assertive sound of the poem, and its haunting plaintiveness contrasts gorgeously with the quiet, contented contemplation of the night in the earlier lines of each stanza.

The vocal line of Wolf's song enhances this poetic expression and adds an almost mesmerizing effect of serenity, contentment, calm, and peace:

The accompaniment lulls the senses still further with an interweaving pattern in the low register, which allows the words their full effect:

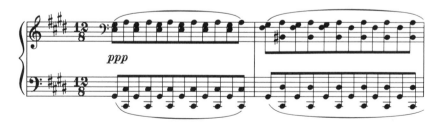

It was a point of artistic honor to Hugo Wolf, fervent disciple of Richard Wagner, that the music of his songs should match the poetic declamation, the word and sentence accent. This concern for the intricacies of word patterns is not necessarily to the advantage of a song, nor even of word-tone fusion, especially when it is carried out to an overly explicit degree and to the detriment of the melodic line, as happens not infrequently in Wolf songs. But in this instance Wolf's effortless mastery of the declamation contributes to the compelling quality of the musical setting. The first two lines of the poem are a rhymed couplet of iambic tetrameter; there follows a rhymed couplet of iambic pentameter with an enjambment that is stunningly mastered by Wolf:

The third rhymed couplet has four accents but is irregular in meter, with dactyls predominating; and the last two lines, the refrain, are quite irregular.[5] The poem thus presents a contrast between the steadier rhythm of the first four lines and the slightly livelier rhythm of the second half of the strophe, which is in perfect accord with the content. This contrast is effortlessly incorporated into the masterly declamation of the song in a manner that permits the rhythm its full effect. The musical movement is somewhat heightened in the second half of each strophe by a shift into a higher register by both voice and accompaniment. The emphasized first "Tage" is highlighted by a subdued discordant major seventh interval between voice and piano, enhancing the remarkable effect of reminiscence and plaintiveness achieved with this word in the poem:

The poem is strophic, and so, by exception, is the song, for Wolf's usual practice was to through-compose even strophic poems.[6] When he did use a strophic musical form, it was often extremely varied. In "Um Mitternacht," by contrast, there are only slight changes in the music to the second strophe. This, too, is a perfect complement to the poem, in which there is no difference at all in mood and only a slight progression in thought between the strophes.

"Im Frühling" is another of Mörike's more advanced poems:

Hier lieg ich auf dem Frühlingshügel:
Die Wolke wird mein Flügel,
Ein Vogel fliegt mir voraus.
Ach, sag mir, alleinzige Liebe,
Wo du bleibst, dass ich bei dir bliebe!
Doch du und die Lüfte, ihr habt kein Haus.

Der Sonnenblume gleich steht mein Gemüte offen,
Sehnend,
Sich dehnend
In Liebe und Hoffen.
Frühling, was bist du gewillt?
Wann werd ich gestillt?

Die Wolke seh ich wandeln und den Fluss,
Es dringt der Sonne goldner Kuss
Mir tief bis ins Geblüt hinein;
Die Augen, wunderbar berauschet,
Tun, als schliefen sie ein,
Nur noch das Ohr dem Ton der Biene lauschet.
Ich denke dies und denke das,
Ich sehne mich und weiss nicht recht nach was:
Halb ist es Lust, halb ist es Klage;
Mein Herz, o sage,
Was webst du für Erinnerung
In golden grüner Zweige Dämmerung?
—Alte unnennbare Tage!

The disarmingly simple opening line is followed by another direct assertion, "Die Wolke wird mein Flügel." Simple as this seems, to the perceptive reader it is highly evocative, even daring. With all its apparent naïveté, it subtly lifts thought and expression into a serene sense of oneness with nature. The third line, "Ein Vogel fliegt mir voraus," does the same thing in an even more surprising way, boldly taking the preceding idea for granted. And so on, through a whole series of splendidly lyrical phrases that defy paraphrase, like "Der Sonnenblume gleich steht mein Gemüte offen."

Further on, to the quiet joy of this pantheistic expansiveness are added typical Mörike touches of ambiguous, fragile longing ("Ich sehne mich und weiss nicht recht nach was") and of vague reminiscence ("Alte unnennbare Tage"). Nothing more specific should be sought for in these lines. The longing and reminiscence will not yield to analysis. Both are intentionally vague, and both are subordinate to the central atmosphere, which is neither future nor past but present.

When one approaches Hugo Wolf's setting of this exquisite poem, one marvels at his sensitivity to its lyric values. Clearly he understood the real sense of the poem. Nonetheless, the uniqueness, the evanescence, and the perfection of the poem are lost in the song. In a strange way, the music, by extending the poetic values into the more abstract musical sphere, robs them of their individuality. The highly evocative poem becomes part of a song which, though it expresses the same moods, deprives them of the insubstantial quality that is their essence.

As in "An eine Äolsharfe," the poem includes certain lines that are probably impossible to set to music in late nineteenth century style. Certainly Wolf was able to do nothing with the magical "Es dringt der Sonne goldner Kuss / Mir tief bis ins Geblüt hinein":

Perhaps the most prominent cause for the failure of this song as a fusion of word and tone is the factor of duration. The exact timing of the successive images contributes to the poem's magic. To be sure, the thrust of the poem is not rapid or assertive (as in Goethe's "Prometheus," for instance), but in its own leisurely way it is insistent and cohesive. A single extra word would throw off the delicate balance. Inevitably, the musical setting slows down this tempo. This change alone is a strain on the fragile juxtaposition of the parts. Moreover, the spacing of vocal entrances, while the voice waits for accompaniment patterns between phrases, beautiful though they are, punctuates and interrupts the subtle continuity of the poem. There are eight such intervals that last more than a full measure of slow-paced 6/4 time; the longest extends over seven measures. Mörike's poem simply cannot tolerate this kind of dilation. The concentrated effect of the poem disintegrates long before the song reaches its conclusion.

Mörike had an enormous range, and most of his lyric poetry is less complex than this. But Wolf, with his sense for poetic beauties, was drawn to the most difficult and advanced poems. Of this category, there are nine other songs, none of them entirely successful as settings of their poems. They are "Der Genesene an die Hoffnung," "Karwoche," "Auf einer Wanderung," "Heimweh," "An die Geliebte," "Peregrina I," "Peregrina II," "Wo find ich Trost?" and "Auf eine Christblume I."

The beloved "Fussreise," in contrast, is another brilliant achievement. The ebullient poem has a breezy walker's rhythm, established immediately in the opening lines:

Am frischgechnittnen Wanderstab,
Wenn ich in der Frühe
So durch die Wälder ziehe,
Hügel auf und ab:

Wolf's skillful declamation does perfect justice to this rhythm. The accompaniment adds a gaily relaxed walking motif, which supplements but does not supplant the rhythm of the poem. The many enjambments, the delightful rhymes ("Gottbeherzte"–"nie verscherzte"; "Wanderschweisse"–"Morgenreise"), the bold compounds ("Erstlings - Paradieseswonne"), the good humor, the infectiousness, the insouciance, the joie de vivre of the poem are translated into irresistible musical terms. Once one has learned the song, it is impossible to read Mörike's poem without hearing it, the two are in such perfect accord.

The virtuoso Mörike was master of many moods and types of lyric. Among these are two brilliant ballads used by Wolf: "Die Geister am Mummelsee" and "Der Feuerreiter." Both poems have an eerie, frightening quality, conjure up dazzling word pictures and sounds, and build to uncanny, even frightening climaxes. No other song composer except perhaps Carl Loewe would have dared to set them to music, yet in his settings Wolf achieved two tours de force. "Der Feuerreiter" in particular has a demonic quality. The Mörike ballad portrays in sharp relief a central action surrounded by uncertainties, ambiguities, mysterious unanswered questions, which gives it a ghostly, spectral quality. The song exploits this powerful situation to the utmost. It is as insistent in its sweeping forward motion as the poem. Frank Walker reports that Wolf once told friends just before performing "Der Feuerreiter," "Now I'll sing you something that will make your hair stand on end,"[7] and he was right. It is a fearfully difficult song to perform, for singer and accompanist both.

"Die Geister am Mummelsee" is less overwhelming, though filled with dazzling effects. The poem itself is not so concentrated as "Der Feuerreiter." To some extent the musical setting dissipates the effect of the poem by placing too much emphasis on detail.

Though both ballads are strophic, they are through-composed by Wolf. Each stanza of the ballads has striking, refrainlike final lines. In "Der Feuerreiter," Wolf's setting of the repeated "Hinterm Berg, / Hinterm Berg / Brennt es in der Mühle!" and variants serves to give the otherwise diffuse musical setting a sharper contour and a strophic feeling. Although the poem "Die Geister am Mummelsee" has an equally arresting refrain, "O nein! So sage, was mag es wohl sein?" with variants, in the song these do not impart the same strophic feeling.

"Seufzer" is a poem of great pathos:

Dein Liebesfeuer,
Ach Herr! wie teuer
Wollt ich es hegen,
Wollt ich es pflegen!

Habs nicht geheget
Und nicht gepfleget,
Bin tot im Herzen—
O Höllenschmerzen!

There is a slow piano introduction of eight measures, full of dissonance, which poignantly expresses the lamentation of the self-accuser. A tortured melodic line to the first four verses, with harsh intervals, over a softer version of the discordant introduction, continues the sense of awful guilt at the soul's weakness, despite its efforts to be strong:

The admission of failure in the last four lines builds to an intense climax, followed by a powerfully discordant piano epilogue that retains the oppressive atmosphere to the end.

"Zitronenfalter im April" and "Auf eine Christblume II" are exquisite miniatures. The poems, though slight and precious, avoid the danger of cuteness, which the composer avoided as well in his settings. "Jägerlied" is a charming song with an interesting difference: the verses of the poem have five accents each, for which Wolf ingeniously uses a 5/4 measure into which the lines fit snugly:

Numerous Mörike poems use folk motifs, though he never attempted the deliberate approximation of folk song in style and language that Heine did, and Goethe in a few instances. "Das verlassene Mägdlein" is an intensely felt poem, which Wolf succeeded brilliantly in making into a powerful song.[8] "In der Frühe" is another brief but poignant expression of the agony of a soul:

Kein Schlaf noch kühlt das Auge mir,
Dort gehet schon der Tag herfür
An meinem Kammerfenster.
Es wühlet mein verstörter Sinn
Noch zwischen Zweifeln her und hin
Und schaffet Nachtgespenster.
—Ängste, quäle
Dich nicht länger, meine Seele!
Freu dich! schon sind da und dorten
Morgenglocken wach geworden.

It is set in the ambiguous time that Mörike so favored, between darkness and daylight, and depicts tortured sleeplessness. As so often with Mörike, the poem describes a state of soul with great clarity, providing a sudden flash of insight into a situation, while leaving the periphery blurred and undefined. The reason for the torment is neither given nor even hinted at. Though the last four lines imply relief, it is by no means fully assured. The morning bells bring only a hope of ease ("Freu dich!"). The ambiguity of the new mood of relief is strongly suggested by the fact that the first line expressing it is "Ängste, quäle"; the thought is not completed until the next line, "Dich nicht länger, meine Seele!". The intriguing indefiniteness and uncertainty remain.

In Wolf's sinuous vocal line, especially in the poignant minor second intervals, he portrays this agonized soul with great intensity:

The accompaniment is an insistent varied repetition of a single motif in the minor:

A stunning continuity is achieved by the persistence of this accompanying motif through the entire song. In the second section, where the intensity is somewhat alleviated, it shifts to a higher register and to the major, but it is still the same figure:

The voice line becomes diatonic:[9]

Äng - st'ge,   quä- le dich nicht län - ger, mei - ne See - le!

The climax is reached in both poem and music on "Freu dich!" which in the song falls on a half note on a high pitch over the insistent leitmotif in the accompaniment. The ambiguity is strengthened by a somewhat strident quality, a suggestion of agitation and frantic uncertainty as to whether the relief will in truth come (though singers usually do not interpret it this way).

"Auf ein altes Bild" is a justly celebrated song which provides the precise musical frame to enhance the lovely but poignant picture of the Christ child playing in his mother's lap in the summer meadow, while behind them in the woods a tree is growing from which the cross will come. The beginning figure in the accompaniment has a modal feeling, expressive of the old picture and projecting a timeless beauty and serenity with just a touch of potential pathos. The voice line and the accompanying figure interweave closely. The description in the poem is restrained and objective up to the point of the single exclamation "Ach" in the last line. This unexpected interjection of the poet's sympathetic reaction shifts the perspective. It adds a new dimension and increases the significance of the simple but awesome final line fraught with tragedy: "Ach, grünet schon des Kreuzes Stamm!" The music highlights the word "ach" by setting it apart on a high note on the fourth beat of the measure over a half-note chord in the piano and then delaying the next word, "grünet," so that there is an eighth-note rest in the melody on the down beat of the next measure. The final word, "Stamm," is set to a meaningful dissonance, which is soon resolved and the song ends with the modal frame much as it began.

"Der Gärtner" is a recital favorite, for understandable reasons, but it contains a major word-tone flaw that usually goes unnoticed. The delightful poem generates an irresistible cantering rhythm as it describes the princess riding along the garden path:

U — U   U — U
Auf ihrem Leibrösslein,

U — U U —
So weiss wie der Schnee,

U — U U — U
Die schönste Prinzessin

U — U U —
Reit't durch die Allee.

In the song, Wolf substitutes an entirely different cantering figure in the piano accompaniment:

This charming motif, far more prominent than the cantering rhythm in Mörike's poem, dominates the brief song. As the melodic line must accommodate itself to this bouncy rhythm, nothing remains of the gentler lilt of the poem:

Auf ih - rem Leib - röss - lein, so weiss wie der Schnee,

Indeed, there is probably not one person in a hundred familiar with the song who has any idea whatsoever of the original rhythm of the poem.

"Verborgenheit" is undoubtedly the most frequently performed Wolf song, though the composer would not have been pleased about this, for he soon grew to dislike it. Frank Walker reports that the song so irritated Wolf that he once claimed, "It's not by me at all."[10] Though not among his best, the song is not entirely uncharacteristic either, having an overblown quality of pathos out of all proportion to the emotion expressed in the poem. This exaggerated emotional intensity is typical of a number of Wolf's Mörike songs (such as "Neue Liebe," "An den Schlaf," "Lebe wohl," "Denk es, O Seele," and "Wo find ich Trost?").

Mörike had a richly modulated sense of humor, and so apparently did Wolf. More than any other song composer, he can enhance musically the inherent humor of a poem (or its good humor, as in "Fussreise"). "Der Jäger" is a charming lyric with a folk atmosphere. The hunter is trying unsuccessfully to persuade himself that he can forget a lover's quarrel, and finally he rushes back to what will surely be a quick and happy reconciliation. The poem has a humorously ironic undertone, which Wolf chose to convey by all manner of unusual sound effects in his gay accompaniment (a shot, the reverberation, the hunter's sudden precipitous rush homeward). He certainly took liberties, but one feels they are justified by the delightful results, which are very much in the spirit of the words.

"Lied eines Verliebten" humorously depicts a sleepless lover, and "Begegnung" a brief encounter of lovers on the street in a storm, with a flashback to a different kind of "storm" when they were alone the previous evening. "Storchenbotschaft," a jolly poem about two storks who announce to a shepherd that he is the father of twins, is another rollicking song.

Both Mörike's and Wolf's humor could also be much broader. Surely there are no more hilarious songs in all song literature than "Abschied," in which the poet joyfully kicks his critic down the stairs, or "Zur Warnung," cautioning a poet never to try to write poetry with a hangover. In both of these songs Wolf proves himself a virtuoso of comic musical effects.

Goethe

Hugo Wolf was keenly sensitive to the accomplishments of Schubert and Schumann—though, as a fanatical Wagner partisan, he could see little virtue in Brahms.[11] On principle, he would not use any poem his predecessors had set to music unless he felt that they had not done justice to it. This did not limit him much in his choice of Mörike verse, since Schubert had been too early for Mörike, and Schumann had set only five poems. That Brahms had composed "Agnes" and "An eine Äolsharfe" could have been of no concern to him whatsoever. As a result, he had Mörike almost all to himself.

Goethe was a different matter. Wolf's inhibitions undoubtedly prevented him from setting many poems he would scarcely otherwise have been able to resist. They also caused him to search for less well-known Goethe poems, his choice sometimes falling on verse not so promising for musical composition. Consequently, though there are many glorious moments, the Goethe volumes do not provide the continuous charm and delight of the Mörike ones.

The fifty-three Goethe songs can be divided into five groups, unequal in number and uneven in quality. There are the inevitable *Wilhelm Meister* songs, ten in all; four longish ballads, "Der Rattenfänger," "Ritter Kurts Brautfahrt," "Gutmann und Gutweib," and the charming "Epiphanias" ("Es zogen drei Könige"); seventeen songs from the *West-östliche Divan*; the three giants "Prometheus," "Ganymed," and "Grenzen der Menschheit," with which Wolf entered into direct competition with Schubert; and finally, a mixed bag of eighteen songs, mostly brief, containing some of the best as well as the most puzzling of Wolf's compositions. Two more songs, "Beherzigung" and "Wanderers

Nachtlied" ("Der du von dem Himmel bist"), published earlier in Volume Two of his *Lieder nach verschiedenen Dichtern*, can be added to the last group. The Goethe songs came in a characteristic flood of inspiration, only a little less rapidly than the Mörike ones. The first of the fifty-one was written on October 27, 1888, just two weeks after all but one of the Mörike songs had been completed; the fifty-first was finished not quite a year later, on October 21, 1889. They were published in the following year.

Wolf began with the *Wilhelm Meister* songs, undaunted by the literally hundreds of settings that had preceded him. He sensed correctly that no one had yet produced the ultimate settings. This he hoped to accomplish. He did not succeed. Observing that his nineteenth century predecessors had moved away from the sense of the novel, Wolf determined to go back to it.[12] However, it is hard to understand how, with the novel as his point of departure, he could have arrived at these songs. For one thing, he followed the sequence of the poems as they were grouped in Goethe's collected lyrics, which is not at all the order in which they appeared in the novel.[13] Since the songs are numbered and are almost always performed as a group, their sequence is bewildering to the listener who tries to relate them to the novel, as Wolf clearly wanted him to.[14] Nor do the songs relate to the characters in the novel as closely as Wolf intended.

With Wolf, as with other nineteenth century composers, the *Wilhelm Meister* poems again proved so multifaceted as to defy perfect musical translation. Thus, for example, in the first one, "Wer sich der Einsamkeit ergibt," although the pathos and loneliness are reflected in the song, the bitterness and austerity are entirely absent. The poem (like the harpist himself) has both distance and dignity:

Wer sich der Einsamkeit ergibt,
Ach! der ist bald allein;
Ein jeder lebt, ein jeder liebt
Und lässt ihn seiner Pein.

Ja! lasst mich meiner Qual!
Und kann ich nur einmal
Recht einsam sein,
Dann bin ich nicht allein.

Es schleicht ein Liebender lauschend sacht,
Ob seine Freundin allein?
So überschleicht bei Tag und Nacht
Mich Einsamen die Pein,
Mich Einsamen die Qual.
Ach, werd ich erst einmal
Einsam im Grabe sein,
Da lässt sie mich allein!

This dignity and distance disappear in Wolf's intense setting. The poignant but measured five-bar introduction and the opening line are an impressive beginning:

But immediately afterward, the mood slips into first a soft and then a pitiful pathos, which builds to an almost maudlin climax in a high register:

To be sure, the words "einsam," "Pein," and "Qual" are a powerful combination, but careful study of the poem shows that their emotional intensity is held in check by the aesthetic, essentially intellectual and conceptual, repetitions of words and ideas. By succumbing to the pathos in the lines, as was almost unavoidable for a nineteenth century composer, Wolf failed to achieve exactly what he set out to do—to portray the true stature of the mysterious, enigmatical, half-crazed, tragic harpist.

"An die Türen" is set in a surprisingly restrained manner. In the novel, the poem is ostensibly only the last strophe of a longer song, which Wilhelm overhears the harpist singing—a song that the novel describes as containing "the consolation of an unhappy man who sensed that he was on the verge of madness."[15] Although Wolf's setting projects consolation, it affords not the faintest glimpse of the near madness of the harpist, who is so incoherent in conversation with Wilhelm immediately afterward and acts so strangely that he has to be put under special psychiatric care. The third song, "Wer nie sein Brot mit Tränen ass," is again highly emotional, reaching a shattering climax on "Dann überlasst ihr ihn der Pein," which is far too much for the sense of the poem. The setting reveals not a trace of the bitterness and epigrammatic quality of the poem.

There are four Mignon songs. One hears Goethe's Mignon best in the first one, "Heiss mich nicht reden." The first stanza is set simply and wonderfully expresses Mignon's puzzling naïveté as expressed in the words:

Heiss mich nicht reden, heiss mich schweigen,
Denn mein Geheimnis ist mir Pflicht;
Ich möchte dir mein ganzes Innre zeigen,
Allein das Schicksal will es nicht.

The slight breakdown of restraint beginning with "ich möchte dir" builds with a crescendo to a near hopeful sense of communication, but breaks off suddenly as though the girl realizes that it must not be. There follows the subdued put poignant and enigmatical "Allein das Schicksal will es nicht":

Sehr getragen

ich möch - te dir mein gan -zes Inn - re zei - gen,

p

al - lein das Schick - sal will___ es nicht.

The second stanza had baffled Schubert and Schumann, and Wolf fares little better. The impersonal images seem to offer little that can be expressed in music, at least in the nineteenth century idiom:

Zur rechten Zeit vertreibt der Sonne Lauf
Die finstre Nacht, und sie muss sich erhellen;
Der harte Fels schliesst seinen Busen auf,
Missgönnt der Erde nicht die tiefverborgnen Quellen.

The final stanza returns again to the personal and emotional, building up to a fine climax, which gives the composer more to work with:

Ein jeder sucht im Arm des Freundes Ruh,
Dort kann die Brust in Klagen sich ergiessen;
Allein ein Schwur drückt mir die Lippen zu,
Und nur ein Gott vermag sie aufzuschliessen.

Goethe's Mignon is unrecognizable in the other three Mignon songs. In the novel, "Nur wer die Sehnsucht kennt" is actually sung as a duet by the harpist and Mignon, though composers after Reichardt and Zelter gave it to Mignon as a solo.[16] Under the circumstances, as the words do not really fit Mignon's personality, one might have expected a duet from Wolf, but he too makes it a solo for her. His setting contains several long piano interludes that stretch the poem beyond the limits of its tolerance.

"So lasst mich scheinen, bis ich werde," the poem that most needs the context of the novel to be understood, could theoretically have been the triumph of Wolf's approach to the *Wilhelm Meister* songs. It is in fact nothing of the sort. In the novel Mignon sings this delightfully naïve but poignantly meaningful song "with unbelievable charm." One thinks of a simple, direct delivery. Wolf's vocal line, however, is tortuous and sophisticated; there is little charm and no naïveté.

The fourth of the Mignon songs is the famous "Kennst du das Land." A recital favorite, it is nevertheless much removed from the character of Mignon. It is a big song, which portrays the longing and exotic quality of the verse with great force, but tears apart the tight structure of the poem in an attempt to squeeze the emotional juice out of each phrase. The music leaves far behind the timid, curious, puzzling, and intriguing character of the girl, to say nothing of the fascinating context in which the song is introduced in the novel.[17]

There are three other *Wilhelm Meister* songs. Wolf's setting of Philine's ditty "Singet nicht in Trauertönen" is surpassed by Schumann's in freshness and gaiety. "Der Sänger" ("Was hör' ich draussen vor dem Tor?") is the best example of Wolf's failure to pursue his resolve to relate his songs more closely to the novel and its characters. It is through-composed, long, rambling, and hence as pointless as Schubert's, Schumann's, and Loewe's settings. [18] The remaining song, "Ich armer Teufel, Herr Baron," which Wolf was the only major composer to set,[19] represents a minor comic interlude in the novel. Its humor, wit, and irony come out well in Wolf's setting. The piano accompaniment is the chief source of interest, however, for the vocal part is strangely devoid of charm.

All four of the large-sized ballads in the second group are comic. Two of these songs are superb. "Der Rattenfänger" is, to be sure, a minor poem of Goethe, but it is full of sparkle, charm, and good humor. The rat-catcher speaks for himself. In the first stanza he is "der wohlbekannte Sänger," who rids towns of mice and even weasels with a song, in the second stanza he is "der gut gelaunte Sänger," who can lure children, too; and in the third, he is "der vielgewandte Sänger," who is irresistible to women:

Und wären Mädchen noch so blöde,
Und wären Weiber noch so spröde,
Doch allen wird so liebebang
Bei Zaubersaiten und Gesang.

In the song these words rush merrily along, after a whimsical
piano introduction, to a charming tune:

The strophic feeling is strong. The playful rhymes are accentuated
in the music, though at times the declamation is subordinated to
the pronounced rhythm. Each of the first two strophes ends with
a delightful flourish:

which overlaps with a repetition of the merry introduction. In the
third stanza, this figure is replaced by a mockingly lovesick motif
on "doch allen wird so liebebang":

The first stanza is then repeated, as Goethe suggested it should be
by a printed direction at the close of the poem, and the piece

is finished long before the listener wishes it to be. This jaunty song leaves Schubert's rather colorless setting in the shade.

The near-nonsense verses of "Epiphanias"[20] are equally engaging. The lines were written in reaction to the Weimar police ban on the traditional street procession of three boys dressed as the three kings on the night of Epiphany. Goethe introduced the custom at court, for which he wrote this hilarious parody:

> Die heilgen drei König' mit ihrem Stern,
> Sie essen, sie trinken, und bezahlen nicht gern;
> Sie essen gern, sie trinken gern,
> Sie essen, trinken, und bezahlen nicht gern.
>
> Die heilgen drei König' sind kommen allhier,
> Es sind ihrer drei und sind nicht ihrer vier;
> Und wenn zu dreien der vierte wär,
> So wär ein heilger drei König mehr.

The part of the first king was taken by the attractive singer and actress Corona Schröter, a fact one must know to enjoy the delightful joke in the last line of the third stanza:

> Ich erster bin der weiss und auch der schön,
> Bei Tage solltet ihr erst mich sehn!
> Doch ach, mit allen Spezerein
> Werd ich sein Tag kein Mädchen mir erfrein.

After each king has made a speech in turn, they march off to the words of the eighth and final stanza:

> Da wir nun hier schöne Herrn und Fraun,
> Aber keine Ochsen und Esel schaun,
> So sind wir nicht am rechten Ort
> Und ziehen unseres Weges weiter fort.

Wolf's song, as the composer himself reveals in a footnote on the title page, was written as a birthday observance for a good friend, Frau Melanie Köchert, and performed on Epiphany by her three children. It is sheer delight, paralleling the silliness of the words with irresistibly inane and often intentionally banal music. The musical characterization of each of the three child-kings is a comic triumph. The long piano march at the end, during which the kings depart separately, each to his distinctive music, then disappear together in the distance, is a fitting close.

The other two ballads show the results of Wolf's deliberate search for lesser known poems of Goethe. "Ritter Kurts Brautfahrt" is hardly a major accomplishment as a poem, and the song is tediously elaborate, pointless, and overly long. For "Gutmann und Gutweib" Wolf had gone to a section called "Translations and Adaptations" among Goethe's posthumous poems. It was not worth the trouble, for the ballad is unattractive, and so is the song. A composer should always remember that a dull song is a lot longer than a dull poem.

Wolf composed seventeen songs from the *West-östliche Divan.* Schubert, it will be remembered, had composed four in 1821, two years after the collection first appeared, and Schumann used six. They both had selected poems that were largely free of any direct eastern idea or association (except for Schumann's "Talismane") and had composed the songs singly. Wolf characteristically made a unified collection of his seventeen, grouping them together as nos. 32–48 of his Goethe songs, and they include numerous oriental allusions. Since they appear in a group, clearly labeled *Divan* poems, the frequent oriental references are not out of place, but it is sometimes hard to understand why Wolf chose the particular poems he did.

At best, the *Divan* collection is a hazardous one for a composer to use. There is a bewildering variety of over two hundred and fifty poems—some as short as two lines, others very elaborate; some slight indeed, others among Goethe's greatest lyrics ("Selige Sehnsucht," "Wiederfinden," "In tausend Formen," to name but a few). The poems bear abundant evidence of the detachment of mature contemplation, of serenity, and often of irony, which one might expect from an aging poet, while they also contain the famous vitality that radiated from Goethe to his dying breath. Technically they are the virtuoso performances of a relaxed poet who has long since learned the lyric process and who has the confidence to take liberties and to make daring experiments in form and content. Many poems in the collection are either abstract or tend toward the epigrammatic, and it is difficult to see what affinity they could possibly have for music.

Goethe himself cannily sensed their unsuitability for musical treatment. In a letter to Zelter at the end of May 1815 he makes two comments which composers would do well to heed. "In order to send you a new poem I have been looking over my oriental Divan, but I have discovered how reflective this type of poem tends to be; I have found nothing singable in it." Later in the same letter: "I have looked through my Divan again and find a second reason why I can't send you anything from it, a reason which in itself is a commendation of the collection. Every single segment is permeated with the sense of the whole, is intensely oriental, relates to customs, usages, religion, and must be explicated by a preceding poem if it is to have an effect on the imagination or emotion. I myself had not realized what a marvelous unity I had made of it."[21]

"Phänomen" is a beautiful contemplative poem which begins:

Wenn zu der Regenwand
Phöbus sich gattet,
Gleich steht ein Bogenrand
Farbig beschattet.

The question is: where can music find a point of connection with such language? Wolf preserves the mood of contemplation in his setting, but the vocal line and the harmonies seem rather pointless.[22]

The second stanza speaks of a white rainbow appearing during a heavy mist. For this, Wolf can do no better than to call for pianissimo singing and playing and add the direction "geheimnisvoll" (mysteriously). The third stanza draws a venturesome analogy with great charm:

So sollst du, muntrer Greis,
Dich nicht betrüben
Sind gleich die Haare weiss,
Doch wirst du lieben.

This comparison gives the musician something to develop, and the song ends with gently increased warmth and a beautiful sense of the vitality of the aging but still dynamic poet.

"Erschaffen und Beleben" is a comic myth about the creation of Adam which, according to the poem, was really completed only after Noah provided wine to animate him. Tippling is associated throughout the *Divan* with lyric creativity and the Persian poet Hafiz, whom the last lines of this poem apostrophize as the drinker-singer. The poem is not particularly funny, and Wolf seems at some disadvantage trying to make it more amusing by means of the music. It is only with mention of Hafiz in the final stanza that the poem offers the composer something to expand. Wolf takes full advantage, with a puzzling change of atmosphere from comic to hymnic. The composer has tried to make the comic too comic and the apostrophe to the poet at the end too expansive.

There follow five outright drinking poems. In the first, "Ob der Koran von Ewigkeit sei," Wolf again runs into the problem of a mildly comic parody which he treats as funnier than it is. The second, "Trunken müssen wir alle sein," is a dazzling tour de force. The music whips the already bacchanalian lines into a riot of bibulousness. If one can preserve sufficient detachment when hearing this bravura song, one detects wider implications to the words than the song takes into account ("Liebe ist Trunkenheit ohne Wein," for instance), but it is a carping critic who can deny the impact of this piece of technical virtuosity, which clearly conveys the main import of the two poems that Wolf here combines into one song. The piano accompaniment contributes not a little to the effect of this bacchanale.

"Solang man nüchtern ist" is a considerable letdown. It is an epigrammatic poem of less than top quality, which plays with the assertion, "If you can't drink, you shouldn't love, and if you can't love, you shouldn't drink." There seems little that music could do with this concept, and little that Wolf in fact does. With the next poem, "Sie haben wegen der Trunkenheit," the composer faced another difficult problem. There is extreme virtuosity in Goethe's use of rhyme in this humorous poem. It is in free imitation of the elaborate ghasel form Hafiz used. The word "Trunkenheit" or a compound of it ends nine of the twenty lines, and all ten of the even-numbered lines end with a rhyme in "−agt" ("tagt," "plagt," "ragt," "zagt"). This construction is not served by the music, and since the point of the poem demands awareness of the overly deliberate rhyme scheme, any musical setting would seem bound to distort it. Wolf's surely does, and without supplying an interesting substitute. Its only pleasure consists in the piano accompaniment. The vocal line is remarkably unattractive. The last four lines of the poem show the pitfalls with which Wolf had to contend:

Lieb', Lied und Weines Trunkenheit,
Ob's nachtet oder tagt,
Die göttlichste Betrunkenheit
Die mich entzückt und plagt.

The drinking songs end appropriately with a rousing one in which Wolf calls on all his virtuosity to dramatize musically the tumultuous scene depicted in the poem:

Was, in der Schenke, waren heute
Am frühsten Morgen für Tumulte?
Der Wirt und Mädchen! Fackeln, Leute!
Was gab's für Händel, für Insulte?

Here was something Wolf could plunge into, and the vivid music portraying the confusion has overtones and undertones of drunkenness, just as the poem does. Poem and music both end on a defiant note. The piano accompanist must be a virtuoso to play this song.

The ten love poems from the book of Suleika can be treated more briefly. This is the book from which Schubert had selected his west-wind and east-wind poems, for which he provided beautiful settings. Wolf chose less wisely, beginning with an intellectual play of wit between Hatem and his beloved Suleika in the two poems "Nicht Gelegenheit macht Diebe" and "Hochbeglückt in deiner Liebe." The first takes its departure from the German proverb "Gelegenheit macht Diebe," which it artfully turns into a song of love. But the poem, like most of the love poems in this book, is not passionate. It is contemplative, witty, sublimated, and not a little playful, reflecting the restrained love relationship between the old poet and his young beloved The song is cool and unconvincing, not to say tedious. The same is true of all but three of the other nine. The three exceptions are "Hochbeglückt in deiner Liebe," "Locken, haltet mich gefangen," and "Nimmer will ich dich verlieren." In spite of the sound of their first lines, which could well have misled Wolf, the poems are not passionate but intellectualized and full of wit. Wolf has given them tempestuous settings. One example will show how inappropriate these settings are.[23] The final lines of the last poem are:

Denn das Leben ist die Liebe,
Und des Lebens Leben Geist.

Wolf's setting is:

If Schubert's "Prometheus" was grandiose, Wolf's is titanic; if Schubert's was daring, Wolf's is sensational; if Schubert's was experimental, Wolf's is unprecedented. Nowhere else in song literature are the resources of piano and voice pushed to such extremes. Wolf is known to have felt that Schubert had failed to understand the great poem. Ironically, in one important point it is Wolf who misinterprets. His Prometheus is clearly Prometheus bound, as Schubert's was not, nor was Goethe's.[24] Fortunately, the shift in basis is not crucial, for the poem can adjust to the change, and Wolf's song is so overwhelmingly convincing that one need not cavil.

The Prometheus of the poem and of both settings is powerfully and scornfully defiant, but Wolf's assumes the classic posture of the rebel reviling the powers who have reduced him to helplessness. Goethe's Prometheus, however, is far from helpless. He scorns the enemy gods as weak, impotent, and harmless. Thus, the opening image compares Zeus's fury with a small boy who knocks the heads off thistles. This image can be adapted to Wolf's more epically defiant posture of Prometheus. Even the contemptuous "Ich kenne nicht Ärmeres / unter der Sonne als euch, Götter!" works in musical terms. The one place which, more than any other, might have alerted Wolf to the basic difference between Goethe's conception and his own is the reference to Zeus as "dem Schlafenden da droben." But it did not, and Wolf's setting actually sweeps over this phrase without seeming to notice it.

The dynamics and tempo are adjusted to the varying situations and attitudes depicted in the poem, but the essential point is the massive energy displayed throughout the setting. The listener is swept into the spell of the song, often reacting with a kind of dazed acquiescence. Analysts have differed over Wolf's heavy accentuation of the word *mir* in the phrase "Ein Geschlecht, das mir gleich sei," where Schubert puts the stress on *gleich*. Schubert is surely right within the original context of the poem, but the change Wolf made is a master stroke in accord with his own conception of the poem.

For all their differences, Schubert's "Prometheus" and his "Ganymed" are basically similar in style. Wolf's "Ganymed," however, is worlds away from his "Prometheus." All energy is forgotten, a quiet lassitude is the dominant note, an ethereal contentment, to which is added a touch of sweet, gentle longing. Even the climactic "Hinauf strebts, hinauf" is sung with a sense of rich contentment. If his "Prometheus" went too far in the direction of energy and defiance, this setting is perhaps excessive in its blissfulness and quietude. But the poem is flexible enough to adjust, and the result is exquisite. It is a mark of Wolf's effortless mastery of declamation that the long line which gave Schubert so much trouble—"Mit tausendfacher Liebeswonne / Sich an mein Herz drängt / Deiner ewigen Wärme / Heilig Gefühl, / Unendliche Schöne"— is set with attention to the intricacies of both rhythm and meaning:

"Grenzen der Menschheit," a reflective philosophical poem of Goethe's Weimar period, is surely less immediately accessible to composition, but Wolf's command is such that he can provide the measured words of the poem with music of sonorous impersonality.

Philosophical though the poem is, it is far from abstract, as evident in stanza one:

Wenn der uralte
Heilige Vater
Mit gelassener Hand
Aus rollenden Wolken
Segnende Blitze
Über die Erde sät,
Küss ich den letzten
Saum seines Kleides,
Kindliche Schauer
Treu in der Brust.

The poem must be read slowly. Although the lines seem short on the printed page, the enjambment joins the first six verses into one continuous thought without pause, and the entire first stanza is but a single sentence. The rhythm is measured and stately but free:

(1) ∪ ∪ — — ∪
(2) — ∪ ∪ — ∪
(3) ∪ ∪ — ∪ ∪ —
(4) ∪ — ∪ ∪ — ∪
(5) — ∪ ∪ — ∪
(6) — ∪ ∪ — ∪ —

The affirmation of the benevolent omnipotence of the eternal god is conveyed within a poetic structure that arches smoothly and unhurriedly throughout.

The beautiful imagery calls forth gently pictorial music. Restraint is hardly the quality one associates with Hugo Wolf's settings, but here the musical effects are difficult to describe and analyze for the very reason that they are understated, in keeping with the elegance of the poem. Word and tone become a unity in this great song. It opens with a sequence of soft, measured introductory chords in A minor. In the opening phrases a surprising lowering of pitch from the tonic to A-flat has an archaic effect, which supports the meaning of "uralte."

The A-flat receives a syncopated accent on the second beat of the measure, anticipating the six chord (with a lowered A) which follows on the third beat. Wolf's use of quarter-note triplets for the three dactylic feet that follow makes the declamation smoother and more measured than it could possibly be in the poem alone, and increases the sense of beneficence implied in the words "segnende Blitze":

Farther on, Wolf commands amazing effects. A rolling accompaniment artfully expresses the uprootedness of the human who reaches too high. Then comes a less subtle, firmly diatonic chordal structure to underline the reverse limitations of the human who remains earthbound.[25] After the thematic question "Was unterscheidet Götter von Menschen?" pianissimo ascending arpeggio chords give a rich musical expression to the words "ein ewiger Strom." A long succession (sixteen measures) of sonorous sustained chords ends this majestic extension into music of the poetic imagery of one of Goethe's great poems.

Wolf's eighteen miscellaneous short songs offer the most unfortunate evidence of his hunt for poems that had not been composed previously. For various reasons, most of these verses are far from easy to set to music. In eleven of the seventeen, the composer's overly explicit attempt to realize the individual images and ideas, his predilection for a through-composing that destroys the strophic patterns, and his indulgence in a fussy subtlety of declamation, which weakens or destroys rhythmic effects and rhyme patterns, result in the largest quantity of not just unsatisfactory word-tone combinations but unsatisfactory songs in his whole production. Included in this category are "Cophtisches Lied I," "Cophtisches Lied II," "Frech und froh I," "Frech und

froh II," "Beherzigung," "Genialisch treiben," "Der neue Amadis,"
"Dank des Paria," and "Königlich Gebet," to which may be added
the other song with the title "Beherzigung" from the *Lieder nach
verschiedenen Dichtern*, as well as "Wanderers Nachtlied" ("Der
du von dem Himmel bist") from the same collection.

On the other side of the ledger are miniature gems like
"Blumengruss," "Gleich und Gleich," "Die Spröde," "Die
Bekehrte," and the exquisite "Frühling übers Jahr." Their success
rests in large measure on an absence of the fussiness that infects
the others. "St. Nepomuks Vorabend," a fragilely beautiful poem
describing the Festival of St. Nepomuk in Prague, with its lights,
bells, and children's chorus, is given a jewel-like setting. Simple
chords in a very high register throughout enclose the song in a
virtually synesthetic atmosphere, as they seem to evoke the lights
and stars as well as the bells and children's voices:

Langsam und durchweg mit äusserster Zartheit

The setting is kept simple and pristine, to give an effect both
childlike and godlike, while the song achieves a mystical quality
that suggests the religious celebration. The unusual 6/4 measure
contributes to the sense of mystery and perfectly frames the lines
of the poem:

Lichtlein schwimmen auf dem Strome, Kinder singen auf der Brücken

This miniature masterpiece is unfortunately rarely performed.

"Anakreons Grab," on the other hand, is certainly not a neglected
song. Although it is exquisitely beautiful, it does not bring out the
flowing dactylic hexameters and pentameters of Goethe's three

distichs, despite the fact that the classical form is a significant part of the meaning and spirit of the poem:

> Wo die Rose hier blüht, wo Reben um Lorbeer sich schlingen,
> Wo das Turtelchen lockt, wo sich das Grillchen ergetzt,
> Welch ein Grab ist hier, das alle Götter mit Leben
> Schön bepflanzt und geziert? Es ist Anakreons Ruh.
> Frühling, Sommer und Herbst genoss der glückliche Dichter;
> Vor dem Winter hat ihn endlich der Hügel geschützt.

In the beginning of the song, the classical form is reinforced by the music. The first distich is perfectly communicated in the musical line, even to the difference in the third foot of the hexameter and pentameter:

The hexameter of the very next line, however, is obliterated by the developing musical idiom, as is the beginning of the next pentameter:

The objection that Wolf does not preserve the form of the distichs is by no means academic, since content and form are so interrelated in this poem.

Joseph von Eichendorff

The twenty Eichendorff songs of Wolf present a problem from the word-tone perspective. Although they are delightful songs, in only a few of them is there a feeling of rapport with the poet. Eichendorff, romantic poet par excellence, was the master of the simple nature poem ("Es war, als hätt' der Himmel / Die Erde still geküsst") and the minstrel-like wandering song ("Wem Gott will rechte Gunst erweisen, / Den schickt er in die weite Welt"). A freshness characterizes most of his poems, which is amazing in view of the persistence with which the same ideas, even the same expressions, recur in his verse. The limpid melodiousness of his language distinguishes his poems from the thousands of similar ones his generation produced. He was the ideal poet for the romantic temperament of Schumann, who wrote to Clara that his Eichendorff cycle, op. 39, was "mein Romantischstes"

Wolf, who greatly admired Schumann's op. 39, stayed away from the poems Schumann had used and for the most part hunted out the more vigorous or more humorous verses. His decision was sound, but even so he was inclined to make his songs too elaborate for the poetic material. Again and again in the twenty songs the involved musical pictorialization of details clashes with the straightforward poetic structure. The through-composing of most of them fights with the poem's simple strophic pattern and its unity of mood. This is so in the very first song, "Der Freund." Wolf sets the first strophe, which begins "Wer auf den Wogen schliefe / Ein sanft gewiegtes Kind," with a placid melodic line to a gently undulating accompaniment marked dolce:

Wer auf den Wo-gen schlie-fe, ein sanft ge-wieg - tes Kind,

This in itself is misleading, as suggested by the third line, "Kennt nicht des Lebens Tiefe," and even the subjunctive verb "schliefe" of line one. For all three remaining stanzas Wolf plunges fortissimo into a boisterous accompaniment and extremely dynamic vocal line in sharp contrast to what preceded, in order to portray the sense of "Doch wen die Stürme fassen" and what follows. The succession of simple stanzas is thus engulfed in the musical portraiture of stormy seas and a difficult passage through life, which blows up the ideas of the poem out of all proportion. There is much of Wolf in this song, but very little Eichendorff.

In "Der Musikant," no 2, there is a much greater rapport. Eichendorff's title was "Der wandernde Musikant," and the first line sets the tone for the whole poem: "Wandern lieb' ich für mein Leben." The melodious, minstrel-like accompaniment and the vocal line supplement the poem splendidly:

The insouciance is sustained right through to the mildly humorous ending, where one learns that the minstrel keeps himself free from feminine entanglements so that he can continue his singing and wandering. The song ends exactly as it began.

"Verschwiegene Liebe," no. 3, is such a fragilely gorgeous song that it is unfortunate to have to point out that the infinite subtlety and sophistication of the music are simply not the right complement to the words. "Das Ständchen," no. 4, is the word-tone masterpiece of the Eichendorff songs. An old minstrel who hears a young man serenading his beloved is reminded of the joys of his own youth when he had done the same. But the touching first two lines of the fourth and last stanza reveal that his beloved has died.

Aber von der stillen Schwelle
Trugen sie mein Lieb zur Ruh—,

The poignancy is foreshadowed in the very first line, which speaks of the moon shining through pale clouds. The poem is a subtle blend of the pain of memory and the beauty of the present moment. And so in the song. The accompaniment is again minstrel-like, but this time not nearly so gay as in no. 2. In the measures that immediately precede the voice a motif is introduced in the left hand:

As the song progresses, this motif undergoes wondrous changes. High above it is another touchingly delicate melody:

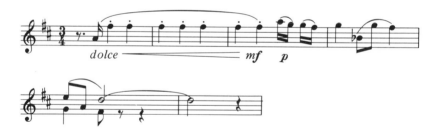

The vocal line rests between these two themes. Wolf's treatment of the rhyming word "blassen" at the end of the first line is a stroke of genius:

Later in the song the sense of poignant reminiscence is increased through daringly dissonant transformations of these motifs:

Both poem and song achieve their effect through understatement, with the sadness of the old minstrel's memories constantly balanced by their sweetness, coupled with the prevalence of the motif of serenading.

The waggish "Der Soldat," no. 5, is also a fine blend of word and music. In the remaining fifteen songs there are only two that achieve a reasonable degree of rapport between poem and music: "Heimweh," no. 12, and the boisterous "Seemans Abschied," no. 17. This last song is blustering and noisy, as is the poem. The sailor bids a buoyant good-by to the girl who has scorned him and sings of the delights of the sea (including mermaids). Then he says farewell to the soldiers and describes the dangers encountered at sea by the courageous sailor. Though in this stanza Wolf goes to an extreme in depicting the snapping jaws of the shark and the shrieking of the sea gulls, still the music faithfully realizes the implicit exaggerations of the sailor. The last bravura stanza boasts that when God sends the deluge to engulf all landlubbers, the sailors will outride it. The vocal line of this stanza, marked "Sehr flott," is the perfect complement to the words:

Gottfried Keller

Six poems of Gottfried Keller are grouped together as "Alte Weisen, sechs Gedichte von Keller" in Volume One of Wolf's *Lieder nach verschiedenen Dichtern*. There is a cycle of twelve poems called "Alte Weisen" in Keller's *Gesammelte Gedichte,* which are slightly revised versions of the early poems previously published under the title "Von Weibern." Brahms had created two delightful songs, "Therese" and "Salome," from this earlier collection, and a direct comparison with Wolf is possible, because the same poems are among the six he selected for composition.

Keller's poems, both the early and later versions, are in two equal groups, the first half portraying women in the ascendancy in the "battle of the sexes," followed by an equal number portraying women later in life in pathetic situations. Wolf chose three from each group. He begins with the defiantly mocking "Tretet ein, hoher Krieger," whose second stanza reads:

Und der Marschalk muss lernen
Wie man Weizenbrot backt,
Wie man Wurst und Gefüllsel
Um die Weihnachtszeit hackt.

This poem is followed by the two set by Brahms. In revising the poems, Keller omitted the women's names originally used as titles, so that "Salome" becomes "Singt mein Schatz wie ein Fink" and "Therese" is now "Du milchjunger Knabe." No. 4 in Wolf's group, "Wandl' ich in dem Morgentau," is a lonely woman's pathetic lament that love is everywhere in nature and only she will die unkissed. No. 5 is the brutal "Das Köhlerweib ist trunken." A woman who has been beautiful and had many suitors delayed too long in choosing and fell victim to wine. She is now a hopeless drunkard. The last song is the ethereal "Wie glänzt der helle Mond," in which a presumably lonely old woman takes comfort in a vision of her life to come in Heaven.

What opportunities these six poems opened up to the genius of Hugo Wolf, and what hazards they contained! Not the least of the hazards are the simple folklike language and verse forms. Wolf through-composed them all, taking such liberties with the regular metrical patterns in the verse that it is hard to believe from the songs that the verse form of each is straightforward and simple. A heaviness, augmented by the very elaborate accompaniments, replaces the light touch of the poems. Three of the six—the two Brahms had already used, plus "Wie glänzt der helle Mond"—are disappointing, as the settings seem fussy and lumbering.

The bravura setting of "Das Köhlerweib ist trunken," no. 5, is
a tour de force. It begins with a vocal line and accompaniment
that are inspired evocations of the ugly words:

The closing line, to the words "wie durch die Dämmerung gellend
ihr Lied erschallt," is overwhelming, as is the brilliant piano
epilogue. But the intervening passages are hardly successful. After
the sordid first glimpse of the drunken woman, the poem turns to
her youth and an account of her deterioration. Here Wolf's music
attempts to maintain the intensity of the opening lines but the
sense of immediacy is gone. The poem has slipped into the past
tense.

The opening and closing songs are the outstanding numbers in
the group. Although "Tretet ein, hoher Krieger," the first song,
comes close to being through-composed, it has a symmetry and

recurrence of musical phrasing that give the listener a pleasing, relaxed sense of recognition, which is close to the folk idiom of the verse. The vocal line is melodious, with sly overtones of the girl's self-assurance:

A tuneful accompanying line supports this mood:

The last song, "Wie glänzt der helle Mond," is ethereal and sustained, with constant quarter-note chordal accompaniment beginning in a very high register. There is a remote, detached quality to the vocal line, which is in perfect accord with the text:

For the picture of Mary on her throne with Jesus sleeping on her knees and God the Father sitting nearby, Wolf produces a line that has the same simplicity and sincerity as the verse:

The songs of Hugo Wolf represent both the culmination and the conclusion of the extraordinary era of the German lied that began in the mid-1700's. Though there has been a continued production of songs in the twentieth century, just as there had been many in the seventeenth and early eighteenth centuries, the later songs do not belong to the same cohesive development. A few of the approximately 150 songs of Richard Strauss might be considered a continuation of the nineteenth century tradition—such as the exquisite setting of Goethe's "Gefunden" ("Ich ging im Walde/So für mich hin")—but the symphonic songs of Gustav Mahler definitely move the lied away from the intimacy of chamber music into the concert hall. To examine these and later compositions, such as the great cycle by Hindemith to Rilke's "Marienleben," or his "Die junge Magd" to poems by Georg Trakl, or Schönberg's epochal "Buch der hängenden Gärten" to poems by Stefan George, not to speak of his "Pierrot Lunaire," requires a separate study, because in this century the assumptions of both poetry and music have changed radically. The production of that extremely intimate chamber form known as the German lied, which at its most exalted moments achieves so close a rapport between poem and music as to approach a union, came to an end when Hugo Wolf's last songs were written.

A Note on Recordings

Bibliography

Notes

Indexes

A Note on Recordings

Many of the songs discussed in this book can be heard on records. However, since new recordings appear constantly and older ones are withdrawn frequently, to provide a listing would be of dubious value. Now that monaural recordings are disappearing from the market, a large number of the recordings I used have become unavailable. Most of the recordings of the less standard repertory are German imports, not generally carried by record stores.

To complicate the listener's task, determining which songs are included on a record entitled, for instance, "A Schumann Song Recital" or "Fischer-Dieskau Sings Beethoven" becomes more irritating every day. Not only are the records sealed, but gaudy pictures and often insipid blurbs at times replace the list of contents that used to appear on front or back and be visible through the transparent sealer.

The best procedure, therefore, is first to consult the current monthly *Schwann Catalog* for available records. For further details, note the date on which a recording was first listed (if included, the date is given in numbers; that is, 2–66 means February 1966). Copies of the back issues of the *Schwann* catalog may ordinarily be located in a library, and under the heading "New Listings" the full contents of the records are usually given. Deutsche Grammophon-Gesellschaft and Telefunken are regularly listed in Schwann. For other foreign imports, Schwann issues a special quarterly *Supplementary Catalog*. Be sure to get the Schwann supplement, not ones prepared by DGG or Telefunken, which contain only their own records. Many imports are eventually reissued under domestic labels.

Bibliography

The number of books and articles on the poets and song writers treated in this study is legion. Listed here are only those works that in one way or another have been of direct assistance or are mentioned in the text. Editions of songs or poems are included only when the apparatus of the edition has proved useful.

Abert, Anna Amalie. *Christoph Willibald Gluck*. Munich: Bong, 1959.

Abert, Hermann, "Wort und Ton in der Musik des achtzehnten Jahrhunderts." *Archiv fur Musikwissenschaft*, 5 (1923), 31-70. (Also in Hermann Abert. *Gesammelte Schriften und Vorträge*. Halle: Niemeyer, 1929.)

Abraham, Gerald, ed. *Schubert: A Symposium*. London: Drummond, 1946.

——, ed. *Schumann: A Symposium*. London: Oxford University Press, 1952.

Austin, Frederic. "The Songs of Hugo Wolf," *Proceedings of the Musical Association*, 38 (1912), 161-169.

Batka, Richard, and Heinrich Werner, eds. *Hugo Wolfs musikalische Kritiken*. Leipzig: Breitkopf und Härtel, 1911.

Bauer, Moritz, ed. *Karl Friedrich Zelter: Fünfzehn ausgewählte Lieder*. Berlin: Breslauer, 1924.

——*Die Lieder Franz Schuberts*. Leipzig: Breitkopf und Härtel, 1915.

Baum, Günther. "Wort und Ton im romantischen Kunstlied," *Das Musikleben*, 3 (1950), 136-140.

Beckmann, Gustav, ed. *Klopstocks Oden für eine Singstimme und Klavier von Christoph Willibald Gluck*. Veröffentlichung der Gluck-Gesellschaft. Leipzig: Breitkopf und Härtel, 1917.

Benn, Gottfried. *Probleme der Lyrik*. Wiesbaden: Limes, 1951.

Benz, Richard E. *Die Welt der Dichter und die Musik*. 2nd ed. Düsseldorf: Diedrich, 1949.

Bieri, Georg. *Die Lieder von Hugo Wolf*. Bern: Haupt, 1935.

Blom, Eric, ed. *Grove's Dictionary of Music and Musicians*. 5th ed. New York: Macmillan, 1954—1961.

Blume, Friedrich, ed. *Die Musik in Geschichte und Gegenwart: Allgemeine Enzyklopädie der Musik*. 14 vols. Kassel: Bärenreiter, 1949—1968.

Böschenstein, Bernhard. "Zum Verhältnis von Dichtung und Musik in Hugo Wolfs Mörikeliedern," *Wirkendes Wort*, 19 (1969), 175-193.

Boettcher, Hans. *Beethoven als Liederkomponist*. Augsburg: Filser, 1928.

Boetticher, Wolfgang. *Robert Schumann: Einführung in Persönlichkeit und Werk*. Berlin: Hahnefeld, 1941.

Bosch, Hans. *Die Entwicklung des Romantischen in Schuberts Liedern*. Leipzig: Noske, 1930.

Brahms, Johannes. *Briefwechsel.* 16 vols. Berlin: Deutsche Brahms Gesellschaft, 1910–1922.

Braunstein, Joseph, ed. *Thematic Catalog of the Collected Works of Brahms.* New York: Ars Musica, 1956.

Bridges, Robert. "On the Musical Setting of Poetry," *Collected Essays, Papers, etc.,* XXI-XXVI, 3-16. London: Oxford University Press, 1935.

Brooks, Cleanth. *The Well Wrought Urn.* New York: Harcourt, Brace, 1947.

Brown, Calvin. *Music and Literature: A Comparison of the Arts.* Athens: University of Georgia Press, 1948.

——"The Poetic Use of Musical Form," *Musical Quarterly,* 30 (1944), 87-101.

Brown, Maurice J. E. *Essays on Schubert.* New York: St. Martin's, 1966.

——*Schubert: A Critical Biography.* New York: St. Martin's, 1958.

Bücken, Ernst. *Das deutsche Lied: Probleme und Gestalten.* Hamburg: Hanseatische Verlagsanstalt, 1939.

——*Geist und Form im musikalischen Kunstwerk.* Handbuch der Musikwissenschaft, vol. 7. New York: Musurgia, 1929.

——"Die Lieder Beethovens: Eine stilkritische Studie," *Neues Beethoven Jahrbuch,* 2 (1925), 33-42.

——*Die Musik des Rokokos und der Klassik.* Handbuch der Musikwissenschaft, vol. 4. New York: Musurgia, 1927.

——*Robert Schumann.* Cologne: Staufen, 1941.

Busch, Gudrun. *Carl Philipp Emanuel Bach und seine Lieder.* Kölner Beiträge zur Musikforschung, vol. 12. Regensburg: Bosse, 1957.

Capell, Richard. *Schubert's Songs.* 2nd ed. New York: Macmillan, 1957.

Castelnuovo-Tedesco, Mario. "Music and Poetry: Problems of a Song-Writer," *Musical Quarterly,* 30 (1944), 102-111.

Cone, Edward T. "Words into Music: The Composer's Approach to the Text." In Northrop Frye, ed. *Sound and Poetry,* pp. 3-15. English Institute Essays. New York: Columbia University Press, 1957.

Cooke, Deryck. *The Language of Music.* London: Oxford, 1959.

Cooper, Martin. "Liszt as a Song Writer," *Music and Letters,* 19 (1938), 171-181.

Crist, Bainbridge. *The Art of Setting Words to Music.* New York: Fischer, 1944.

Davison, Archibald T. *Words and Music: A Lecture.* Louis Charles Elson Memorial Lecture. Washington, D.C., 1954.

Decsey, Ernst. *Hugo Wolf.* 4 vols. 2nd ed. Berlin: Schuster und Loeffler, 1903–1906.

Detweiler, Alan. "Music and Poetry," *British Journal of Aesthetics,* 1 (1960–1961), 134-143.

Deutsch, Otto Erich. *Schubert: Thematic Catalogue of All His Works in Chronological Order.* London: Dent, 1951.

Douliez, Paul, and Hermann Engelhard, eds. *Das Buch der Lieder und Arien.* Munich, 1958.

Drager, Hans Heinz. "Zur Frage des Wort-Ton-Verhältnisses im Hinblick auf Schuberts Strophenlied," *Archiv für Musikwissenschaft,* 11 (1954), 39-59.

Eggebrecht, Hans Heinrich. "Das Ausdrucks-Prinzip im musikalischen Sturm und Drang," *Deutsche Vierteljahresschrift für Literaturwissenschaft und Geistesgeschichte,* 29 (1955), 323-349.

Egger, Rita. *Die Deklamationsrhythmik Hugo Wolfs in historischer Sicht.* Tutzing: Schneider, 1963.

Einstein, Alfred. *Gluck: Sein Leben, seine Werke.* Zurich: Pan, 1954.

——*Gluck.* Tr. Eric Blom. London: Dent, 1936.

——*Schubert: A Musical Portrait.* New York: Oxford University Press, 1951.

Eismann, Georg. *Robert Schumann: Ein Quellenwerk über sein Leben und Schaffen.* 2 vols. Leipzig: Breitkopf und Härtel, 1956.

Erny, Richard. "Lyrische Sprachmusikalität als ästhetisches Problem der Vorromantik," *Jahrbuch der deutschen Schillergesellschaft,* 2 (1958), 114-144.

Fairley, Barker. *Heinrich Heine: An Interpretation.* Oxford: Clarendon, 1954.

Felber, Rudolf. "Schumann's Place in German Song" *Musical Quarterly,* 26 (1940), 340-354.

Feldmann, Fritz. "Zur Frage des 'Liederjahres' bei Robert Schumann," *Archiv für Musikwissenschaft,* 9 (1952), 246-269.

Fisch, Samuel. *Goethe und die Musik.* Frauenfeld: Huber, 1949.

Fischer-Dieskau, Dietrich. *Texte deutscher Lieder: Ein Handbuch.* Munich: Deutscher Taschenbuchverlag, 1968.

Fox Strangways, Arthur Henry. "Brahms and Tieck's 'Magelone,' " *Music and Letters,* 21 (1940), 211-229.

——"Schubert and Wolf," *Music and Letters,* 23 (1942), 126-134.

——"Some of the Less-Known Songs of Schubert," *Proceedings of the Musical Association,* 54 (1928), 115-129.

——"Words and Music in Songs," *Essays and Studies by Members of the English Association, Oxford,* 7 (1921), 30-56.

Friedlaender, Max. *Brahms's Lieder: an Introduction to the Songs for One or Two Voices.* Tr. C. L. Leese. London: Oxford University Press, 1928.

——*Das deutsche Lied im 18. Jahrhundert: Quellen und Studien.* 2 vols. Stuttgart: Cotta, 1902.

——, ed. *Gedichte von Goethe in Compositionen seiner Zeitgenossen.* Schriften der Goethe-Gesellschaft, 11. Weimar, 1896.

——, ed. *Gedichte von Goethe in Kompositionen.* Schriften der Goethe-Gesellschaft, 31. Weimar, 1916.

——"Goethes Gedichte in der Musik," *Goethe-Jahrbuch,* 17 (1896), 179-194.

Frotscher, Gotthold. "Die Ästhetik des Berliner Liedes in ihren Hauptproblemen," *Zeitschrift für Musikwissenschaft,* 6 (1923/24), 431-448.

Frye, Northrop. "Introduction: Lexis and Melos." In Northrop Frye, ed. *Sound and Poetry,* pp. ix–xxvii. English Institute Essays. New York: Columbia University Press, 1957.

——"Music in Poetry," *University of Toronto Quarterly,* 11 (1941–1942), 167-179.

Gatz, Felix. *Musikästhetik in ihren Hauptrichtungen.* Stuttgart: Enke, 1929.

Geiger, Ludwig, ed. *Briefwechsel zwischen Goethe und Zelter in den Jahren 1799 bis 1832.* 3 vols. Leipzig: Reclam, n.d.

Geiringer, Karl. *Brahms: His Life and Work.* 2nd ed. London: Allen and Unwin, 1963.

Georgiades, Thrasybulos. *Musik und Sprache: Das Werden der abendländischen Musik dargestellt an der Vertonung der Messe.* Berlin: Springer, 1954.

——*Schubert: Musik und Lyrik.* Göttingen: Vandenhoeck und Ruprecht, 1967.

Gerber, Rudolf. "Formprobleme im Brahmsschen Lied," *Jahrbuch der Musikbibliothek Peters für 1932.* 39 (1933), 23-42.

Gessler, Luzius. *Lebendig begraben: Studien zur Lyrik des jungen Gottfried Keller.* Basler Studien zur deutschen Sprache und Literatur, vol. 27. Bern: Francke, 1964.

Giebeler, Konrad. *Die Lieder von Johannes Brahms: Ein Beitrag zur Musikgeschichte des neunzehnten Jahrhunderts.* Münster: Kramer, 1959.

Goldschmidt, Hugo. *Die Musikästhetik des achtzehnten Jahrhunderts und ihre Beziehungen zu seinem Kunstschaffen.* Zurich: Rascher, 1915.

Gudewill, K. "Lied: A. Das Kunstlied im deutschen Sprachgebiet," *Musik in Geschichte und Gegenwart,* vol. 8, col. 746-775. Kassel: Bärenreiter, 1949−1968.

Hall, James *The Art Song.* Norman: Oklahoma University Press, 1953.

Hammermann, Walter. *Johannes Brahms als Liedkomponist:Eine theoretisch-ästhetische Stiluntersuchung.* Leipzig: Spamer, 1912.

Heinen, Clemens. "Der sprachliche und musikalische Rhythmus im Kunstlied: Vergleichende Untersuchung einer Auswahl von Mörike-Vertonungen." Ph.D. diss., University of Cologne, 1958.

Heuss, Alfred. "Der geistige Zusammenhang zwischen Text und Musik im Strophenlied," *Kongress für Aesthetik und allgemeine Kunstwissenschaft,* 1913, pp. 444-455.

——"Haydns Kaiserhymne," *Zeitschrift für Musikwissenschaft,* 1 (1918−1919), 5-26.

Hirth, Friedrich, ed. *Heinrich Heines Briefe.* 6 vols. Mainz: Kupferberg,1950−1951.

Höllerer, Walter. *Zwischen Klassik und Moderne.* Stuttgart: Klett, 1958.

Höweler, Caspar. *Rhythme in vers en muziek.* s'Gravenhage: Mouton, 1952.

Holländer, Hans. "Franz Schubert's Repeated Settings of the Same Song-Texts," *Musical Quarterly,* 14 (1928), 563−574.

Hopkinson, Cecil. *A Bibliography of the Works of C.W. von Gluck, 1714−1787.* London: privately printed, 1959.

Hughes, Edwin. "Liszt as Lied Composer," *Musical Quarterly,* 3 (1917), 390-409.

Ibel, Rudolf. *Gestalt und Wirklichkeit des Gedichtes.* Munich: Heimera,1964.

Istel, Edgar. "Schubert's Lyric Style," *Musical Quarterly,* 14 (1928), 575-595.

Jaskola, Heinrich. "Vom Geheimnis des Liedes: Theoretische Erwägungen Goethes und der Seinen zur Wort- und Tonkunst des Liedes," *Aurora: Eichendorff Almanach,* 26 (1966), 66-81.

Jelinek, Werner. "Schubert und die poetische Lyrik seines Klavierliedes." Ph.D. diss., University of Vienna, 1939.

Jensen, F. Gustav, ed. *Robert Schumanns Briefe: Neue Folge.* Leipzig: Breitkopf und Härtel, 1904.

Jolizza, W. K. von. *Das Lied und seine Geschichte.* Vienna: Hartleben, 1910.

Jonas, Oswald. "Das Verhältnis von Wort und Ton," *Das Wesen des musikalischen Kunstwerks: Eine Einführung in die Lehre Heinrich Schenkers,* appendix A, pp. 199- 214. Vienna: Saturn, 1934.

Just, Klaus Günther. "Musik und Dichtung," *Deutsche Philologie im Aufriss,* ed. Wolfgang Stammler, 2nd rev. ed., vol. 3, col. 699-750. Berlin: Schmidt, 1960−1962.

——"Wilhelm Müllers Liederzyklen 'Die schöne Müllerin' und 'Die Winterreise'," *Zeitschrift für deutsche Philologie,* 83. 4 (1964), 452-471. (Also "Wilhelm Müller und seine Liederzyklen" in Klaus Günther Just, *Übergänge: Probleme und Gestalten der Literatur.* Bern: Francke, 1966.)

Kalbeck, Max. *Johannes Brahms.* 4 vols. Berlin: Deutsche Brahms Gesellschaft, 1904–1914.

Kaulhausen, Marie-Hed. *Das gesprochene Gedicht und seine Gestalt.* 2nd ed. Göttingen: Vandenhoeck und Ruprecht, 1959.

Keller, Gottfried. *Gottfried Keller: Gesammelte Gedichte.* Ed. Jonas Fränkel. Vol. 2, in two parts, of *Gottfried Keller, Sämtliche Werke,* ed. Jonas Fränkel and Carl Helbling. Zurich: Benteli, 1931–1938.

Klein, Hans. "Musikalische Komposition in deutscher Dichtung," *Deutsche Vierteljahresschrift für Literaturgeschichte und Geisteswissenschaft,* 8 (1930), 680-716.

Koehler-Deditius, Annemarie. "Mignon: Untersuchungen über die Struktur eines Goetheschen Gedichtes und seiner Kompositionen," *Zeitschrift für Ästhetik und allgemeine Kunstwissenschaft,* 16 (1922), 145-200.

Komma, Karl M. "Probleme der Hölderlin-Vertonung," *Hölderlin Jahrbuch,* 9 (1955–1956), 201-218.

Krabbe, Wilhelm. "Das deutsche Lied im 17. und 18. Jahrhundert," *Handbuch der Musikgeschichte,* ed. Guido Adler, vol. 2, pp. 691-703. Berlin: Keller, 1930.

Kravitt, Edward F. "The Influence of Theatrical Declamation upon Composers of the Late Romantic Lied," *Acta Musicologica,* 34 (1962), 18-28.

Kreisig, Martin, ed. *Gesammelte Schriften über Musik und Musiker von Robert Schumann.* 5th ed., 2 vols. Leipzig: Breitkopf und Härtel, 1914.

Kretzschmar, Hermann. *Geschichte des neuen deutschen Liedes.* Vol. 1. Leipzig: Breitkopf und Härtel, 1911.

Kruse, Georg Richard. *Zelter.* Reclam Musikerbiographien, vol. 34. Leipzig, 1915.

Lang, Paul Henry. *Music in Western Civilization.* New York: Norton, 1941.

Lanier, Sidney. "The Centennial Cantata," *Music and Poetry,* pp. 80-90 New York: Scribner's, 1914.

Le Massena, Clarence, and Hans Merx. *The Songs of Schubert.* New York: Schirmer, 1928.

Lindlar, Heinrich. "Zu Schumanns Eichendorff-Zyklus," *Aurora: Eichendorff Almanach,* 22 (1962), 82-88.

Lindner, Dolf. *Hugo Wolf: Leben, Lied, Leiden. Mit einem Anhang: Das Liedwerk.* Bergland Österreich-Reihe, vol. 96-97. Vienna, 1960.

Luntz, George E. "Musical-Literary Expression in Songs from Goethe's 'Wilhelm Meister.' " Ph.D. diss., University of Iowa, 1953.

Mackworth-Young, G. "Goethe's Prometheus and Its Setting by Schubert and Wolf," *Proceedings of the Royal Musical Association,* 78th session, 1951–1952, pp. 53-65.

Meyer, Leonard B. *Emotion and Meaning in Music.* Chicago: University of Chicago Press, 1956.

Mies, Paul. *Johannes Brahms: Werk, Zeit, Mensch.* Leipzig: Quelle und Meyer, 1930.

——"Goethes Harfenspielergesang 'Wer sich der Einsamkeit ergibt' in den Kompositionen Schuberts, Schumanns und Hugo Wolfs: Eine vergleichende Analyse," *Zeitschrift für Ästhetik und allgemeine Kunstwissenschaft,* 16 (1922), 383-390.

——, ed. *Lieder für eine Singstimme mit Begleitung des Klaviers: Haydns Werke.* Vol. 1, series XXIX. Munich: Henle, 1960.

——"Mehrfache Bearbeitung gleicher Texte bei Schubert," *Bericht über den internationalen Kongress für Schubertforschung,* pp. 117-124. Augsburg, 1929.

——*Franz Schubert.* Leipzig: Breitkopf und Härtel, 1954.

——*Schubert, der Meister des Liedes: die Entwicklung von Form und Inhalt im Schubertschen Lied.* Berlin: Hesse, 1928.

——*Stilmomente und Ausdrucksstilformen im Brahmsschen Lied.* Leipzig: Breitkopf und Härtel, 1923.

Miller, Philip L. *The Ring of Words: An Anthology of Song Texts.* Garden City, N. Y.: Doubleday, 1963.

Mittenzwei, Johannes. *Das Musikalische in der Literatur: Ein Überblick von Gottfried von Strassburg bis Brecht.* Halle (Saale): VEB Verlag, 1962.

Mohr, Wolfgang. "Wort und Ton," *Bericht über den internationalen musikwissenschaftlichen Kongress, Hamburg, 1956,* pp. 157-162. Hamburg, 1957.

Moser, Hans Joachim. *Christoph Willibald Gluck: Die Leistung, der Mann, das Vermächtnis.* Stuttgart: Cotta, 1940.

——*Das deutsche Lied seit Mozart.* 2nd ed., 2 vols. Tutzing: Schneider, 1968.

——*Das deutsche Sololied und die Ballade.* Das Musikwerk, vols. 14-15. Cologne: Arno Volk, 1957.

——*Goethe und die Musik.* Leipzig: Peters, 1949.

——"Karl Friedrich Zelter und das Lied," *Jahrbuch der Musikbibliothek Peters, 39 (1933), 43-54.*

——"Kleine Beiträge zu Beethovens Liedern und Bühnenwerken," *Neues Beethovenjahrbuch,* 2 (1925), 43-65.

Müller-Blattau, Josef. *Goethe und die Meister der Musik.* Stuttgart: Metzler, 1969.

——*Das Verhältnis von Wort und Ton in der Geschichte der Musik.* Stuttgart: Metzler, 1952.

Muncker, Franz, and Jaro Pawel, eds. *Friedrich Gottlieb Klopstocks Oden.* 2 vols. Stuttgart, 1889.

Newman, Ernest. *Hugo Wolf.* London: Methuen, 1907.

Nowak, Leopold. *Joseph Haydn: Leben, Bedeutung und Werk.* Zurich: Amalthea, 1959.

Oliphant, E. H. C. "Poetry and the Composer," *Musical Quarterly,* 8 (1922), 227-241.

Ophüls, G. *Brahms-Texte.* 2nd ed. Berlin: Deutsche Brahms Gesellschaft, 1908.

Pamer, Fritz Egon. "Das deutsche Lied im neunzehnten Jahrhundert," *Handbuch der Musikgeschichte,* ed. Guido Adler, vol. 2, pp. 939-955. Berlin: Keller, 1930.

Pauli, Walther. *Johann Friedrich Reichardt: Sein Leben und seine Stellung in der Geschichte des deutschen Liedes.* Musikwissenschaftliche Studien, vol. 2. Berlin: Ebering, 1903.

Peacock, Ronald. "Probleme des Musikalischen in der Sprache," *Weltliteratur: Festschrift für Fritz Strich zum 70. Geburtstag.* Bern: Francke, 1952.

Perle, George. "Woyzeck and Wozzeck," *Musical Quarterly,* 53 (1967), 206-219.

Porter, Ernest G. *Schubert's Song Technique.* London: Dobson, 1961.

Prawer, S. S. *Heine: Buch der Lieder.* Studies in German Literature, vol. 1. London: Arnold, 1960.

——*Heine, the Tragic Satirist: A Study of the Later Poetry, 1826–1856.* Cambridge, Eng.: Cambridge University Press, 1961.

——*Mörike und seine Leser: Versuch einer Wirkungsgeschichte.* Stuttgart: Klett, 1960.

——*The Penguin Book of Lieder.* Baltimore: Penguin, 1964.

Rehberg, Walter and Paula. *Johannes Brahms: Sein Leben und Werk.* Zurich: Artemis, 1947.

——*Robert Schumann: Sein Leben und sein Werk.* Zurich: Artemis, 1954.

Reichert, Georg. "Literatur und Musik," *Reallexikon der deutschen Literaturgeschichte,* 2nd ed., vol. 2, pp. 143-163. Berlin: De Gruyter, 1964.

Salmen, Walter. *Johann Friedrich Reichardt: Komponist, Schriftsteller, Kapellmeister und Verwaltungsbeamter der Goethezeit.* Freiburg: Atlantis, 1963.

——, ed. *Johann Friedrich Reichardt: Goethes Lieder, Oden, Balladen und Romanzen mit Musik.* Das Erbe deutscher Musik, vol.58. Munich: Henle,1964.

Sams, Eric. *The Songs of Hugo Wolf.* London, 1961.

——*The Songs of Robert Schumann.* New York: Norton, 1969.

Schauffler, Robert Haven. *Florestan: The Life and Work of Robert Schumann.* New York: Holt, 1945.

Schering, Arnold. "Metrische Studien zu Beethovens Liedern," *Neues Beethoven Jahrbuch,* 2 (1925), 23-32.

Schleich, Carl Ludwig. *Besonnte Vergangenheit: Lebenserinnerungen.* Berlin: Rowohlt, 1922.

Schmidt, Walther F. "Promusikalität und Musikalität der lyrischen Dichtung," *Zeitschrift für Ästhetik und allgemeine Kunstwissenschaft,* 20 (1926), 219-234.

Schnapp, Friedrich. *Heinrich Heine und Robert Schumann.* Hamburg: Hoffmann und Campe, 1924.

—— "Robert Schumann and Heinrich Heine," *Musical Quarterly,* 11 (1925), 599-616. (Condensed version, in English, of preceding title.)

Schnapper, Edith. *Die Gesänge des jungen Schubert vor dem Durchbruch des romantischen Liedprinzips.* Bern: Haupt, 1937.

Schnebel, Dieter. "Sprache als Musik in der Musik," *Schweizer Monatshefte,* 46. 6 (1966), 560-575.

Schottländer, Johann-Wolfgang. "Zelters Beziehungen zu den Komponisten seiner Zeit," *Jahrbuch der Sammlung Kippenberg,* 8 (1930), 134-248.

Schuh, Willi. *Goethe-Vertonungen: Ein Verzeichnis.* Zurich: Artemis, 1952.

Schulz, J. A. P. *Lieder im Volkston.* Berlin, 1782.

Schwab, Heinrich W. *Sangbarkeit, Popularität und Kunstlied: Studien zu Lied und Liedästhetik der mittleren Goethezeit, 1770–1814.* Studien zur Musikgeschichte des neunzehnten Jahrhunderts, vol. 3. Regensburg: Bosse, 1965.

Seelig, Harry E. "Goethe's 'Buch Suleika' and Hugo Wolf: A Musical-Literary Study." Ph.D. diss., University of Kansas, 1969.

Sieber, Paul. *Johann Friedrich Reichardt als Musikästhetiker: Seine Anschauungen über Wesen und Wirkung der Musik.* Sammlung musikwissenschaftlicher Abhandlungen, ed. K. Nef, vol. 2. Strasbourg: Heitz, 1930.

Staiger, Emil. *Goethe.* 3 vols. Zurich: Atlantis, 1952–1959.

——*Goethes Gedichte mit Erläuterungen.* 3 vols. Zurich: Manesse, 1949.

——*Musik und Dichtung: Aufsätze, Vorträge, Reden.* 2nd ed. Zurich: Atlantis, 1959.

Steglich, Rudolf. "Zum Kontrastproblem Johannes Brahms–Hugo Wolf," *Kongressbericht: Gesellschaft für Musikforschung,* pp. 140-143. Kassel, 1950.

Stein, Franz A. *Verzeichnis deutscher Lieder seit Haydn.* Dalp Taschenbücher, no. 385G. Bern: Francke, 1967.

Stein, Jack M. "Musical Settings of the Songs from *Wilhelm Meister,*" *Comparative Literature,* 22 (1970), pp. 125-146.

——"Poem and Music in Hugo Wolf's Mörike Songs," *Musical Quarterly,* 53 (1967), 22-38.

——"Poetry for the Eye," *Monatshefte für deutschen Unterricht, deutsche Sprache und Literatur,* 55 (December 1963), 361-366.

——"Schubert's Heine Songs," *Journal of Aesthetics and Art Criticism,* 24 (1966), 559-566.

——*Richard Wagner and the Synthesis of the Arts.* Detroit: Wayne State University Press, 1960.

——"Was Goethe Wrong about the Nineteenth Century Lied? An Examination of the Relation of Poem and Music," *PMLA,* 77 (1962), 232-239.

Sternfeld, Frederick W. *Goethe and Music.* New York: New York Public Library, 1954.

Stevens, Denis, ed. *A History of Song.* New York: Norton, 1960.

Storz, Gerhard. "Die Lieder aus *Wilhelm Meister,*" *Der Deutschunterricht,* 1 (1949), 36-52.

Tausche, Anton. *Hugo Wolfs Mörikelieder in Dichtung, Musik, Vortrag.* Vienna: Amandus, 1947.

Tenschert, Roland. "Das Verhältnis von Wort und Ton in Hugo Wolfs Goethe-Liedern," *Rondo, Österreichische Musikzeitschrift,* 8 (1953), 53-58.

Thomas, R. Hinton. *Poetry and Song in the German Baroque: A Study of the Continuo Lied.* Oxford: Clarendon, 1963.

Thomas, Werner. "Der Doppelgänger von Franz Schubert," *Archiv für Musikwissenschaft,* 9 (1954), 252-267.

Todoroff, Kosta. "Beiträge zur Lehre von der Beziehung zwischen Text und Komposition," *Zeitschrift für Psychologie,* Erste Abteilung, 63 (1913), 401-441.

Tovey, Donald. "Words and Music," *The Main Stream of Music and Other Essays.* New York: Oxford University Press, 1949.

Treanor, Paul Arthur. "Goethe's Mignon Poems: Their Literary Interpretation and the Musical Illustration of Their Poetic Devices." Ph.D. diss., Princeton University, 1963.

Walker, Ernest. "The Songs of Schumann and Brahms: Some Contacts and Contrasts," *Music and Letters,* 3 (1922), 9-19.

Walker, Frank. *Hugo Wolf: A Biography.* New York: Knopf, 1952.

Weihs, Herta. "Die physiologischen Grundlagen des musikalischen Ausdrucks am Beispiel von Goethes 'Erlkönig' in seiner Vertonung durch Schubert dargestellt," *Musikerziehung,* 11 (1957–1958), 78-82.

Wellek, Albert. "The Relationship between Music and Poetry," *Journal of Aesthetics and Art Criticism,* 21 (1962–1963), 149-156.

Wendriner, K. G. *Wilhelm Meisters Lehrjahre.* 4 vols. 1914. Goethe: Werke in Form und Text ihrer Erstausgabe. Berlin: Morawe und Scheffelt, 1914.

Werner, Th. W. "Beethovens Komposition von Goethes 'Nur wer die Sehnsucht kennt,' " *Neues Beethoven Jahrbuch,* 2 (1925), 66-75.

Wittmann, Gertraud. *Das klavierbegleitete Sololied K. F. Zelters.* Berlin: Triltsch und Huther, 1936.

Wörner, Karl. *Robert Schumann.* Zurich: Atlantis, 1949.

Wolff, Viktor Ernst. *Lieder Robert Schumanns in ersten und späteren Fassungen.* Leipzig, 1914.

Notes

Introduction

1. Berg's work is called *Wozzeck* because he used an earlier, faulty edition of Büchner's posthumous drama. One must be careful to say "Wozzeck" to musicians and "Woyzeck" to Germanists. See George Perle, "Woyzeck and Wozzeck," *Musical Quarterly*, 53 (April 1967), 206-219.

2. Carl Orff is the exception that proves the rule. In his two stage works *Antigonae* (1949) and *Oedipus der Tyrann* (1959) he in fact sets every word of the tragedies by Sophocles in Hölderlin's translations. Undoubtedly he has done the same thing in his newest work (1968), a setting of the original Greek text of Aeschylus' *Prometheus Bound*. (*Der Spiegel*, in reporting this latest work by the Bavarian composer, titled its article "Urworte Orffisch.")

3. This example is from an Electrola jacket, printed in Germany. Throughout my book, poems and song text appear only in the original German. Translations of many of the poems can be found in S. S. Prawer, ed., *The Penguin Book of Lieder* (Baltimore: Penguin, 1964), or Philip L. Miller, comp., *The Ring of Words: An Anthology of Song Texts* (Garden City: Doubleday, 1963). I have translated all prose quotations from German sources.

4. See Edward T. Cone, "Words into Music: The Composer's Approach to the Text," in Northrop Frye, ed., *Sound and Poetry*, English Institute Essays (New York: Columbia University Press, 1957), pp. 3-15.

5. See Jack M. Stein, "Poetry for the Eye," *Monatshefte für deutschen Unterricht, deutsche Sprache und Literatur*, 55. (1963), 361-366.

6. Novalis' comment is apropos here: "If poems are set to music, why not set them to poetry?" (Wenn man die Gedichte in Musik setzt, warum setzt man sie nicht in Poesie?).

7. Submitted to the Department of German, University of Kansas, 1969.

8. Donald Tovey, "Words and Music," *The Main Stream of Music and Other Essays* (New York: Oxford University Press, 1949), p. 212.

9. "There is a plenitude of problems to be investigated in all epochs, since word-tone research is still in its infancy." Klaus Günther Just, "Musik und Dichtung," *Deutsche Philologie im Aufriss*, 2nd ed. (Berlin: Schmidt, 1960–1962), III, cols. 699-750.

I. Problems of Combining Poem and Music

1. Two recent books that deal impressively with this problem are Deryck Cooke, *The Language of Music* (London: Oxford, 1959), and Leonard B Meyer, *Emotion and Meaning in Music* (Chicago: University of Chicago Press, 1956). Cooke attempts to establish a core of melodic, harmonic, and rhythmic phrases that intrinsically convey precise shades of emotion and which composers intuitively turn to when wishing to express these emotions. The argument is persuasive but not definitive. It could perhaps be verified by examining the entire corpus of eighteenth and nineteenth century lieder,

since the presence of a text in most instances would indicate the emotion that the composer wished to express.

2. Robert Haven Schauffler tries to argue, in his popularized biography *Florestan: The Life and Work of Robert Schumann* (New York: Holt, 1945), the aesthetic unacceptability of the lied as a union of word and music (pp. 384-388). E. H. C. Oliphant in "Poetry and the Composer," *Musical Quarterly*, 8 (1922), 227-241, also exhibits a curiously dogmatic intolerance, demanding (though seldom finding) exact equivalence between the meter, rhythm, and accentuation of poems and music, even to the point of insisting that the composer not repeat any words or phrases.

3. This point of view is not acceptable to many. I argue my case in some detail in my article "Poetry for the Eye," *Monatshefte*, 55 (1963), pp. 361-366.

4. An interesting proof of the need for greater precision in pitch than in rhythm was provided by the singing of the outstanding Wagnerian Heldentenor Lauritz Melchior. Melchior frequently allowed himself subtle liberties with the musical rhythm, which enhanced the effect of the word-tone communication by bringing out more clearly the dramatic and lyric effect of the poetry. (It is not widely known that Wagner himself encouraged his singers to do just that.) On the other hand, especially in the years after Melchior had passed his prime, he occasionally sang slightly off pitch. The rhythmic deviations were exciting, the deviations from pitch excruciating.

5. Sound values in lyric poetry are often incorrectly called "musical" values by literary critics. Northrop Frye has shown once and for all that the term "musical" is badly misused in discussions of literature. See his "Introduction: Lexis and Melos," to *Sound and Poetry,* pp. ix-xxvii. A longer version appeared earlier as "Music in Poetry," *University of Toronto Quarterly,* 11 (1941–1942), 167-179.

6. Calvin Brown, in his *Music and Literature: A Comparison of the Arts* (Athens, Ga.: University of Georgia Press, 1948), pp. 73, questions whether the accompaniment in fact gallops, suggesting that, if Schubert had intended to portray galloping, "he could have easily done it much better." This would be true if Schubert had wanted to portray galloping alone, and as unmistakably as possible. But both he and Goethe had more subtle intentions.

7. See Alfred Heuss, "Der geistige Zusammenhang zwischen Text und Musik im Strophenlied," *Kongress fur Aesthetik und allgemeine Kunstwissenschaft,* 1913, pp. 444-455.

8. Max Friedlaender, *Gedichte von Goethe in Compositionen seiner Zeitgenossen,* Schriften der Goethe Gesellschaft, 11 (Weimar, 1896), 137. A second volume, *Gedichte von Goethe in Kompositionen,* Schriften der Goethe Gesellschaft, 31 (Weimar, 1916), is not restricted to Goethe's contemporaries, though containing many additional songs by them.

9. Heinrich Schwab, *Sangbarkeit, Popularität und Kunstlied: Studien zu Lied und Liedästhetik der mittleren Goethezeit, 1770–1814* (Regensburg: Bosse, 1965), p. 71.

10. See Rudolf Gerber, "Formprobleme im Brahmsschen Lied," *Jahrbuch der Musikbibliothek Peters für 1932,* 39 (1933), 23-42.

11. Friedlaender, *Gedichte von Goethe in Compositionen seiner Zeitgenossen* (1896), p. 141.

12. Since Schubert's setting is considerably more elaborate, it is not possible to reproduce the accompaniment. It will be described as necessary in the course of the analysis.

13. Earlier in the same year (1815) Schubert had composed a different setting, a strophic one. Its melody, too, grouped the stanzas of the poem into pairs, so he had no choice but to leave one out.

II. The Lied Before Schubert

1. Josef Müller-Blattau, *Das Verhältnis von Wort und Ton in der Geschichte der Musik* (Stuttgart: Metzler, 1952).

2. Herder, too, is on record as wishing "our lyric songs, odes, lieder, or however they are called, could be simplified . . . freed from such oppressive decoration as has become almost mandatory these days." Quoted in Heinrich Jaskola, "Vom Geheimnis des Liedes: Theoretische Erwägungen Goethes und der Seinen zur Wort- und Tonkunst des Liedes," *Aurora: Eichendorff Almanach,* 26 (1966), p. 68.

3. Eight, possibly only seven Klopstock odes were used. Two of them were set twice: "Die Sommernacht" ("Wenn der Schimmer von dem Monde") and "Der Jüngling" ("Schweigend sahe der Mai"). The other odes used by Gluck are: "Vaterlandslied" ("Ich bin ein deutsches Mädchen"); "Wir und Sie" ("Was tat dir, Tor, dein Vaterland"); "Schlachtgesang" ("Wie erscholl der Gang des lauten Heers"); "Die frühen Gräber" ("Willkommen, o silberner Mond"); "Der Tod" ("O Anblick der Glanznacht"); and "Die Neigung" ("Nein! Ich wiederstrebe nicht mehr"). The authenticity of this last ode is very cautiously questioned by Muncker and Pawel in their critical edition of Klopstock's odes. "If the ode, which in content and form is not above question, really is by Klopstock, which is likely in view of the close connection between him and Gluck, it probably was written about 1766." Franz Muncker and Jaro Pawel, ed., *Friedrich Gottlieb Klopstocks Oden* (Stuttgart, 1889), II, 182. The Matthison song is not listed in Grove but is reproduced in Hans Joachim Moser, *Christoph Willibald Gluck: Die Leistung, der Mann, das Vermächtnis* (Stuttgart: Cotta, 1940), p. 323.

4. There is minor uncertainty about the date. See Gustav Beckmann, ed., *Klopstocks Oden für eine Singstimme und Klavier von Christoph Willibald Gluck,* Veröffentlichung der Gluck-Gesellschaft (Leipzig: Breitkopf und Härtel, 1917), pp. iv-v.

5. Klopstock's letters show that he was greatly concerned that musical compositions of his odes should conform to their metrical patterns. See Schwab, *Sangbarkeit, Popularität und Kunstlied,* p. 37. Gluck's compositions surely fulfill this wish.

6. In *Die Lieder von Hugo Wolf* (Bern: Haupt, 1935), p. 26, Georg Bieri quotes Reichardt as failing to comprehend why such great composers as Haydn and Mozart "made so little use of our best poets, and had no real contact with the true nature of song." Although this remark certainly reflects Reichardt's thinking, I cannot locate any reference to it in Walter Salmen's undoubtedly definitive book on Reichardt, *Johann Friedrich Reichardt: Komponist, Schriftsteller, Kapellmeister und Verwaltungsbeamter der Goethezeit* (Freiburg: Atlantis, 1963).

7. Quoted in Samuel Fisch, *Goethe und die Musik* (Frauenfeld: Huber, 1949).

8. Heinrich Schwab points out in his *Sangbarkeit, Popularität und Kunstlied,* p. 30, that the inclusion of the melodies had a significance far beyond the mere desire to produce a deluxe edition. Schwab also calls attention to the astonishing fact that all other editions since 1795, critical editions included, omit the music altogether. A single exception is the reprint in K. G. Wendriner, ed., *Goethe: Werke in Form und Text ihrer Erstausgabe* (Berlin: Morawe und Scheffelt, 1914).

9. Willi Schuh, *Goethe-Vertonungen: Ein Verzeichnis* (Zurich: Artemis, 1952).

10. The melodic line alone was given in the novel, though Reichardt later published all the songs with piano accompaniment in his *Goethes Lieder, Oden, Balladen und Romanzen* (Leipzig, 1809). As the later versions are only slightly different from those in the novel, the songs are discussed here as they appeared in their full form.

11. Ludwig Geiger, ed. *Briefwechsel zwischen Goethe und Zelter in den Jahren 1799 bis 1832* (Leipzig: Reclam, n.d.), II, 58. Zelter's conservative influence on Goethe in matters musical is often decried. But Goethe was a man with an independent mind. One should not overemphasize his helplessness when judging music. Because he knew little musical theory, it is not surprising that he was unable to understand the changes music was undergoing at the hands of Beethoven and Schubert. See Jack M. Stein, "Was Goethe Wrong about the Nineteenth Century Lied? An Examination of the Relation of Poem and Music," *PMLA*, 77 (June 1962), 232-239.

12. *Briefwechsel*, II, 56.

13. *Briefwechsel*, III, 159.

14. Quoted in Gertraud Wittmann, *Das klavierbegleitete Sololied K. F. Zelters* (Berlin: Triltsch and Huther, 1936), p. 20.

15. This statement is made, amazingly, in a letter to Goethe, dated October 18, 1827. See *Briefwechsel*, II, 551. A little later in the same letter Zelter assures his celebrated friend that he handles Goethe's words more cautiously ("vorsichtiger, ja keuscher"), though in fact Zelter altered even Goethe's verse on occasion. "After all," he comments on August 13, 1821 (*Briefwechsel*, II, 121), "the melody has its rights too."

16. *Briefwechsel*, I, 360.

17. Friedlaender points out in *Gedichte von Goethe in Compositionen seiner Zeitgenossen*, p. 136, that Zelter achieves an archaic quality by avoiding a G-sharp in the melody and thus transforming what would be felt as the key of A minor into the late medieval Aeolian mode.

18. Until recently, it was thought that a fine setting of Goethe's "Heiss mich nicht reden," included in a handwritten manuscript entitled "Lieder beim Clavier zu singen von Joseph Haydn" in the Austrian National Library in Vienna, was by Haydn. Ernst Bücken, in his *Das deutsche Lied: Probleme und Gestalten* (Hamburg: Hanseatische Verlagsanstalt, 1939), discusses the setting at length. Grove's *Dictionary* lists it as "doubtful," and it is not even mentioned in the more recent fourteen-volume *Musik in Geschichte und Gegenwart* (Kassel: Bärenreiter, 1949—1968). Nor does it appear in the new edition of Haydn's *Werke*, Series 29, vol. I: *Lieder für eine Singstimme mit Begleitung des Klaviers,* ed. Paul Mies (Munich: Henle, 1960), not even in the appendix of doubtful songs. The song contains some musical clichés and

shows operatic influence; nevertheless, it is one of the better contemporary settings of this *Wilhelm Meister* poem. But it is apparently not by Haydn, which deprives him of the one possible claim to attention in this discussion of word-tone relationship.

19. Hans Boettcher, *Beethoven als Liederkomponist* (Augsburg: Filser, 1928), reports that in a preliminary draft of a song, never completed, to an Anacreontic poem of Johann Wilhelm Gleim, "Flüchtigkeit der Zeit," Beethoven changed the last two lines of the second stanza from:

Ich will mich vergnügen
So lang ich noch bin.

to:

Drum will ich nutzen
So lang ich noch bin.

20. Over half a century earlier, Carl Philipp Emanuel Bach had set the same Gellert poem in his *Geistliche Arien und Lieder* (1752). The surprising similarity in melodic treatment of the lines quoted here is often pointed out. The gentler, more restrained tone of the earlier setting, however, makes the similarities more apparent than real. The parallel passages, in fact, show how much more emotionally expressive the song becomes in Beethoven's idiom.

21. Hans Joachim Moser reports once having tried to sing all the stanzas, with a predictable lack of success. See his "Kleine Beiträge zu Beethovens Liedern und Bühnenwerken," *Neues Beethovenjahrbuch*, II (1925), 43-65.

22. This melodic figure recurs four more times in the song, each time to words on which the added emphasis is precisely appropriate: "Und Freud und Wonne aus jeder Brust"; "Du segnest herrlich das frische Feld"; "O Mädchen, Mädchen, wie lieb ich dich"; and "Wie ich dich liebe mit warmem Blut."

23. Bücken, *Das deutsche Lied*, p. 70. Neither Bücken nor anyone else gives these settings more than a few sentences, except for a brief article by Theodore W. Werner in the *Neues Beethoven Jahrbuch*, II (1925), 66-76, which does not address itself to this question.

24. Martin Kreisig, ed., *Gesammelte Schriften über Musik und Musiker von Robert Schumann*, 5th ed. (Leipzig: Breitkopf und Härtel, 1914), I, 273.

25. Originally part of Wenzel Tomaschek's autobiography in Paul Alois Klar, ed., *Libussa: Jahrbuch für 1850* (Prague,) IX, 331. Reprinted in Friedlaender, *Gedichte von Goethe in Compositionen seiner Zeitgenossen*, p. 145.

26. Another example of the tendency toward musical dominance may be the dynamic markings at the beginning of the song and of each new stanza. In each case, the first four words are marked to be sung forte, with an abrupt change to piano for the following phrases. There seems to be no basis in the text for this alternation in dynamics, which was a favorite instrumental device of Beethoven.

III. Franz Schubert

1. It is impossible to treat all 251 songs here; therefore, a goodly number go unmentioned. But all of those that in my view achieve an unusual degree of word-tone rapport are discussed, or at the very least mentioned. The omission of any song thus implies that I do not consider it an appropriate example.

2. Schiller would surely have approved of Schubert's version, could he have heard it, though perhaps Tennyson, who did not have a good musical ear, would not have. "Why do those damned musicians make me say a thing twice when I said it only once!" he is reported to have complained.

3. Werner Jelinek, "Schubert und die poetische Lyrik seines Klavierliedes" (Ph.D. diss., University of Vienna, 1939), p. 8.

4. For a discerning and detailed analysis of this song, see Calvin Brown, *Music and Literature* (Athens: University of Georgia Press, 1948), pp. 70-80.

5. Schubert's expression mark is not vulnerable to the witty comment in Goethe's *Xenien* distich: "Frostig und herzlos ist der Gesang, doch Sänger und Spieler / Werden oben am Rand höflich zu fühlen ersucht." The jibe was in all probability directed toward Reichardt.

6. Ernst Bücken, *Geist und Form im musikalischen Kunstwerk,* Handbuch der Musikwissenschaft, vol. 7 (New York: Musurgia, 1929), p. 133.

7. Witty parodies of Schiller, usually in the form of inept schoolboy paraphrases, are numerous.

8. "Gretchen am Spinnrade" is op. 2; "Erlkönig," though labeled op. 1, was written a year later. More than twenty songs preceded "Gretchen am Spinnrade," and over a hundred intervened between it and "Erlkönig." Opus numbers are never useful for dating Schubert's songs, since they reflect date of publication, which was often long delayed. Many of the songs were not even published during his lifetime. Otto Erich Deutsch, *Schubert: Thematic Catalog of All His Works in Chronological Order* (London: Dent, 1951), dates the composition of each one with considerable accuracy. *Grove's Dictionary of Music and Musicians* gives a chronological list of all the songs.

9. This situation is quite different from that of "Erlkönig," which was to be actually sung at the beginning of *Die Fischerin.* Goethe's poem "Meine Ruh ist hin" is an entire dramatic scene in *Faust,* introduced by the stage direction, "Gretchens Stube. Gretchen am Spinnrade allein." It is unthinkable that the words to this lyric poem should be sung in the drama. However, "Es war ein König in Thule," from the previous scene, is sung by Gretchen. Thus, "König in Thule" and "Erlkönig" are parallel, whereas "Meine Ruh ist hin" is entirely different.

10. Schubert wrote "mit Entzückung füllest," probably just a careless transcription.

11. Though Schubert includes a brief balladlike interlude, to indicate the supposed song performed by the minstrel, there are no words to go with it.

12. S.S. Prawer, *Heine: Buch der Lieder* (London: Arnold, 1960), and *Heine, the Tragic Satirist: A Study of the Later Poetry* (Cambridge, Eng.: Cambridge University Press, 1961); Barker Fairley, *Heine: An Interpretation* (Oxford: Clarendon, 1954).

13. Schubert's mastery of this intricate passage in 1815 is especially surprising in view of his difficulties with similarly complicated syntax in "Ganymed," composed two years later.

14. Schubert's E-flat in this chord should be written D-sharp.

IV. Robert Schumann

1. Robert Schumann to Hermann Hirschbach, June 30, 1839, in F. Gustav Jensen, ed., *Robert Schumanns Briefe: Neue Folge* (Leipzig: Breitkopf und Härtel, 1904), p. 158.

2. Martin Kreisig, ed., *Gesammelte Schriften über Musik und Musiker von Robert Schumann,* 5th ed., I, 495. On Schumann's attitude toward poetry in the lied I must take issue with Eric Sams. Referring to the composer's remark cited in my n. 1 above, Sams states in *The Songs of Robert Schumann* (New York: Norton, 1969), p.3: "Schumann himself implied that he believed poetry to be an inferior art-form." This is a highly inaccurate conclusion to draw from Schumann's remark. Sams nevertheless continues, "Nothing suggests that he ever changed his mind. On the contrary, all his recorded comments on the relation of words to music instinctively award pride of place to the latter. The poem, he said, must be crushed and have its juices expressed like an orange; it must wear the music like a wreath, or yield to it like a bride." Even these remarks are not so unequivocal as Sams implies. More important, there are many statements in the *Gesammelte Schriften* that express a high regard for the place of the poem in the lied. For example, in a review of new songs by Norbert Burgmüller in 1840, Schumann declared, "To weave the finest features of the poem into the more delicate musical fabric was for him the supreme task, as it should be for all." And later in the same essay, "[W.H.] Veit too exercises the most loyal care in the faithful rendering of the words by the musical expression." In 1843, in another article, appear the words, "Along with the expression of the poem as a unit, its more delicate features should also be given prominence." *Gesammelte Schriften,* I, 494, II, 123. To these could be added many other comments in Schumann's works and letters, showing that from the time of the Liederjahr he was by no means inclined to treat poetry as an inferior form of art.

3. Friedrich Schnapp, *Heinrich Heine und Robert Schumann* (Hamburg: Hoffmann und Campe, 1924), p. 19. A shorter version in English translation appeared in *The Musical Quarterly*, XI (1925), 599-616.

4. Twenty poems were composed in all. Four of them were not included in the "Dichterliebe" cycle and were published only later: "Dein Angesicht," op. 127, no. 2 (poem no.5 of "Lyrisches Intermezzo"); "Es leuchtet meine Liebe," op. 127, no. 3 (poem no. 46); "Lehn deine Wang," op. 142, no. 2 (poem no. 6); and "Mein Wagen rollet langsam," op. 142, no 4 (poem no. 54).

5. Kreisig, ed., *Gesammelte Schriften über Musik und Musiker von Robert Schumann,* I, 272.

6. Friedrich Hirth, ed. *Heinrich Heine Briefe* (Mainz: Kupferberg, 1950), I, 244.

7. Heine later changed this word to "schön."

8. Schumann uses an ingenious pattern of repetition. Each of the two musical phrases in each strophe has three subdivisions. Thus, one of each pair of lines must be repeated. In the first stanza the second and fourth lines are heard twice, and in the second stanza, the first and third lines. In each case these are the most expressive lines in the stanza.

9. The poem as Schumann used it is considerably different from the version found in current Heine editions. In view of Schumann's notorious inclination to alter texts of poems, it should be noted that in this particular case he used an earlier version, later revised by Heine, and stuck to it faithfully.

10. Heine's title is "Die Grenadiere."

11. Wagner also used the "Marseillaise" at the climax of "Die Grenadiere," in a French version composed in Paris in the same year.

12. Heine's title is "Zwei Brüder."

13. Originally Schumann almost completed a setting of the three poems for chorus and orchestra, but gave it up in favor of these settings, op. 64, no. 3.

14. See Karl Wörner, *Robert Schumann* (Zurich: Atlantis, 1949), pp. 213-215; Sams, *The Songs of Robert Schumann*, p.92.

15. Eichendorff's title is "Waldgespräch."

16. The repetition is in the poem. To use this line for the vocal climax of the song ingeniously underscores the legendary quality of the work. For some reason, perhaps only carelessness, Schumann altered the line, which in the original is "Es ist schon spät, es *wird* schon kalt."

17. "Sich" in the second line receives an incorrect emphasis. But this is a splendid example of how much more important it is to match the precise implication of the poetic line than to set the poetic rhythm meticulously.

18. Eichendorff's title is "Die zwei Gesellen."

19. Yet one surely cannot object to his suppression of an embarrassing stanza from one of the middle poems, "Süsser Freund, du blickest mich verwundert an," and the substitution of a touching piano interlude to convey the mood of the passage. The omitted stanza is:

Hab' ob manchen Zeichen
Mutter schon gefragt,
Hat die gute Mutter
Alles mir gesagt,
Hat mich unterwiesen,
Wie, nach allem Schein,
Bald für eine Wiege
Muss gesorget sein.

Carl Loewe, whose many songs are forgotten today except for a few of his remarkable ballads, composed the whole cycle, including the final poem and the stanza just quoted, in sweetly sentimental style.

20. This is the weakest and the most colorless of Schumann's often splendid piano epilogues. It begins with an awkward, abrupt modulation from the despair of the final song into the key and mood of the first song. What follows is literally the piano accompaniment of the first half of the opening song.

21. Kreisig, ed., *Gesammelte Schriften über Musik und Musiker von Robert Schumann*, II, 147.

22. An additional poem from the *West-östliche Divan* appears in op. 51, composed in 1842. Schumann calls it "Liebeslied," though Goethe gave it no title (the first words are "Dir zu eröffnen"). It is curious that Schumann selected this poem from the extensive "Noten und Abhandlungen zum Divan" which Goethe appended to his collection. Neither verse nor setting is noteworthy.

23. "Kennst du das Land" was composed as the last of twenty-two songs in *Album für die Jugend*, op. 79, and taken over unchanged as no. 1 of op. 98a. Willi Schuh is incorrect in listing two settings by Schumann in his *Goethe-Vertonungen*.

24. No music for this song appeared with the novel, though there is a later setting by Reichardt.

25. No. 1, "Lied eines Schmiedes," is the only cheerful one.

26. American performers often miss the point of the "Hauskreuz." Literally it means "domestic trouble"; here it is a humorous reference to her intention to be the boss of the family.

V. Johannes Brahms

1. Reported in Rudolf Gerber, "Formprobleme im Brahmsschen Lied," *Jahrbuch Peters*, 39 (1932), 23-42.

2. See Gerber, "Formprobleme im Brahmsschen Lied," for detailed analyses of the formal musical structure of Brahms's songs.

3. See Jack M. Stein, *Richard Wagner and the Synthesis of the Arts* (Detroit: Wayne State University Press, 1960).

4. Paul Mies, *Stilmomente und Ausdrucksstilformen in Brahmsschen Lied* (Leipzig: Breitkopf und Härtel, 1923), p.33.

5. Yet it is hard to see how the famous "Wie bist du, meine Königin" fits this explanation. Walther Hammermann's attempt in his *Johannes Brahms als Liedkomponist: Eine theoretisch-ästhetische Stiluntersuchung* (Leipzig: Spamer, 1912), pp. 66-68, is not convincing.

6. It will be seen that the case was exactly the reverse with Hugo Wolf. Indeed, in this distinction lies the single most important difference between the songs of Johannes Brahms and Hugo Wolf. Brahms's opposition to Wagner and his theories of declamation, as contrasted with Wolf's enthusiastic acceptance of those principles, is a decisive factor.

7. Konrad Giebeler, *Die Lieder von Johannes Brahms: Ein Beitrag zur Musikgeschichte des neunzehnten Jahrhunderts* (Münster: Kramer, 1959), p.12.

8. The second stanza of the text is a curious mixture of an earlier and later version of the poem. There are other minor changes. All instances of changes in text made by Brahms in his songs are given in Max Friedlaender, *Brahms's Lieder: An Introduction to the Songs for One and Two Voices,* tr. C. Leonard Leese (London: Oxford University Press, 1928).

9. *Johannes Brahms, Briefwechsel,* vol. XVI: *Johannes Brahms im Briefwechsel mit Philipp Spitta und Otto Dessoff,* ed. Carl Krebs (Berlin: Deutsche Brahms Gesellschaft, 1920-1922), p. 200.

10 *Johannes Brahms, Briefwechsel,* vol. VIII: *Briefe an Joseph Widmann, Ellen und Ferdinand Vetter, Adolf Schubring,* ed. Max Kalbeck (Berlin: Deutsche Brahms Gesellschaft, 1915), p.214.

11. Karl Geiringer, *Brahms: His Life and Works,* 2nd ed. (New York: Oxford University Press, 1947), p. 275.

12. Indeed, as Friedlaender demonstrates, the poem as used by Brahms would have been unrecognizable to its author. The blame rests not on the musician but on another poet, Johann Heinrich Voss, a friend of Hölty's noted for his translation of Homer, who published the poems of his late friend in 1783 but altered some of them considerably. Friedlaender *Brahms's Lieder,* pp. 23-24, gives the original poem and shows the differences.

13. Goethe's poem originally had no title. "Unüberwindlich" was added in a later edition of Goethe's verse.

14. If proof were needed that songs are not selected for recording with reference to the poem or to the word-tone relationship, Brahms's op. 59 would provide it. There are four songs in the first set, of which "Dämmrung senkte sich von oben" is the first. This masterpiece is not on records, but the other three, to inferior poems by Carl Simrock and Klaus Groth, are. Similarly, of the four songs in the second set, the three by Georg Daumer and Klaus Groth are on records, but "Agnes," to a poem by Mörike, is not.

15. Two very minor changes were made by Brahms in these lines. He changed "im" to "am" and omitted the hyphen before "Glut."

16. The repetitions of the stanzaic pattern are transmitted musically by the strophic voice line, the different words by the nonstrophic accompaniment. This is an ingenious means of introducing into musical strophic form the variations provided in the successive poetic stanzas by the different words and concepts.

17. Brahms spelled the name with two m's—Flemming—following Wilhelm Müller, the romantic poet, who edited an eight-volume series of seventeenth century poets.

18. In both of these songs Brahms took the words directly from the Schumann songs without checking the originals, adopting slight variants exactly as Schumann had them. See Friedlaender, *Brahms's Lieder,* pp. 6 and 251.

19. There is no connection whatsoever between these two poems and the title role of Keller's uncompleted play, *Therese,* or the Salome of his late work *Das Sinngedicht.* Jonas Fränkel, editor of Keller's lyric poetry, states in Jonas Fränkel and Carl Helbling, eds., *Gottfried Keller: Sämtliche Werke,* vol. II 2: *Gesammelte Gedichte* (Berne: Benteli, 1938), p. 198, that Brahms also composed "Crescenz" ("Wie glänzt der weisse Mond"), but I find no record of this in *Musik in Geschichte und Gegenwart;* in Joseph Braunstein, *Thematic Catalog of the Collected Works of Brahms* (New York: Ars Musica, 1956); nor in the complete edition of the songs, *Johannes Brahms, Sämtliche Werke,* vols. XXII-XXVI: *Lieder und Gesänge für eine Singstimme mit Klavierbegleitung,* ed. Eusebius Mandyczewski (Leipzig: Breitkopf und Härtel, n.d.).

20. Carl Helbling, ed. *Gottfried Keller: Gesammelte Briefe* (Bern: Benteli, 1950-54), I, 305.

21. Reported in Carl Ludwig Schleich, *Besonnte Vergangenheit* (Berlin: Rohwohlt, 1922), p. 129; Luzius Gessler, *Lebendig begraben: Studien zur Lyrik des jungen Gottfried Keller* (Bern: Francke, 1964), p. 101.

VI. Hugo Wolf

1. S.S. Prawer, *Mörike und seine Leser: Versuch einer Wirkungsgeschichte* (Stuttgart: Klett, 1960), p. 36.

2. Cleanth Brooks, *The Well Wrought Urn* (New York: Harcourt, Brace, 1947), esp.ch. I.

3. Walter Höllerer, *Zwischen Klassik und Moderne: Lachen und Weinen in der Dichtung einer Übergangszeit* (Stuttgart: Klett, 1958), pp. 321-356.

4. Frank Walker, *Hugo Wolf: A Biography* (New York: Knopf, 1951), p. 207.

5. It is usually pointed out that these last two lines, if written as a single line, would form an additional, largely dactylic hexameter. Though true, this is irrelevant, since they are not written as a single line, and there is a long pause between the lines. Wolf discerningly follows the poet's lead here.

6. Examples of through-composed strophic poems among the Mörike songs are "Der Genesene an die Hoffnung," "Karwoche," "An die Geliebte" (a sonnet), "Peregrina I," "Peregrina II," "Wo find ich Trost?" and "Auf eine Christblume I."

7. Walker, *Hugo Wolf*, p. 306.

8. "Das verlassene Mägdlein" is one of the Mörike songs that Schumann had already set to music. Walker, *Hugo Wolf*, pp. 203-204, reports Wolf as having said to his friend Friedrich Eckstein, "On Saturday I composed, without having intended to do so, 'Das verlassene Mägdlein,' already set to music by Schumann in a heavenly way. If in spite of that I set to music the same poem, it happened almost against my will, but perhaps just because I allowed myself to be captured suddenly by the magic of this poem, something outstanding arose, and I believe that my composition may show itself beside Schumann's."

9. Wolf substituted the more normal form "ängst'ge" for Mörike's original "ängste." In view of Wolf's great respect for the poet, this was probably inadvertent.

10. Walker, *Hugo Wolf*, p. 288.

11. In a typical concert review that appeared on December 13, 1885, Wolf wrote: "We heard . . . the serenade by Brahms, sung by Herr Winckelmann. In view of Winckelmann's clear diction it is not surprising that we failed to make sense out of the poem. Presumably the lover is lamenting to his beloved his boredom, his desolation, and his toothache. Here Brahms, whose equal in the characterization of such moods and suffering would be hard to find, has once again given a splendid example of his eminent ability to master a situation with a few bold strokes. How charmingly boredom is expressed in the serenade! The effect was amazing. There was a veritable orgy of yawning. And with what sovereignty the transition from boredom to desolation was prepared for, with what mastery it was executed! One was tempted to tear one's hair with delight. It went along, now desolate, now boring, and this with a degree of perfection that only a master of the stature of Brahms can achieve." Richard Batka and Heinrich Werner, eds., *Hugo Wolfs musikalische Kritiken*(Leipzig: Breitkopf und Härtel, 1911), p. 225. It is not certain which song is being reviewed here, as Wolf does not give the word "Ständchen" (serenade) as a title. The well-known "Ständchen," op. 106, no. 1 ("Der Mond steht über dem Berge"), was not published until 1889. The words, from a poem by Franz Kugler, are not sung by a lover. Wolf could be referring to an earlier "Ständchen" with the subtitle "Volkslied," op.14,no.7.

12. "In conversation with his friends Wolf stressed the fact that in his *Wilhelm Meister* songs he had not simply written music for the poems as they stood, but had tried to realize in his music the characters of the singers as they appear in Goethe's novel." Walker, *Hugo Wolf*, p. 240.

13. "Was hör' ich draussen vor dem Tor" and "Kennst du das Land," the songs sung respectively by the harpist and Mignon on their first appearance in the novel, are the last two of the entire group of ten. The other harpist's songs are grouped together, but in the order 3–4–2; Mignon's in the order 3–2–4.

14. With Schubert it is not possible to establish a logical sequence for the *Wilhelm Meister* songs, nor is it important, since he returned to individual poems repeatedly from 1815 to 1826, and for most of them contributed more than one version. Schumann, who wrote all his compositions in 1849, apparently was guided only by musical considerations in his arrangement, though even this would be hard to establish.

15. No music was provided for this song in the novel. There is a later setting by Reichardt.

16. Of Schubert's four settings, the third is a duet.

17. Here is the passage, which contains definite hints to any composer who would relate his setting to the novel: "Wilhelm soon discerned the tones of a zither, and the voice which began to sing was Mignon's. He opened the door, the child came in and sang the song we have just given.

"Melody and expression pleased our friend greatly, although he could not understand all the words. He had her repeat and explain the stanzas, wrote them down and translated them into German. But the originality of the turns of phrase he could only remotely imitate. The childlike innocence of expression disappeared when the broken phraseology was smoothed out and the disjointed was connected. The attractiveness of the melody was also incomparable.

"She began each verse solemnly and in a stately manner, as if she had something of special importance to communicate. At the third line the song became darker and more somber; the 'Kennst du es wohl?' she expressed mysteriously and with deliberation; in the 'Dahin! dahin!' lay an irresistible longing and she was able to modify the 'Lass mich ziehn!' at each repetition in such a manner that it was now pleading and urgent, now impelling and alluring.

"After she ended the song a second time, she paused a moment, looked at Wilhelm piercingly and asked, 'Kennst du das Land?' – 'It must be Italy,' answered Wilhelm, 'Where did you hear the song?' – 'Italy!' said Mignon meaningfully, 'If you go to Italy, take me with you. It's cold here.' – 'Have you been there, child?' asked Wilhelm.–The girl was silent, and nothing further could be gotten out of her."

18. Wolf uses the poem as it appeared in the collected lyrics, which is considerably different from the earlier version in the novel.

19. It is not even composed by Reichardt in the first edition of the novel.

20. Goethe's title is "Epiphaniasfest."

21. *Goethe-Zelter Briefwechsel*, I, pp. 419, 421-422. Yet seven years later, Goethe wrote, in *Kunst und Altertum*, III, sec. 3: "The compositions of my Divan have given me much pleasure. To hear Zelter's and Eberwein's songs sung well . . . will surely put anyone capable of enjoyment in the best of spirits."

22. Eric Sams, *The Songs of Hugo Wolf,* p. 145, draws a dubious analogy between the color chromaticism of a rainbow and the iridescent harmony in this song.

23. Seelig, "Goethe's 'Buch Suleika' and Hugo Wolf: A Musical-Literary Study," offers a detailed analysis of the ten poems and their settings, which argues a close parallel between words and music and claims for Wolf a phenomenal sensitivity to the nuances of the verse. The evidence is impressive, but I feel that the music is keyed to a high pitch of intensity in the three songs mentioned here that is not in accord with the poems, so that much of the rapport between word and tone is vitiated.

24. See G. Mackworth-Young, "Goethe's 'Prometheus' and Its Settings by Schubert and Wolf," *Proceedings of the Royal Musical Association,* 78th session (1951–1952), pp. 53-65.

25. One thinks of "Ganymed" and "Prometheus" respectively.

Index of Titles and First Lines
of Poems and Songs

Dagger (†) indicates quotation from poem
Asterisk (*) indicates musical quotation

General Index

Absolute poetry, 156
Aeschylus: *Prometheus Bound,* 214n*1*
Album für die Jugend (Schumann), 222n*23*
Alcaic ode, 93
Alceste (Gluck), 30
"Alte Weisen" (Keller), 198
"Alte Weisen, sechs Gedichte von Keller" (Wolf), 198
Amphibrach, 63
Anapest, 132
"An die ferne Geliebte" (Beethoven), 57
Antigonae (Orff), 214n*1*
Aristotle: *Nicomachean Ethics,* 6
Asclepiadic ode, 3, 93, 142-144

Bach, Carl Phillipp Emanuel:*Versuch über die wahre Art das Klavier zu spielen,* 29; *Geistliche Oden und Lieder,* 29, 218n*20*
Bach, Johann Sebastian, 58
Ballad: Goethe–Reichardt, 35-36; Goethe–Zelter, 43-45; Goethe–Mozart, 47; Schiller–Schubert, 59-60; Goethe–Schubert, 63-69, 77-78, 219n*11*; Heine–Schumann, 104-109; Eichendorff–Schumann, 112-114; Goethe–Schumann, 123; Mörike–Wolf, 167-168; Goethe–Wolf, 174, 180-183, 188-189
Baudelaire: *Les fleurs du mal,* 156
Beethoven, Ludwig van, 48-57, 58, 125; Ninth Symphony, 1; as transitional figure, 2, 48; influence on song, 17, 217n*11*; quality of verse secondary to message, 48-49, 218n*19*; Gellert songs, 49-51, 218n*20*; Goethe songs, 51; *Die Sehnsucht von Goethe mit vier Melodien,* 53; *Leonore* Overture no. 3, 53; *Pastoral* Symphony, 53; E-flat String Quartet, op. 74, 53; "An die ferne Geliebte," 57
"Bekenntnislyrik," 27, 80
Berg, Alban: *Lulu,* 1; *Wozzeck,* 1, 214n*1*
Berlioz: *Eight Songs from Faust,* 42
Biedermeier, 98, 110, 120, 121
Brahms, Johannes, 2, 29, 58, 97, 155, 159-160, 174, 222n*5*, 222n*6*, 223n*14*; favored cyclic form, 16; "Vier ernste Gesänge," 50; and Hölty, 93, 142; and Platen, 94, 132; on composing songs, 129-130; Platen songs, 131-135; Heine songs, 131, 135-138; "Die schöne

Magelone," 131, 138; Tieck songs, 131, 138-141; Hölty songs, 131, 142-144; Goethe songs, 131, 145-149; Mörike songs, 131, 150; Eichendorff songs, 131, 151; Fleming songs, 131, 151; Liliencron songs, 131, 152-153; Brentano song, 131, 153; Storm song, 131, 153; Keller songs, 131, 153-154; Uhland songs, 151; and Gottfried Keller, 153-154; review by Hugo Wolf, 224n*11*
Brentano, 131, 153
Brooks, Cleanth, 156
Brown, Calvin: *Music and Literature,* 215n*6*
Brun, Friederike, 45
"Buch der hängenden Gärten" (George-Schönberg), 202
Buch der Lieder (Heine). *See* Heine, Heinrich
Büchner, Georg: *Woyzeck,* 1, 214n*1*
"Buch Suleika" (Goethe), 74-76
Buch von der deutschen Poeterey (Opitz), 9
Bücken, Ernst, 51, 53, 68
Bürger, Gottfried August, 28, 59

Candidus, Carl, 131
Capell, Richard: *Schubert's Songs,* 5
Chamisso, Adalbert von, 103; "Frauenliebe und -leben," 97, 119-120, 221n*19*
"Chinesisch-deutsche Jahres- und Tageszeiten" (Goethe), 146
Claudel, Paul, 1
Claudius, Matthias, 28, 58
Confessional lyric, 27, 80
Cooke, Deryck: *The Language of Music,* 214n*1* (ch. I)
Cornelius, Peter, 58
Cyclic song: defined, 15, 16-17; in Brahms, 16; in Schubert, 71, 84, 94

Dactyl, 9, 62, 63, 135, 140, 163, 191, 192, 224n*5*
Dante: *Divine Comedy,* 61
Daumer, Georg, 131, 223n*14*
Declamation, 20, 23, 37, 52, 63, 66, 67-68, 70, 78, 113, 122, 129, 135, 139, 163, 167, 181, 189, 190-191, 221n*17*, 222n*6*
"Deklamationsstücke" (Reichardt), 33-34

233